READING BETWEEN DESIGNS

FRONTISPIECE. *Above,* Harry Pottle's drawing for the sitting room of Sir Clive's house in "The Master Minds" from **The Avengers** *(1965). Courtesy of Denise Pottle.* **Below,** *a scene from "The Master Minds" using this set, with,* **left to right,** *Manning Wilson as Major Plessy, Diana Rigg as Emma Peel, John Wentworth as Sir Jeremy, and Patrick Macnee as John Steed.* © *Canal + Image UK Ltd.*

Visual Imagery and the
Generation of Meaning
in **The Avengers,**
The Prisoner,
and **Doctor Who**

B
E
T
READING T DESIGNS
W
E
E
N

PIERS D. BRITTON
AND
SIMON J. BARKER

University of Texas Press
Austin

First edition, 2003

Requests for permission to reproduce material from this work
should be sent to Permissions, University of Texas Press, Box 7819,
Austin, TX 78713-7819.

⊗ The paper used in this book meets the minimum requirements
of ANSI/NISO Z39.48-1992 (R1997) (Permanence of Paper).

LIBRARY OF CONGRESS CATALOGING-IN-PUBLICATION DATA

Britton, Piers D.
Reading between designs : design and the generation of meaning
in The Avengers, The Prisoner, and Doctor Who / Piers D. Britton
and Simon J. Barker.
        p.   cm.
Includes bibliographical references and index.
ISBN 0-292-70926-9 (alk. paper) —
ISBN 0-292-70927-7 (pbk. : alk. paper)
1. Television—Stage-setting and scenery.   2. Costume.
3. Avengers (Television program)   4. Prisoner (Television
program)   5. Doctor Who (Television program)   I. Barker,
Simon J.   II. Title.
PN1992.8.S7 B75   2003
791.45′026—dc21
                                                                    2002013300

Dedicated to the memory of
HARRY POTTLE
—as remarkable a human being
as he was an artist

C
O
N
T
E
N
T
S

As I recall those days of overlapping pressures for all of us in television design, our overriding daily concern was to get the sets and costumes made and built to meet the relentless studio deadlines.

We designed on "the hoof" with often three programs in hand—one in the studio, one on the drawing board, one at the planning stage—relying on technical know-how supported by our training at art school, which in turn was enriched by a designer's preoccupation with the shape and size and color of the world around us . . . "from then until now."

Analysis and diagnosis of our creativity was not in the forefront of our minds during the haste of the working day. These considerations would surface as we briefly relaxed round the lunch table, our discussions left in the air as we returned to the studio to help make another program. Those essential concerns were, however, discussed and given a thorough airing by delegates from around the world at the three International Design Conferences mounted by the BBC during these years.

Having been a television designer and subsequently Head of Design at

BBC Television during the period covered by the central thesis of this book, I am pleased to contribute this foreword. This study puts a perceptive critical line around the creativity that we struggled to bring to our commitment to offer worthwhile television to our audience.

Clifford Hatts
April 2002

ACKNOWLEDGMENTS

June Hudson has provided every kind of assistance in the preparation of this volume, facilitating our work in innumerable ways. Her enthusiasm for the project, her humor, and her boundless energy have propelled us through a number of dark nights of the soul. Miss Hudson's generosity is exceeded only by her talent; it has been a pleasure and a privilege to work with her.

We are also deeply grateful to Barry Newbery for giving unstintingly of his time and hospitality and allowing us unlimited access to a variety of materials that have been crucial to our research. His wife Zena has repeatedly been the kindliest of hostesses and has also routinely served as Barry's "memory" when dates and names proved elusive.

Clifford Hatts has in many ways been the midwife of this project. We have depended upon his sagacity and expertise throughout the preparation of this volume. His agreeing to write the foreword of the book was the last in a long line of kindnesses for which there is no adequate recompense.

The late Harry Pottle, his widow Denise Exshaw, Christine Ruscoe, Dee Robson, and David Myerscough-Jones have all been generous with their time and have graciously permitted us to examine and borrow their collections of drawings and photographs. It is a source of considerable regret to us that coverage of their work is not in every case as intensive as we would ideally have wished, and we mean to rectify this in a future volume.

James Acheson, Roger Murray-Leach, Graeme Story, Tom Baker, Daphne Dare, Raymond P. Cusick, Stuart Craig, David Murphy, Bill Alexander, and Barbara Kidd were kind enough to grant us extensive interviews, and their contributions have all had a considerable impact on the final realization of this study.

We have benefited greatly from the expertise, advice, and criticism of Ian Potter and John Trenouth, both of the National Museum of Photography, Film and Television in Bradford, England. Ian Potter's and Charles Tashiro's comments on early versions of the manuscript were particularly useful in honing our ideas and focusing our attention to detail. However, it should be stressed that any lacunae, solecisms, or pedantries that remain in the text are entirely our own. We are also particularly indebted to Brian Statham and Katie Schneider for acting as "control" readers and offering trenchant remarks at a crucial stage.

Among the many other people who have contributed valuable ideas, information, technical support, and advice during our research, special thanks are due to Martin Lees Baugh, John Bloomfield, Derek Dodd, Patrick Downing, the late Jon Pertwee, Jacki Pinks, Christine Rawlins, Peter Seddon and Elizabeth Waller, and also to Alex and Sarah Barker, Monte Bassow, Frances Bay, Paul Binski, David and Pauline Bride, Rachel Buck, Peter Burton, Suzy Butters, Andrew Causey, Dick Coles, Mark Crinson, Laura Crow, Rebecca Crum, Caroline Davidson, Andy Fairhurst, Jacqueline Faulkner, Samantha Finn, Graham Guest, Diane Gies, Chloë Golden, Chris and Sharron Goldie, Stella Halkyard, Alan and Alys Hayes, Barbara Hatts, Carrie Hines, Philip Hinchcliffe, Patrick Hogan, Mary Hollingsworth, Celeste Hotaling-Lyons, David J. Howe, Sarah Hyde, Dawn and Tony Jagger, Ludmilla Jordanova, Julian Ketel, Naomi Kosten, Axel Lapp, Peter LePage, Ray Majerski, Rick Majerski, Steve Milkis, Robert Murphy, Barry O'Dwyer, John Onians, Marcia Pointon, Michael Pollard, Tom Rasmussen, Nick Ross, Joe Saber, Benet Simon, Robin Skeates, Geoffrey Tozer, Michael Uzick, Valentina Vulpi, Lynne Walker, Josh van Gelder, Amy West, Michael Wilson, and Karl Wurst.

Too long an exposure to the ravages of postmodern irony ought to prevent us from ingenuously thanking our editor, Jim Burr, for "believing in the dream." Still—thanks for believing in the dream, Jim.

David K. Smith's willingness to assist us by providing a painstakingly constructed composite image of Steed's apartment for the chapter on *The Avengers* was of great importance to our morale as well as our discursive purpose.

Julia Willcock, for many years the departmental secretary (and bedrock) of the School of Art History and Archaeology at the University of Manchester, has furnished tireless and uncomplaining support during several key phases of the research and collation of this volume. We are most thankful to her.

Finally, we owe an immeasurable debt of gratitude to our parents, Rosemary and John Britton and Sue and Keith Barker, and also to Jo and Brian Statham. Without their beneficent support and patience, this book would certainly never have been completed.

READING BETWEEN DESIGNS

I
N
T
R
O
DESIGN D FOR TELEVISION AS A SUBJECT FOR STUDY
U
C
T
I
O
N

AIMS AND LIMITS OF THIS STUDY

This book is about design for television. No serious, sustained examination of the role of scenic or costume design in the medium has been attempted.[1] The exploratory chapter that follows this introduction is, therefore, the first essay into a hitherto unexplored area. The present volume has no pretensions toward comprehensively filling the gap. The chief concern of this study is the drama series, and even here our perspective is limited.

While no other critical account of design for television has yet been written, there are a few significant volumes dealing with the subject of design in the cinema. To documentary works, such as Vincent LoBrutto's corpus of interviews with film production designers[2] and Beverly Heisner's meticulous chronicle of the work of art directors within the Hollywood studio system,[3] have been added several valuable critical studies of production design or costume for film in the last decade. In 1995, Charles and Mirella Jona Affron published their pioneering interpretation of the way production design relates to film narrative,[4] and three years later C. S. Tashiro brought out a thoughtful study of the nature and uses of design in the history film.[5] Costume in the British history film was one of the subjects of a 1994 book by Sue Harper,[6] while the significance of dress in various movie genres has been considered in greater depth by Stella Bruzzi in a more recent volume.[7]

The critical studies by the Affrons, Harper, and Bruzzi might be regarded as foreshadowing this book. After all, film and television have more in common with each other than with any other form of entertainment, and, superficially, creating a costume or a set is the same in either medium. While this last point is broadly speaking true (we will not linger here on the impact of the different techniques of film and video recording on the work of the scenic designer), a book on film does not constitute a precedent for a book on television. First, film design, like film itself, enjoys a higher status. This prejudice should not be glossed over by ignoring the difference between film and television. More important, television has spawned specific types of entertainment, such as the long-running drama series, for which there are no parallels in film. Such medium-specific forms make unique demands on the designer.

It is important to define precisely what we mean by design. In this book, design refers, quite simply, to all material objects, spaces, and costumes created or selected to appear in front of the camera—all visible phenomena, that is, except the actors themselves.

It must be added that design in the present study excludes graphics. Nor do we give much attention to visual or special effects and make-up. This reflects our belief that the design of settings and costumes is paramount in furnishing the overall aesthetic character of a program. Of course, there are important exceptions. The make-up designer, for example, plays a major part in establishing the plausibility both of historical dramas and of sci-fi shows dealing with weird, nonhuman beings, as in *Babylon 5* (TNT, 1993–1998). Nevertheless, even given the extravaganzas of prosthetics, animatronics, and computer-generated imagery seen today, we believe that costume and scenery contribute most to the visual ethos or character of a production.[8]

A brief rider about nomenclature: When we speak of "costume designers," we use the term to encompass all those who, for reasons entirely extraneous to their art (such as union requirements), are designated in on-screen credits as "costume supervisors" and "wardrobe supervisors."[9]

Whether selecting off-the-rack clothes, recreating modes from the past, inventing futuristic dress, or devising "practical" outfits for comedy routines, all those responsible for costume are engaged in essentially the same creative activity.

Although the terminology used to describe those involved in designing sets is very precise in the film world, in television it was, until recently, capricious.[10] For the sake of clarity, we have chosen to use the title "scenic designer" for those who are credited variously as "art director," "set designer," "production designer," and, in the case of BBC employees, simply "designer."

FROM SKETCH TO SCREEN: DESIGN FOR TELEVISION AS MANUFACTURING PROCESS AND MENTAL PROCESS

As well as limiting our field of inquiry in terms of the areas of design we explore, we have also restricted the ways in which we approach our material. We examine costume and scenic imagery from a conceptual and aesthetic standpoint rather than a practical one: our concern is with design as a vehicle for ideas rather than design as process. Yet because most designed images on television are products of collaboration and compromise, it is important to indicate some of the changes that a design may undergo between conception and finished work.

The activities of those working in scenic and costume design for television are hedged about with contingencies. What appears on the screen may not be exactly what the creative artist had envisaged at the drawing board. Anything from the cost of building materials to the overriding predilections of actors and directors may dilute the designer's original vision.

In television, compromise may be substantial. Except for futuristic sci-fi/fantasy series or particularly unusual period pieces, very few productions will be entirely stocked with an array of new costumes or specially made furnishings. Thus, for the clothing of minor characters or extras, the best fit (in the aesthetic as well as the literal sense) usually has to be found in costumiers' stock, and these stock items must then be harmonized as fully as possible with the designer's overall conception.

This study is primarily concerned with three dramas that had a higher than usual amount of specially conceived design imagery. In some cases, expert craftsmen and manufacturers were involved in the construction. For

2

example, when June Hudson designed costumes for the *Doctor Who* episode "Warriors' Gate" (1981), creating the monstrous Tharils (fig. I.1) was a major practical and aesthetic challenge. For one thing, she was reliant on hints rather than explicit descriptions in the script. Her initial conception was tempered from an early stage by budgetary constraints, and the finished outfits combined custom-made items with cheap, ready-made ones for the less obvious parts of the ensemble.

Hudson was also part of a chain of patronage.[11] While she was a BBC staff designer, she regularly worked with a freelance maker, Roger Oldhamstead, to create special clothing, jewelry, and even full-body suits for monsters in *Doctor Who*. The use of such external contractors, though less common among BBC scenic designers during this period (sets were primarily constructed at the corporation's in-house workshops), was relatively widespread among costume designers. Working with Oldhamstead reduced costs,[12] and Hudson says that he "was prepared to take on just about anything, which gave me a lot of creative freedom."

According to Hudson's recollections:

When I read the script, I instantly pictured the Lion People [Tharils] as pirates, because they were described as sailing on the winds of time, and had made their empire by plundering all the civilizations which they encountered on their travels. The other reason that [seventeenth-century] pirate dress seemed right is that it's tremendously masculine and swashbuckling, with a very strong, big silhouette—it takes the human form half way to meet the bushy, powerful, rounded forms of the big cat. In the end, though, I toned down the buccaneer echoes, partly because I wanted the Lion People to have a great dignity and pathos, which a lot of plumes and fringes and silks would slightly have spoilt, and partly because there wasn't actually that much money to spend.

The basic Tharil costume was meant to suggest the creatures' leonine nature and "to enhance subtly" the lion's-mane wigs and facial prosthetics. Hudson recalls that the chief fabric for

their jerkins was a very strong, surprisingly cheap simulated suede, a cotton fabric with a lovely velvety finish [and] a good cotton backing. It was a sort of stone-buff color, which suggested the lion's pelt, and I wanted the shape of the jerkin to enhance this. A lion's body, if you think about it, is full at the top, going into a little waist with

FIGURE I.1. *June Hudson's design drawing for the Tharil in* **Doctor Who**, *"Warriors' Gate" (BBC TV, 1981). Courtesy of June Hudson.*

very full flanks below. To create the effect of the big chest and big neck, I had the jerkins padded and cut very full, with box-pleats all the way round the skirts to give a flared effect which would suggest the lion's bulky flanks.

Hudson continued to refine her initial image after Oldhamstead had actually produced the costumes. As she herself stresses, a design begun at the easel can in some cases only be finalized when it has taken shape in three dimensions:

When I draw something, I'm always aware that the real test is the first fitting. . . . In this case, when I saw the jerkin [made up], I realized that it didn't feel quite complete—it was bland. I went back to my drawings and in some of them I found I had done diagonal lines across the [foreparts], which were really only my way of suggesting the huge, strongly defined rib cage of the Lion. So I thought the best thing was to make a feature of this. I simply had some . . . cut-out strips of velveteen applied in a diagonal row to each of the foreparts, which was a cheap solution and gave the richer, denser effect I was looking for.

Other accoutrements for the Tharils had to be inexpensively done because of the cost of their jerkins and custom lion's-head belt buckles (molded in resin by Oldhamstead). Their cummerbunds and loose, full trousers were cut from a durable, low-priced, black faux silk that "was virtually indestructible [and] hung beautifully." Chemises and footwear also had to be bargains:

A lot of the costume designer's work is actually foraging: rummaging around in odd little boutiques, second-hand shops, and surplus stores. For the Lion People's shoes, I made a lucky find: There was a whole batch of used fireman's boots in a government and army surplus shop on the Tottenham Court Road. They were perfect—heavy, butch, strong—I could actually never have had anything made which was so effective. The shirts, too, were bought from a surplus store. At that time you could still pick up lots of 1970s New Age stuff, with loose, romantic, ballet-dancer kind of shirts, and I managed to find a whole bunch of them, all more or less the same.[13]

Hudson's keen recall of the practical challenges involved in realizing the Tharil costumes is, in our experience, typical of designers' retrospective accounts of their work. Less characteristic of designers is her very full and crisp account of the formation of the basic Tharil image. Her colleagues are seldom articulate about the shaping of the details of a design. They consistently disavow that they think in a logical or even sequential fashion. In our early conversations with designers, they were generally bemused if asked to explain the meaning of their work the way one might interpret poetry or prose. June Hudson described her initial approach to a design thus:

When I read a script and start to think about a character, a hazy picture forms in my mind which I then try to clarify on paper, working around it until I get the effect that I want. I see the character first of all in shapes and colors, and the details come later. It's often easier for me to recognize the inspirations for a costume in retrospect— beforehand I don't necessarily reason it through unless I'm working with someone like the director Don Taylor, who sets me deliberate challenges.[14]

This statement should be taken very seriously, and certainly *not* regarded as a disingenuous attempt to mystify the creative process. Rather it should be recognized that the "syntactical" tidy mindedness and analytical clarity for which the academic strives are, if not actually foreign to designers, then certainly not their conceptual mainstays.

Scholars in the field of the humanities, especially in this postmodern, poststructuralist age, nurture their critical faculties to the point where skepticism is the almost automatic response to any assertion such as Hudson's. Historians and critics are trained to look for dissimulation (and self-deception) in others, for a powerful assumption within the humanities is that everyone must have an ideological position, an "agenda." Yet the possibility must be borne in mind by the reader of this book, as it has been by the writers, that not everyone possesses the scholar's well-honed suspiciousness and heightened self-awareness. A certain amount of imagery that designers create is, according to their own claims, charged with identifiable, carefully thought-out connotations. Nevertheless, the nature of their art means that designers, unlike scholars, are not intellectually bound by language systems: they do not need to think in a syntactical or critical fashion. By the same token, not all their aesthetic choices can be marshaled by the eager interpreter into sequential—and consequential—patterns. This is a matter to which we will return in Chapter One, in relation to the question of how designs acquire "meaning."

We have noted that critical studies of design for television are nonexistent. Why has this state of affairs come about? Why, until the 1990s, was design for screen media entirely neglected by all but a few distinguished practitioners within the profession itself, writing about their own art?[15]

There are no simple answers to this question, but a few suggestions may be put forward. Consider the character of the scholarly literature generated by the discipline of screen studies. The first humanistic field of study of the twentieth century that has engaged wholly with populist, mass-communication culture (or, some might say, subculture), screen studies is still regarded with a measure of contempt by some both inside and outside academia. This intellectual snobbery, though not defensible, is not surprising either. Screen studies appears to be, almost by definition, a "Mickey Mouse" discipline. For many, the idea of expending intellectual energy in earnestly discussing *Ellen* or *Star Trek* as one might discuss *Electra* or *Sons and Lovers* is inherently laughable.

Given this kind of prejudice, scholars working within the field have fashioned screen studies in a normative, even traditional, way. Literary and linguistic studies have provided many of the conceptual models used in the discipline. Even the more substantial accounts of different kinds and genres of screen entertainment tend to concentrate on narrative or on the sign systems that operate within and around screen productions.[16] Of course, some film studies have dealt with the "iconography" of cinema as part of the study of cinematography.[17] Yet the lion's share of attention has been given to narrative structure, dialogue, and—especially since the rise of deconstruction and gender studies—the metanarratives that determine or underpin the narratives themselves.[18] Rather perversely, screen studies has established itself as what might be called a "linguacentric" discipline.[19] That is to say, film and television productions—like so much else in the larger field of cultural studies—are considered primarily in terms of linguistic structures: *narrative* form, not *visual* form, has taken precedence in scholarly analysis.

This general tendency of screen studies toward words and away from images has been exacerbated by the surprising shortage of interdisciplinary links with those who are engaged wholly in the study of visual and material culture. While scholars who work within the field of literary and linguistic studies often hop with alacrity into the arena of screen studies, art and design historians have, for the most part, remained cautiously within their own sphere.[20] True, one art historian has recently observed that art history and film studies should be regarded as "significant others," but this clarion call has hardly been met with a storm of enthusiasm.[21] Some architectural critics and historians have been willing to interest themselves in set design for film, but historians of painting, sculpture, and the graphic arts have stayed with their traditional concerns.[22]

This widespread unwillingness among historians of twentieth-century art, architecture, and design to pay attention to design for screen media is not hard to understand. Modernist art detached itself more completely from the quotidian than the art of any previous era. A largely gallery-oriented sensibility and the influence of powerful critics such as Clement Greenberg promoted the rise of an increasingly recherché, rarefied artistic avant-garde over the last fifty years, with a massive increase in the aesthetic intractability and conceptual "difficulty" of art.[23] Meanwhile, designers working in theater, film, and television have steadily perpetuated a figurative tradition, which has none of the philosophizing pretensions of fine art. This popular art presumably lacks interest for specialists in twentieth-century high art partly because it has not been deemed progressive. Design imagery in screen entertainment, especially television, can readily be perceived as middlebrow rather than highbrow, easy rather than difficult, spectacular rather than thought-provoking.[24]

This characterization of television and film as lightweight and populist principally explains the general neglect of design in both media by those working in the fields of visual studies and screen studies. This seems to be a case of the ancient prejudice against all visual arts—that they lack intellectual substance. The inclusion of painting among the liberal arts rather than the manual trades is recent.[25] Only during the last century did certain contemporary artists—Picasso and van Gogh spring immediately to mind[26]—achieve a kind of heroic status in popular awareness. Painters and architects of the so-called High Renaissance, a cultural epoch now regarded as a glistering pinnacle of human achievement, were most decidedly "jobbing" artists: the now-exalted Leonardo da Vinci, for example, spent a fair proportion of his career designing costumes and sets for court masques and other diversions, as extant drawings bear testimony.[27] Nor would Leonardo have seen anything unduly demeaning about working in what we would now call show business.[28] The discrimination against screen art seems, in short, to be due to a split between the fine and applied arts, the latter having taken on the stigma of being mechanical that had so long dogged the former.

The present volume is meant to help establish design for television as a subject for serious scholarly discussion. In light of recent changes within art history that have led some to prefer the more catholic term "visual studies,"[29] it should not be necessary to defend bringing populist material within the purview of the discipline. Strenuous efforts have been made during the last two decades to shake off the lingering influence of connoisseurship-based art history, which segregated major and minor arts and artists, favoring the progressive, serious, and avant-garde while shunning the allegedly derivative and slight.[30] Art historians now pay attention to popular media of the period 1500–1900, such as mass-produced woodcuts and engravings.[31] A similar lack of elitism should allow students to consider the imagery of television, the most potent and popular means of visual expression in the twentieth century.[32]

Two final points should be made apropos our choice of material and approach. First, our treatment of design for television concentrates on programs whose design can be considered unusual, even subversive. Design imagery that was not conceived in such a way as to render subject matter problematic, or to excite the viewer's active thought (sometimes beyond the immediate concerns of the narrative), is not considered at any length here. Second, we are interested in the cumulative meanings acquired by designs or design concepts over the course of the run of a series and with the ways in which specific images contributed to the overall character of a series.

*Design for
Television in
the Arena of
Cultural Studies*

C
H
A
P
T
E
R

O
N
E

MAKING A SPECTACLE

MEANINGS AND MODALITIES OF DESIGN FOR THE SCREEN

As the title of this book indicates, our prime concern is with the ways in which design may be said to become "meaningful" in the context of screen drama. This is not a straightforward project. The meanings of design imagery are many, and some are fugitive or indefinable. We offer neither a formula for interpreting design nor a handbook for deciphering it. Instead, we explore some of the ways in which design imagery interacts with narrative, particularly in the television series.

As viewers, we tend to respond to design imagery at an emotional rather than an intellectual level. Designs must be either unusual or strongly appealing for spectators to pay conscious attention to them. It is no coincidence that films and television programs from the genres of period drama and fantasy tend to receive most of the awards for costume and production design.[1] More clearly than contemporary drama, historical reconstruction reflects imaginative effort on the part of the designer. In period pieces and fantastical dramas, design also has a defining role, for it is an immediate and powerful expression of "otherness."

Because design imagery for drama tends to engage attention much less readily than plot, dialogue, and performance, most audience members lack a well-developed critical vocabulary for discussing and evaluating design. The identification of meaning and significance is also more difficult for design imagery than for aspects of storytelling. Designs are not expected to be overtly meaningful, so finding tangible, stable significance in them can be fraught with difficulties. Nor, conversely, will designers load imagery with arcane or recherché ideas, for there is little guarantee that these will register with the audience.

In spite of these epistemological problems, it is possible to identify three distinct kinds of meanings for design imagery in screen drama. Most obviously and most important, design supports the integrity of plot and characterization. Characters' homes and décor, for example, bespeak differences in social status, and designers must accommodate this kind of meaning for the drama to be plausible. Explicit information in the script about the appearance of a set or outfit is rare and unlikely to be detailed. Nevertheless, plot and characterization provide the main referent for understanding what design is "signaling" to us.

A second kind of significance for design can be discovered by talking to designers and program-makers themselves. The motives, precedents, and associative ideas that went into the creation of a design may not be discernible in the finished costume, set, or artifact. Yet knowledge of such particulars often helps explain aspects of a design that are not clearly defined in or deducible from the narrative. Inferring from the narrative why one character has a grander domicile than another is usually easy, but determining why a designer chose the particular décor or furnishings for a given residence is more complicated. Any supplementary information gleaned from the creator is extrinsic to the finished work, but this category of meaning should not be undervalued. A popular television series that is widely considered stylish often excites the audience's curiosity over the origin and evolution of its "look." Newspaper and magazine coverage will fuel this interest, and journalistic discussion of a design idea may render an image even more potent than it was in its original dramatic context.

An audience's imaginative response to screen imagery generates a third kind of meaning for design: one, unlike the other two kinds, not subject to fixed definition. While certain associations may be well understood by members of the target audience (e.g., teens or sci-fi buffs), the factors that condition individual viewers' sympathies, or antipathies, are not predictable.[2]

A single example will serve to demonstrate the three kinds of significance for design that we have outlined above. For the sake of clarity, we will take a design that is boldly conceived rather than finely nuanced, by virtue of its generic context. The teenage heroine in *Buffy the Vampire Slayer* (Sandollar/Fox/Mutant Enemy Inc., 1997–) is supervised in her battles with the undead by a "Watcher," Rupert Giles (fig. 1.1), who is also the librarian at her high school in Sunnydale, California.

Giles is British, and because the series is on one level a spoof, he is quintessentially the diffident, upper-crust Englishman. There is nothing ingenuous about the invocation of the cliché: it is frequently acknowledged in the scripts, which are dryly deconstructive in tone. In one episode, for example, Giles is brought a cup of coffee by Xander, one of Buffy's friends, who asks him teasingly if he wouldn't prefer tea. When Giles demurs, Xander replies, "Okay, but you're destroying a perfectly good cultural stereotype here." This kind of knowing humor hints at the response that Giles' clothing is meant to elicit. For the first two seasons of the series, he was invariably dressed in a tweed jacket, generally with a striped or checked shirt, corduroy pants, and (with studied inappropriateness for the California setting) a cardigan. This evocation of British fustiness was the target of frequent witticisms from the younger members of the cast. For example, when asked if she thought Giles was ever less of a fuddy-duddy, Buffy responded, "Are you kidding? His diapers were tweed."

The overt, scripted signaling of Britishness as a meaning for Giles' attire does not explain the precise choice of garments; nor does it explain the significance of the gradual metamorphosis of his costume image. For explanations at this level, we must turn to statements made by the designer. Tweed was not the only possible signifier of Britishness, as the programmakers demonstrated in the third season, when Giles was temporarily supplanted as Buffy's Watcher by another Englishman, Wesley Wyndham-Price. Although younger, Wesley was even stuffier and more anal-retentive. His crisp, buttoned-up image—in marked contrast to Giles' endearingly rumpled appearance—was based on another British cliché, namely the pinstripe-clad toff or city gent. Wesley's sober suits, white-collared shirts, striped ties, and highly polished shoes epitomized the correct grooming of conservative members of the "Upper Ten."

FIGURE 1.1. *"Three-piece-suit guy": Anthony Stewart Head as Giles. Publicity photograph for* **Buffy the Vampire Slayer** *(Sandollar/Fox/Mutant Enemy, 1998). Costume designed by Cynthia Bergstrom. © Twentieth Century Fox.*

By the time of Wesley's arrival, Giles' wardrobe had undergone a slight change. Cardigans and cords were gone, and during the third season he was generally dressed in soft three-piece suits, mostly in quiet herringbone, barleycorn, or pick-and-pick fabrics (see fig. 1.1). As well as affording him greater dignity, since Wesley was now the butt of jokes about the British, this attire gave Giles an aspect of old-fashioned warmth that the clinical, unyielding, and crass younger Watcher lacked. This seems to have been the intent of the costume designer, Cynthia Bergstrom, who has commented that she wanted Giles to have "that old-world feel—sort of a forties-type feel."[3]

If Bergstrom's account of her reasoning adds a dimension to the meaning of Giles' third-season costumes, her comments are indispensable for properly understanding the major revision of his wardrobe in the next season. Bergstrom describes him as "no longer the three-piece-suit guy: He's wearing nubby, loose-knit sweaters, corduroys, and jeans. He's just sort of exploring himself, I think."[4] Since Giles has become unemployed (as a result of Buffy's blowing up the school at the end of the third season), his newly casual clothing might, without Bergstrom's hint, simply be regarded as off-duty attire. Yet her explanation, once given, can readily be mapped onto the dramatic development of Giles' character in the fourth season. Always something of a dark horse, he begins here to reveal unexpected traits, including a penchant for late-night, bluesy cabaret singing in the local coffee shop.

This analysis of the significance of Giles' costumes as set out in the scripts and in the designer's statement of intent has been interspersed with several examples of the third kind of meaning for design in screen drama, that brought to the image by the viewer's personal outlook and experience. In fact, the foregoing passage is riddled with our own inferences and assumptions. The mere fact that we are English means that our conclusions are probably not the same as an American's would be. Our view of British stereotypes, and even the kind of language we use to define them, are inevitably colored by our own sense of national identity and language. An American commentator probably would not have used the terms "toff," "city gent," and "Upper Ten," the latter a culturally specific term for the upper crust (an abbreviation of "Upper Ten Thousand"). Nor would the average American be likely to react as we do to Giles' initial costume image, conceived by Susanna Puisto. With its viciously clashing combination of fabrics, patterns, and hues, it seems to our "schooled" eyes a coarse and inaccurate cliché of Britishness. Conversely, Giles' three-piece suits in the third season probably have less of an "old world . . . forties-type" look to us than to most Americans, who would not necessarily know that high-fastening three-piece suits enjoyed a renaissance among fashion-conscious Britons during the 1990s.

There is a limit to how far screen narrative can furnish the meaning of design imagery. Information given in the narrative cannot, of itself, restrict the train of associations that a visual image may trigger in the mind of the spectator. These often semiconscious responses by audience members may generate meanings that run tangentially or even contrary to the program-maker's intent.[5] Thus, our response as English viewers to Giles' original costume was presumably the opposite of what the makers of *Buffy* intended: Far from confirming and embodying his Englishness, this outfit struck us as embarrassingly *un*-English by virtue of its sartorial solecisms.

The fact that design and narrative may belie each other is ultimately less interesting than another aspect of their interplay. Design imagery can spark ideas that unfold at a tangent to the spectator's linear experience of a drama. The recognition of this tangential relationship raises an issue that previous commentators on design for screen drama have insufficiently developed. Design imagery and narrative signify differently, for all that the former is necessarily subordinate to the latter.[6] Whereas the plot of a drama must develop logically toward a satisfying conclusion, no such burden of expectation rests on design. While design images must never confound the narrative premise of a drama—viewers would balk at miniskirts or hot pants among crinolines in a mid-nineteenth-century drama—designers can stay true to period authenticity without being seriously restricted in their aesthetic choices. While crinolines may seem right in an adaptation of a Trollope novel, responses to the various costumes in that drama will not be confined to the simple acknowledgment of their rightness. Visual imagery is suggestive on more than one level, and the overall success of a design conceit is perhaps best measured by its evocative richness.

The defining feature of design is its suggestive plurality, whereas the defining feature of narrative is its teleological unity. Narratives may be underpinned with metaphor, and dialogue may be replete with subtexts, but most mainstream screen dramas are meant to portray a chain of events that progress unambiguously to a reasonable conclusion. By contrast, design is inevitably multidimensional and never monolithic in its significance.

To return to Rupert Giles from *Buffy,* a host of associative ideas might be triggered by his costume image, beyond its supposed redolence of stuffy Britishness. Many of these will be furnished by generic precedent. For some, Giles' attire will call to mind Roddy McDowall's tweed-clad caricature of English bookishness, Peter Vincent, "the Great Vampire Killer," in *Fright Night* (Tom Holland, 1985). Behind both Giles and Peter Vincent stands Van Helsing, the eccentric professor of medicine and arcana who defeated Dracula. The associative web may spread further still. Van Helsing is closely associated with the actor Peter Cushing, another of whose famous roles was the tweed-clad Sherlock Holmes, a distant precursor of Buffy's Watcher. Beyond Holmes lie more nebulously related ancestors for Giles—Fu Manchu's quasi Holmesian nemesis, Nayland Smith, perhaps, or the apparently unassuming, bespectacled Albert Campion from Margery Allingham's mystery stories. No members of Giles' "lineage" need surface to consciousness: such referents can comfortably coexist in the viewer's awareness, however dimly, alongside broader, less genre-specific factors such as the evocation of cultural cliché.

The ability of design imagery to generate constellations of associative thoughts in the mind of the spectator, spinning ideas around the linear trajectory of the narrative, is one to which we will return. Since this study is primarily concerned with the transcendent meanings that design can acquire in relation to the overall identity of a series, we now turn to the modalities of design for screen drama.

The relationship between genre and design is, from one point of view, more straightforward and immediately apparent than the relationship between narrative and design. For example, a period drama announces itself at once through its costuming: the clothes, in other words, are a prime signifier for the genre. The same is true of both costumes and sets for westerns and futuristic dramas. In contemporary dramas, too, design can suggest genre. Costumes and props have an obviously denotative function in series about doctors or uniformed policemen, but even among programs that lack such defining visual features, design can help the viewer identify the specific mood and tone of a series. The slick, trendy dress of Crockett and Tubbs, the two cops in the crime series *Miami Vice* (NBC TV, 1984–1989), made it abundantly clear that the program was as much about style and posturing as about the apprehension of criminals. The emphasis on designer machismo helped to distance this flashy thriller from more realistic cop dramas; for example, the "slice of life" character of *Cagney and Lacey* (CBS, 1982–1988) was emphasized by the plain, nondesigner dress of its female protagonists.

One form of idiomatic variation in design imagery cannot be defined simply in terms of genre, namely the degree of its realism or stylization. Since the terms "stylization" and "stylized" occur frequently in this study, it is important to clarify exactly what we mean by these words, which have generally been imprecisely used by authors writing on design for film. To stylize is, according to the primary dictionary definition, to paint or draw in a conventional, nonrealistic style. This is our principal meaning when we deploy the term. Richard Levin, former Head of Design at the BBC, has described stylized design for television as "derived design" representing "an analytical thought process."[7] Stylization means that which manifestly departs from the conventional aim of simulating actuality and presents instead a highly selective version of the real.[8] Stylization always involves a measure of simplification—the use of primary colors instead of secondary, bold contours instead of subtle, a quasi-graphic linearity instead of the complex "patina" of objects in the real world, and so forth.

The stylized should not be confused with the exotic, the unfamiliar, or the unconventional. To say that the genres of science fiction and the history film are innately stylized, as C. S. Tashiro claims, is somewhat misleading.[9] Representation of the past is bound to be stylized in the sense that the designer, however "archaeological" in approach,[10] is working with forms that have no contemporary currency and in some cases are known only via tendentious representations from the period in question. However, the aspiration to realism in period drama, which Tashiro acknowledges in certain instances, should not be underrated.[11] Nor is it necessarily absent from science fiction, even the more fanciful kind. The popularity of such films as Ridley Scott's *Alien* (1979) and *Blade Runner* (1982) can be attributed in large part to their eerie contingency on day-to-day experience—their "lived-in" realism.

No screen imagery is in any absolute sense realistic. One generation's realism may well appear mannered and artificial to the next,[12] and elements of artifice may be selectively introduced into fundamentally realist dramas. Yet throughout the history of film, the vast majority of dramas have been in our terms much closer to the pole of absolute naturalism than to that of overt stylization.[13] Similarly, it is only in avant-garde or "difficult" drama that stylization has been tolerated in television (though, as we will see, this is not true of other kinds of television programming such as light entertainment). The aspiration toward naturalism has become ever greater in television as the medium has sought to ape film. In turn, the benchmark for believability provided by cinema has become ever more demanding as technology has become increasingly sophisticated.

The perceived need for an optimal sense of actuality in film and television drama has greatly discouraged the production of stylized design imagery. In the cinema, stylized projects are now largely the province of films intended for the "art house." In television, antinaturalistic projects such as Neil Gaiman's surreal drama *Neverwhere* (BBC TV, 1996) are unlikely to be shown during prime time on a popular entertainment channel.[14] The unspoken rule for a mainstream film or television drama has always seemed to be that stylization can only be used to inflect naturalistic imagery—used, that is to say, as a "seasoning" rather than a basic ingredient. The three series in this study are unusual in their extensive deployment of stylized imagery.

LINES AND CHECKS: DESIGN FOR TELEVISION — TECHNICAL CONSIDERATIONS

An audience's experience of television is quite different from its experience of cinema, both at a purely sensory level and in terms of other factors that condition the spectator's degree of engagement.

Certain aspects of the picture-making process in television have always constrained scenic and costume designers. For example, costume designers avoid pendulous earrings. Such accessories are likely to be distracting in a close-up shot since their movement will take on exaggerated importance within the frame of the standard television screen.[15] For less obvious reasons, pure white was used sparingly in sets and costumes in the early years of television. Patches of true white (or "peak white") tended to flare and bleed into the adjacent color fields because of the high levels of illumination needed by the less-sensitive television cameras of the 1950s and 1960s.[16] At best, the use of a white element that had not been properly "dipped" (i.e., tinted to pale gray to avoid glare) might result in a slight distraction or the infelicitous lighting of a performer; at worst, it could disrupt the coherence of the picture.[17]

Sometimes, dealing with these technological problems can have unexpected results for the design aesthetic of a program. For example, the use of natty, colored shirts for John Steed, Patrick Macnee's character in *The Avengers* (ABC TV, 1961–1969), actually arose from the practical necessity of employing "tech white" rather than true white in the days when the series was shot on video. (This "tech white" was, in fact, achieved by washing the shirts in a solution of weak tea.)[18] By the time the series was being shot on film and in color,[19] a virtue had been made of necessity. According to Hardy Amies, who provided some of Macnee's clothes, the discerning gentleman always prefers a colored shirt to a run-of-the-mill white one.[20] Thus, the use of low-intensity, high-value colors for the foppish Steed's haberdashery became a matter of good taste, and not merely a response to a technological *force majeure.*

Other difficulties for designers have arisen from the composition of the television picture itself. The screen image is made up of a number of lines: 405 were generally used before the arrival of color (c. 1967), and 625 have been used since then in Britain. The dot of light that traces these lines scans first all the odd lines and then the even ones at a speed where the persistence of vision ensures that the eye sees a coherent picture. However, the movement can give rise to perceptible anomalies, especially in the 625-line system. Certain checked fabrics, for example, produce a stroboscopic effect in the broadcast image and must therefore be avoided. For example, Patrick Troughton wore vividly houndstooth-checked trousers while portraying Doctor Who between 1966 and 1969. When he reprised his performance for cameos in 1973 and 1983, each time the gauge of the check was different from that on his original pair of pants, in accordance with the ever more exacting standard for picture clarity at the BBC.[21]

Interesting as these and similar cases may be, such technological considerations are largely peripheral to the concerns of this book. Of course, it could be argued that technological matters influence all responses to a televised image and should, therefore, be acknowledged in any argument or description. In a sense, this is true, but the mechanics of making an image discernible on screen are no more directly important to the viewer than the workings of the internal combustion engine are to the driver of a car. For this study, it is enough to say that nearly all the images discussed are shot and lit so as to be readily discernible and, in the case of many of the costumes, can be appreciated in a range of visual contexts.

At the same time, it is worth acknowledging that our analyses and observations are the result of our having used home video technology. Unlike the original viewers of the series, we were able to watch episodes of the series repeatedly and intensively, and we made free use of the freeze-frame control. Very occasionally, our interpretations or observations have been germanely affected by this recourse to video's capabilities; where this is true, we have indicated it clearly in the text or notes.

Home video technology allows viewers to watch programs at their leisure, to fast-forward and rewind, thereby releasing them from the necessity of sustained concentration. This points to the other medium-related issue to be considered here, namely, the experiential divergence between watching a film at the theater and watching a broadcast television program. An audience's optical interaction with the cinema screen is quite unlike that with the television screen. Also, television programs and theatrical films are viewed in quite different social settings. These two facts are related.

In a movie theater, the viewer is optically monopolized by the much larger cinematic image. This sensory immersion is strengthened by the social conventions of the experience: lights are dimmed, extraneous noises are minimized, and unnecessary movement or conversation is frowned upon. These restrictions do not apply in the home or in bars or other venues where television is routinely watched. In short, television-watching is not an event in the same way as cinema-going; nor does the medium so comprehensively command attention. Television programs are typically shorter than feature films, and on all commercial networks they are regularly interrupted by advertisements.

A degree of active, participatory intelligence is demanded of the spectator in order for television entertainment to be effective. There are two reasons for this. First, because it is generally viewed in the home, television is in competition with the perpetual sideshow of real life. Second, the television image offers a relative paucity of visual information, in comparison with the much larger and clearer image on the cinema screen. These two factors also have ramifications for the kind of imagery that is effective on the television screen. Television is better suited to the vignette than the grand tableau, which is the province of cinema. So, to a lesser extent than the live theater but to a much greater extent than feature films, television programs demand that viewers augment what they see through their imagination.

In film, design imagery is subsumed in pure spectacle; it is part of the sensory bombardment meant to transfix the viewer. In television, design is part of a conceptual process involving the viewers themselves. The natural tendency of design to stimulate the associative faculties of the mind in many ways comes into its own in television. There, relatively simple visual conceits can take on a redolence that they would not possess as part of the more complex and grandiose film image.

Television entertainment embraces a much greater variety of materials than film.[22] Drama accounts for the vast majority of the output of the world's filmmakers: in television, on the other hand, nondramatic entertainment of various kinds has traditionally accounted for the majority of programming. The variation between types of movies is generic, which is to say primarily a matter of premise and presentation. The difference between a film noir and a musical comedy or gothic fantasy is, in essence, just a difference in kinds of story and modes of storytelling. In television, on the other hand, we must distinguish between productions that differ radically in kind.

A talk show such as *The Tonight Show* (NBC TV, 1962–), a comic revue such as *The Two Ronnies* (BBC TV, 1971–1986), and a hard-hitting crime drama such as *Homicide: Life on the Streets* (NBC TV, 1993–1999) can be differentiated more fundamentally than by genre. The concept of genre, as used in the critical vocabulary of the arts, denotes a basic commonality, which does not exist among such a diverse group of television programs. The disparity is aptly demonstrated by comparing news reports and episodes of a soap opera.

Television journalism is meant to inform. News broadcasts generally present a number of items, those judged more important coming earlier in the report.[23] Soap operas need not be concerned with edification.[24] Their raw material is not "factual" data, and they make no claims to be dispassionate or to encourage rational responses in the spectator. They depict matters of "human interest" rather than political, economical, and ethical importance and often do so in an unabashedly manipulative way.[25] Unlike news reports, soap operas place the most highly charged dramatic elements at the end of the show.[26] And whereas news stories cease to appear in nightly broadcasts once they are no longer deemed newsworthy, the narrative strands of a soap opera are generally carried through until they reach some kind of denouement.[27]

In stressing the intrinsic differences between soap operas and news programs, we are necessarily glossing over certain deep similarities. Both are governed by the ethical values of the society that produces them. Scriptwriters for a British soap opera are no more likely than British television journalists to condone murder, racism, domestic violence, political corruption, and so on. And it could be argued that both grab an audience's interest by dwelling on the more sensational aspects of human frailty. Yet for the concerns of this book, these resemblances are a side issue. That a single worldview may underpin a whole range of forms does not preclude those forms from having many distinct or even irreconcilable characteristics.

The fact that television entertainment encompasses a variety of different species of program has important ramifications for understanding the creative role of the designer.[28] Whereas in the film industry costumes and sets are invariably produced for some form of drama, in television the designer can be called upon to work in radically different idioms from week to week and even at the same time. For example, a scenic designer must in principle be able to cover projects ranging from the simulation of an urban environment for the soap opera *EastEnders* (BBC TV, 1985–) to the invention of heavily abstract set decoration for the current affairs program *Newsnight* (BBC TV, 1980–). While verisimilitude of some sort is almost always the goal of design in film, in television there has historically been no such baseline aim, and designers have had to satisfy a wide range of expectations.

Not all forms of television program require the services of a designer. For example, sports broadcasts demand few, if any, specially made sets and no specially made costumes. This is also true of most of the documentaries that occupy an ever-increasing proportion of the weekly television schedule, from farming magazines and natural history programs to so-called "docusoaps" such as *The Real World* (MTV, 1992–) and *Paddington Green* (BBC TV, 1999–2000). With the expansion of such "reality programming," there has been a correspondingly smaller demand for designers, and many television companies now run a skeleton design department or else have no staff designers at all.

The three forms of television entertainment within which designers work most often are those typically referred to in Britain as drama, light entertainment, and current affairs. While each of these forms has a distinctive visual idiom, the borders between them are somewhat blurred. Situation comedy, for example, is often categorized as light entertainment, for all that it is a kind of drama and more specifically a kind of drama series. These shared traits (talk shows, for example, have at least as much in common with political interviews as with game shows) reflect a larger truth that must be borne in mind in relation to the work of the designer. In many ways, the various species of television program are best viewed as points on a scale, not as the tributary components of three discrete categories. We have outlined this scale in the following table, with lines between the usual divisions of the three areas of programming.

Drama	*One-off plays*
	Serials
	Series

Light Entertainment	*Situation comedies*
	Revue or variety shows
	Game shows
	Cooking programs
	Music magazines
	Talk shows

News & Current Affairs	*Political or ethical debates*
	Lectures and talks
	News (including sports news)

Programs in the lower half of the list (from game shows to news) make fewer practical demands on costume and set designers than those in the upper half. Newsroom sets, for example, are generally used for years at a time, and both guests and presenters in current-affairs programs will almost certainly wear their own clothes. Programs in the upper half of the list, on the other hand, may be design-intensive. Variety shows, even more than dramas, consistently demand a large number of sets, and in a comic revue such as *Goodness Gracious Me* (BBC TV, 1996–1998) or *French and Saunders* (BBC TV, 1987–), costume changes are needed for each new sketch. Furthermore, a single ninety-minute costume drama may require several outfits for each of the principal players and scores more costumes for minor characters and extras.

Our list also describes a polarity between programs that typically call for a high degree of realism and those that are generally characterized by a high degree of abstraction in design. If we consider programming in terms of the three overarching categories on the left of the table, then light entertainment turns out to be the only form within which a wide range of design idioms is contiguously used. Within a single edition of *The Two Ronnies* (BBC TV, 1971–1986, 2000), for example, certain sketches might call for realistic sets while others might require a patently artificial, "music hall" stage environment. By contrast, the norms for drama and current-affairs programs have become increasingly rigid over the years. This is especially truc of drama: Audiences are sure to regard a play or series with nonrealistic sets and strange costumes as "arty" and therefore "difficult." As a consequence, forays into blatant stylization in plays and series have been rare.[29] In fact, the demand for an ever greater sense of realism has increased exponentially, with all-location work taking precedence in the 1980s over the largely studio-based culture that had hitherto been the norm.[30]

In current-affairs programming, stylization has long been the custom, with elements of realism acting only as a foil to the stylized scenery and furnishings. For example, the sets currently used for BBC News programs, which are aesthetically uniform for both national and local bulletins, often incorporate vistas onto the real world; yet the emphasis in these sets remains on abstraction. Each one is dominated by a single motif—overlapping and radiating circles. This conceit is most ostentatiously expressed in the form of the newscaster's huge table, which is generally that of a lemniscate or ellipse. This conceit is drawn from the programs' title sequence, which shows a cluster of radiating pulses that represent the transmission of television waves. It is significant, given the coherence of all this stylization, that the title sequence and the prototypical set (i.e., the one at BBC Television Centre) were devised by a graphic designer, Martin Lambie Nairn.[31] Only in current-affairs programming could graphic forms, and the graphic artist's sensibility, predominate.

For all that television entertainment encompasses such a breadth of imagery and places such heavy creative demands on its designers, the rigors of their discipline are barely acknowledged beyond the confines of the business itself. Compared even with their colleagues in the movies, who enjoy none of the accolades heaped on designers in the fashion world, television designers gain little recognition of any kind. For example, the costume designer James Acheson is known today not for his highly inventive television work at the BBC in the 1970s, but for winning three Oscars after his transition to the movie business (for *The Last Emperor* (Bernardo Bertolucci, 1987), *Dangerous Liaisons* (Stephen Frears, 1988), and *Restoration* (Michael Hoffman, 1995)). Similarly, while the names of a few scenic designers for film such as William Cameron Menzies and Ken Adam are known to aficionados and scholars in the field of screen studies, the same cannot be said of those who work in television. Indicative of this difference of status, and more generally of the low premium placed on design in television programs, is a review by Nancy Banks-Smith, the television critic of the *Guardian,* of the lavish production of *Gormenghast* (BBC TV, 1999). She observes that the serial

has the kind of credits you read from the bottom up. Who designed those shimmering sets? (Christopher Hobbs). Dreamed up these extraordinary costumes? (Odile Dicks Mireaux) . . . Any actor who can both stand up to and suit this magnificence has had plenty of practice.[32]

The clear implication that it is unusual to read the credits "from the bottom up" neatly expresses the prevalent critical attitude to television, which generally takes no account of the designer or, for that matter, any of the other behind-the-camera personnel except perhaps the writer or director. *Gormenghast* is an exception to the general rule because its design is so assertive that, as Banks-Smith notes, the actors have to "stand up" to it.

The heavy "design intensity" of Hobbs' sets and Dicks Mireaux's costumes in *Gormenghast* guarantees them recognition and makes it possible for them to eclipse the story and the actors.[33] It is not only in its artifice that *Gormenghast* exceeded expectations, but also in its costliness. Such BBC productions were not entirely unprecedented—in the field of children's drama, there have been splendid adaptations of fantastical literature like *The Box of Delights* (1984)—but there had never been one that looked, or indeed was, so expensive.[34]

Although made for television, *Gormenghast* is, from a certain point of view, not a television production at all: it is a film in four episodes. By 1999, when the serial was made, no flagship BBC drama of this kind was any longer recorded on video within the studios of BBC Television Centre, as such programs typically had been until the mid-1980s. *Gormenghast,* like many other British costume dramas from the late 1980s and 1990s that were heavily subsidized by American television companies such as A&E and WGBH Boston, was in no real sense an in-house production. Indeed, it was, ironically, not even made in the BBC film studios at Ealing, but in the larger and more prestigious facilities at Shepperton.[35]

The changes in production techniques and production values that *Gormenghast* epitomizes may, in due course, slightly improve the status of the designer working in television, or, at least that of the designer working in television drama. Christopher Hobbs—who has also done well-received work in film, notably with Derek Jarman on *Caravaggio* (1986) and *Edward II* (1991)—and Odile Dicks Mireaux belong to an elite. Talented designers doing sophisticated work on other kinds of television entertainment are likely to remain unacknowledged by critics and the voters for the Emmy and BAFTA awards. Consider, for example, Graeme Story, who designed the sets for the seminal "alternative" comedy series *The Young Ones* (BBC TV, 1982–1984). Since leaving the BBC, Story has gone on to be principal designer for comic and satirical programs such as *Whose Line Is It Anyway?* (Channel 4 TV, 1988–1998), *Drop the Dead Donkey* (Channel 4 TV, 1990–1998), and *Clive Anderson Talks Back* (Channel 4 TV, 1989–1996), all made by the highly successful British television company Hat Trick Productions. Yet Story is unlikely to receive critical recognition for his beautifully conceived sets, at least beyond the confines of such studies as this, because he works in light entertainment rather than "serious" drama.

Here, then, we confront an irony. Television design, so long *en bloc* the country cousin of design for film, is no longer monolithic: from a critical standpoint, at least, design work for television can now be divided into two discrete groupings of material. In one compartment is prestige drama, shot on film and produced in more or less the same way as movies intended for cinematic release. (In fact, releasing "made for TV" movies such as *Four Weddings and a Funeral* first in the cinema has proved highly successful for both the BBC and Channel 4 and has revivified the British film industry.)[36] In the remaining compartment is every other kind of television program that calls for a designer. Nearly all the productions in this category are recorded on video and generally shot in the studio rather than on location. Their design imagery is rarely ascribed any kind of serious importance by the critics.

There is, then, a critical hierarchy—or, in Marxist terms, a "center" and a "periphery"—within the discipline of design for television. The critical exaltation of design for prestige drama relates to the predilection for naturalism in drama for both screen media. Designers themselves are, apparently, not immune to these twin prejudices. The costume designer June Hudson recalls that many designers actively petitioned to work on major contemporary and period dramas—those that were "most likely to be BAFTA winners," as she dryly expresses it.[37] Moreover, the scenic designer Barry Newbery candidly acknowledges that he himself always regarded work on drama as representing the acme of his art, but other kinds of projects, such as game shows, as slighter efforts.[38]

This critical ascendancy of drama and realism has not affected the outlook of all designers. For example, Clifford Hatts, Head of Design at the

BBC from 1974 to 1980, received a BAFTA award in 1960 for his work as scenic designer on *Quatermass and the Pit* (BBC, 1958), but sets little store by this accolade:

My success was hung on other people's pegs. I got my "Designer of the Year" award for Quatermass because of the overall calibre of the show, not my contribution. Thank you, Nigel Kneale [writer]; thank you, Rudolph Cartier [director]. The work— brilliant, innovative; the production—operationally superb, creative and content- enhancing. What did deserve the "Oscar" was the work I did on a revue, On the Bright Side*—twelve weeks of my T.V. life that made 23 years worthwhile, and that passed as a zephyr.*[39]

Hatts' work for the weekly variety show *On the Bright Side* (BBC TV, 1959–1961), as assertively stylized as his *Quatermass* imagery was eerily real- seeming, won him only unofficial plaudits from discerning colleagues at the BBC ("'Loved your sets for *On the Bright Side*,' said Yvonne Littlewood, doyenne of BBC variety, who crossed the building to tell me so").[40] For Hatts, the "sharp, economical, International Style" effects that he sought to achieve in the several sets required each week for *Bright Side* represented excellence and ingenuity more fully than did his contribution to successful programs like *Quatermass*.[41] His argument, in short, would be that design for television is judged by institutions such as BAFTA not on its own terms, but in what is really an alien frame of reference—that is, as a mere adjunct to "legitimate" or "serious" drama.[42]

The implications and ramifications of Hatts' claim cannot all be consid- ered in the context of the present volume. Suffice it to say we endorse his assertion that design for television is judged in an inherently prejudicial manner. However, one issue must be teased out of his polemic. We have noted that the polarization between realism and stylization includes a hier- archy that favors realism. Paradoxically, drama, the only form for which de- sign holds any significance for the critics, is also the one in which designers have generally had the least expressive freedom.[43] The pursuit of natural- ism in design for television drama is not surprising, for theater audiences showed an insatiable thirst for simulation of the real world long before the arrival of television or film; screen media have merely made it easier to sat- isfy this appetite. What needs a little more explanation is the acceptance of stylization as a design idiom for any kind of television program.

Within the BBC (which we may take as exemplary, since it was evi-

FIGURE 1.2. *Set for The Brains Trust (BBC TV, 1959) designed by Natasha Kroll.* © BBC Worldwide.

dently acknowledged as a world leader in design for television during the 1950s and 1960s),[44] the original justification for the use of nonnaturalistic imagery in current-affairs programming was its supposed neutrality. The progressive Head of Design at the BBC in the 1950s, Richard Levin, had arrived direct from overseeing the traveling exhibition for the Festival of Britain;[45] he lost no time in injecting a "Festival style" contemporaneity into both light entertainment and current-affairs shows.[46] In relation to the latter, he clearly stated his belief that programs dealing with contemporary issues should have a setting that "reflects current interest without special emphasis . . . a background positive in style yet neutral in effect."[47]

Sets for BBC current-affairs programming under Levin were produced by the Studio Design Unit run by Natasha Kroll.[48] A former window-display designer for Simpsons (one of London's principal department stores), Kroll's enthusiasm for inventive design and persuasive imagery matched Levin's. Her set design for a weekly discussion program, *The Brains Trust* (BBC TV, 1955–1961), exemplifies the style she encouraged—one that has left an indelible mark on design for both the BBC and television journalism worldwide (fig. 1.2). When describing Kroll's set for *Brains Trust*, Levin observed that "the background is of an abstract nature related to [the] composing of pleasant pictures and the philosophical nature of the programme."[49] Though the sub–W. T. Russell chairs look slightly dated today and the beautifully simple conceit of the foliage-backed translucent screens seems positively antediluvian compared with the virtual-reality newsroom sets of the 1990s, Levin's analysis is still remarkably apropos.

What Levin did not say, because it had no relevance to his quietly evangelizing article, was that Kroll's aesthetic of abstraction replaced a very different design idiom in current-affairs programs, one established before World War II and still prevalent when Levin took over as Head of Design in 1953. According to his successor, Clifford Hatts, Levin imposed such imagery as Kroll's in face of opposition from the forces of conservatism within the BBC. Hatts claims that current-affairs directors typically wanted their programs to be adorned by "a wine table, centre, flanked by a couple of repro' Chippendale armed chairs in front of a Regency library stock set."[50] (As Head of Design in the 1970s, Hatts ruefully remarked of current-affairs design that while "the Regency library belongs in [the] drama department . . . we have only been partially successful in keeping it there.")[51] The ideological overtones of this backward-looking, elitist visual conceit—and, for that matter, the ideology implicit in the Kroll *Brains Trust* set, which in its aggressive modernism was far from neutral and in a different way just as elitist—cannot detain us here. What is important at this juncture is to emphasize that the Kroll aesthetic was in no way the natural choice for current affairs. Clifford Hatts avers that the Levin/Kroll aesthetic eventually gained "the endorsement of reluctant admiration because it felt right—*was* right."[52] In one way, the longevity of Kroll's influence in current affairs may be said to endorse the "rightness" of Levin's and her vision; but it is important to remember that the introduction of a stylized/abstract idiom, even in this context, was not unproblematic.

Abstraction and stylization did not become normative in BBC telejournalism and light entertainment simply because Levin willed that they should. There were overriding reasons why imagery that was selectively simplified or selectively exaggerated could flourish within these areas of entertainment, but not in mainstream, "straight" drama. Although the set design for a current-affairs program may contribute to or even furnish the character of the show, it is not, unlike the set design for a drama, part of a strategy to make viewers suspend their disbelief. In other words, in telejournalism, a set has no sustaining role: there is no fictional diegesis for it to support or confirm. In virtually all current-affairs programs and similar forms, the presence of the viewer (or the viewer's proxy, the camera) is directly acknowledged at least twice, in the introduction and at the close of the program; in some news programs, the audience is addressed throughout.

The audiences of news programs or discussions are not called upon to believe in the set as a "real" space, though they may do so involuntarily from habit. The newsroom set exists purely as a backdrop for the newscaster: it simply fills up the part of the screen unoccupied by a human body. Just as most of us are likely to look at anyone who addresses us, ignoring what is in our peripheral vision, so we are more concerned with the face of the newscaster than with the studio surroundings. With this in mind, it is easy to see the force of Richard Levin's argument in favor of abstract settings, which are "positive in style yet neutral in effect."[53]

For game shows, stand-up comedy, and revue or variety programs, sets are not infrequently meant to draw attention to themselves. Questions of probity and ideology scarcely apply here. The only functions of the set for a musical number in *The Two Ronnies,* for example, are to enhance the wit of the lyrics and to provide an apt context for any sight gags. By the same token, in a monologue by Ronnie Barker for the same program, where the comedian satirically adopts the guise of a political broadcaster or lecturer, the setting and props are likely to have been conceived specifically in relation to the verbal humor, often as "cod" visual aids. Either way—and this would apply equally to the slick, light-and-color-suffused, largely abstract settings used in *Top of the Pops* (BBC TV, 1964–)—the sole intention is to divert. The artifice is deliberate; no one expects viewers to suspend disbelief.

On the other hand, realism prevails in the design of television series, serials, and plays because all are essentially escapist; suspension of disbelief is crucial. The pleasure of watching drama is, conventionally, bound up with viewers' ability to accept what they see as real. They may later reflect on issues and ideas raised in a drama, on questions of plausibility, and so forth, but while they are actually watching, they want to be drawn into the autonomous world of the drama.[54] The power of screen drama to entertain often corresponds to the degree to which it provides a convincing alternative to reality.

As watchers, we are unlikely to be seriously fazed when, in the creative and current-affairs program for children, *Blue Peter* (BBC TV, 1957–), the cameras occasionally pull back beyond the perimeter of the set to reveal, for example, a large group of guests, such as a troupe of carol-singing Girl Scouts, entering through the studio doors. We accept this breach of the visual coherence of the set because we cognize *Blue Peter* as a "real life" program. By extension, we can readily accept that production staff, presenters, guests, and even the scenery itself must have come into the studio through doors that almost certainly do not figure in the designer's creation. The set is understood to be purely decorative, not part of an illusion of reality. Yet viewers would probably object to a similar revelation in a dramatic production—enough so, in some cases, to engender dislike for the drama itself.[55] Any reminder that we are watching a fiction may leave us feeling cheated: it smacks of either incompetence or perversity on the part of the program-makers.

Curiously, audiences for one kind of dramatic entertainment are not averse to being reminded of the presence of things external to the diegesis. When watching a situation comedy, viewers accept that there was a studio audience present at the recording, for all that we only hear that audience's laughter and never actually see them or the space that they occupy. Unpopular though the laugh track may be with some, it is for better or worse a convention of the sitcom.

Viewers will accept as normal those moments when an actor is obliged to pause to accommodate a long or loud burst of hilarity, while such interruptions in the flow of any other kind of drama would be very disturbing. For the duration of an episode of a sitcom, viewers are implicitly invited to imagine themselves as members of a live audience in a theater.

In a rather perverse way, the viewer's enforced affiliation with the sitcom studio audience negates the fact that television, as a medium, inherently demands a high degree of participation. They need no extra encouragement to involve themselves in what they see: the nature of television demands it. As Marshall McLuhan pointed out, low-definition television images, rather like cartoons, provide such limited visual information (compared with films) that spectators are obliged to imaginatively complete what they see.[56]

GET INVOLVED: THE TELEVISION SERIES AS A "COOL" FORM

McLuhan famously divided media into the hot and the cool, the latter being those that require a greater measure of completion by the audience. Having defined television as essentially cool (where film, radio, and the printed word are hot because they "extend one single sense in 'high definition'"),[57] McLuhan went one stage further and indicated that a distinction could be made between different kinds of programs within television—again in terms of hot and cool. By way of example, he contrasted the "broadcast of a symphony performance with a broadcast of a symphony rehearsal," commenting apropos the latter that it was particularly suited to the special properties of television. For McLuhan, "a cool medium like TV, when really used, demands this involvement in process."[58] His ideas can usefully be applied to the series as a form and, by extension, to the role played by design imagery within the series.

Among the various forms of screen drama, the series is, in McLuhan's terms, probably the "coolest." The single play and the serial (e.g., the adaptation of a classic novel) are much "hotter" because both are conceived as "complete packages"—their narratives are closed and finite.[59] Drama series and soap operas are open-ended and, in theory, eternal. Although a series must contain elements of continuity, it need not present a unified, ongoing narrative and may consist of nothing more than a sequence of disparate stories linked only by the presence of regular characters. In other words, the series as a form, like the television medium itself, is elliptical, and it is up to viewers to fill in the lacunae—to work with their imagination in the interstices of the narrative.

Of course, the series has certainly not achieved preeminence as a dramatic form for any reasons as idealized as its "truth to medium." The single play has been eclipsed in Britain (as in the U.S.) for essentially commercial reasons: neither the independent companies nor the increasingly accountable BBC could ignore pressure consistently to win loyal (and large) audiences. Single plays, even when broadcast regularly under an overall title such as "Armchair Theatre," simply cannot generate allegiance in the same way as a successful series—even one that is only erratically produced, such as *Inspector Morse* (Central TV, 1987–2000).[60]

What distinguishes an effective series is, in essence, its formula. Ongoing "story arcs" aside, the individual episodes of most series are variations on a theme.[61] Whether character-driven or action-driven (the former being more usual in the financially constricted sphere of television drama), all series furnish predictable entertainment, which guarantees audience loyalty. The interest for the spectator arises from seeing how the changing elements, which need be no more than superficially varied, are played off against the constant.

Although formulaic, the television series offers greater opportunities for experimentation than any other form of drama, by virtue of the fact that it is open-ended and inherently loose-knit. Once the narrative set-up has been established, the relations between the component elements can be altered in all manner of ways. Narrative conventions can be adopted and put aside; the focus can shift from character to character; the basic premise can even be modified and subverted.[62] For the purposes of this study, the most important consideration is that the series allows aspects like design not only to vary in their interplay with other elements but also, crucially, to take on a defining role.

One qualification: The potency of design in a television series is highest in dramas that use stylized imagery. In television, commonplace imagery is rendered even less engaging than in film. This is not to suggest that less skill is involved in designing for drama with a prosaic, modern-day setting; designers and other creative personnel certainly do not endorse such an idea.[63] However, the fact remains that the television design imagery most likely to be consciously appreciated by the viewer is that which is strikingly stylized, in the strict sense of something that is represented in a conventionalizing, non-realistic manner.

In practice, most series offer relatively little scope for imagery that is strongly antinatural. The use of extreme stylization and abstract forms for scenic design has been as sparse in British television drama as it has been widespread in the live theater since the innovations of Granville Barker and Edward Gordon Craig in the early twentieth century.[64] Nor is stylized dress any more common, except in sci-fi and fantasy programs. Even in sitcoms, where a humorous premise might seem to allow a more permissive approach, the aspiration to the "reality effect," as the Affrons call it, has been well-nigh universal except in the case of series such as *The Young Ones* deliberately conceived so as to poke fun at the genre.[65] Barsacq's dictum that "one of the fundamental requirements of the cinema" is to "give the impression of having photographed real objects" has generally speaking been obeyed in mainstream television drama, too.[66] It is the province of the "arty"—and therefore usually the one-off play—to depart radically from naturalism.[67]

Our three subject series, *The Avengers, The Prisoner,* and *Doctor Who,* are among the few popular television dramas in Britain that have made extensive use of stylized design. These series were chosen because the character of each was heavily conditioned by its design imagery, and in two of the three cases design also played a crucial role in reshaping the conceptual framework of the series.

Because the series form is not only open-ended but inherently mutable, a study of the role of design in a series must take account of this adaptability. It is not, in our view, useful to focus narrowly on the way in which design "serves" the miniature narratives that constitute individual episodes. To do so would in effect be to reduce design for television to a poor man's version of design for film, and to belie the distinctiveness of small-screen entertainment. Certain designs in a television series acquire a cumulative significance; certain others stand out because of the way they deviate from the internal conventions of the series; and so on. Because these accretive meanings are the main focus of attention in the following case studies, there is very little shot-by-shot analysis of material from individual episodes. Within a series, we will argue, design not only multiplies meanings around a particular narrative conceit, but can also reflect the fact that the program as a whole has been steered away from its original narrative, aesthetic, and ideological premise.

What unites our three-subject series is their use of antinaturalistic design in escapist drama. Otherwise, they have little in common except their cult status. *The Avengers* and *The Prisoner* were both nominally espionage-related dramas, and both deconstruct the spy genre, though in different ways and with different intentions. And while they also incorporated sci-fi elements —both, for example, featured strange robotic menaces—this hardly links them with *Doctor Who*, which was a thoroughgoing fantasy.

The three series also differ in how far they strayed from the standards of their genres. *The Prisoner* was aggressively out of the ordinary. *The Avengers* was a little less so: there were other espionage spoofs in the 1960s, including films such as *Our Man Flint* (1966) and the U.S. television series *The Man From U.N.C.L.E.* (NBC 1964–1968). Yet these were cruder and less multifaceted, and they certainly did not espouse the range of discursive conceits used by designers for *The Avengers*.

Doctor Who bears a superficial resemblance to other sci-fi/fantasies in its use of way-out imagery. However, the series sometimes warped its own reality with design imagery that was uncompromisingly antinatural. This was possible because of the bizarre premise of *Doctor Who*, which generously accommodated the anomalous. Although not politically charged or consistently satirical like *The Prisoner* and *The Avengers*, *Doctor Who* resembled and, indeed, outstripped them in the off-kilter nature of its underlying conception.

The common thread that unites these three programs is the emphasis they gave to stylized imagery strikingly juxtaposed with realistic design. And because the three series unfolded quite differently, each offers a unique opportunity to explore various kinds of interactions between design imagery and the developing, cumulative narrative of a series.

*Stylishness and
the Sense of Play
in Design for
The Avengers*

C
H
A
P
T
AGENTS E **EXTRAORDINARY**
R

T
W
O

THE AVENGERS AND THE SIXTIES

Of the three series with which our book is principally concerned, *The Avengers* was unquestionably the most successful in its heyday. The series developed a huge international following during its run in the 1960s, and it has continued to enjoy wide acceptance and recognition among television audiences worldwide. Like a variety of other products of British popular culture from the period—albums such as the Beatles' *Revolver* and *Sergeant Pepper's Lonely Hearts Club Band,* images of Twiggy, Mary Quant's "Chelsea Girl," the boutiques of Carnaby Street, and so on— *The Avengers* has become a prime signifier for the Sixties. Indicative of the ongoing potency of the series as emblematic of the Sixties is that a large portrait of Emma Peel, the *Avengers* superwoman played by Diana Rigg, adorns the cover of *Windows on the Sixties,* a recent collection of essays on eight "key texts of media and culture" from the period.[1] The identification of *The Avengers* as quintessentially "of the Sixties" is justified in terms of simple chronology: The production history of the series spanned the decade, the first episode being recorded in 1960 and the last in 1969.[2]

Like any decade-spanning phenomenon, *The Avengers* was not homogeneous. Compare an early episode, "The Frighteners," with the last to be made, "Bizarre."[3] Except for the presence of special agent John Steed in both, the two productions have virtually nothing in common. Early *Avengers* episodes were shot in black and white and recorded live (i.e., continuously, with the scenes performed in broadcast order, since the editing of videotape was still impracticable in 1960). From 1964 on, the series was shot on film by Independent Artists, and from 1967 it was filmed in color.[4] The difference in organization and tone between early and late episodes is even more striking. Partly because of its rapidly mounted, "live" character, "The Frighteners" has an immediacy, an almost improvised feel not present in "Bizarre." The latter resembles a slickly constructed mini-feature film, its dialogue impeccably delivered and its concluding set piece (a kind of "Keystone Kops" chase) as polished in realization as it was obviously long-rehearsed.

Yet notwithstanding its meticulous craftsmanship, "Bizarre" flaunts its artifice in a way that the earlier, more rudely constructed episode emphatically does not. A tale of commercial terrorism in London's demimonde, "The Frighteners," though using low-key lighting and such rhetorical devices as extreme close-ups, portrays its subject in a way that is clearly meant to be realistic. "Bizarre," on the other hand, tells the highly improbable tale of criminals' faking their own deaths and escaping to a luxurious haven beneath the "Happy Valley" cemetery.[5] As if the silliness of the plot were not enough, the narrative presentation—accelerated-motion shots for the final chase and a cemetery set knee-deep in knowingly schmaltzy sentiment—throws the zany humor into even stronger relief.

The development of British cinema in the 1960s was, roughly speaking, also marked by an overall shift away from social realism towards experimentation, a shift that bespeaks anything but homogeneity.[6] "The Frighteners" hardly mimics the uncompromising idiom of such social-realist films as *The Loneliness of the Long Distance Runner* (Tony Richardson, 1962), and "Bizarre" is amiably undemanding in comparison with surreal fantasies such as Richard Lester's *The Bed Sitting Room* (1969).[7] Nevertheless, the fact that a single series could run the gamut of realism and fantasy within the space of ten years shows how rapidly tastes can shift and how little fashions respect the arbitrary demarcations of our decade-oriented calendrical system.

The massive aesthetic pendulum-swing in *The Avengers* also reflects the inherent flexibility of the drama series as a form. A series can be gradually reshaped during the course of a single season, and in the gap between seasons major renovation can take place without any real danger of alienating viewers. The producers of *The Avengers* regularly availed themselves of these opportunities for change.[8]

Costume design furnished the most obviously avant-garde element in *The Avengers,* especially the startlingly "liberated" clothing worn by the main female protagonists. However, once Honor Blackman's leather fighting suits set a precedent for daring costume effects (fig. 2.1)—which helped make *The Avengers* the most talked-about series on British television—the very success of this image limited the possibilities for further invention. Blackman was the earliest superheroine in *The Avengers.* So potent was her leather-clad image that her successor, Diana Rigg, was at first also obliged to adopt it.[9] Blackman's original look even affected expectations of what Rigg's successor, Linda Thorson, would wear as the third *Avengers* girl, Tara King: though the leather was gone, the tomboyish bodysuits remained.

Experimentation with clothing in *The Avengers* peaked early, for the highly idiosyncratic, studiedly old-fashioned style of clothing worn by the male lead, Patrick Macnee, was fixed before the establishment of Honor Blackman's leather-clad look. Scenic design took a while to catch up with costume, not reaching the height of its flamboyance until the late 1960s. Nevertheless, set design was one of the most progressive elements in *The Avengers,* regularly marking the stages on the way towards the full-blooded antinaturalism that the program ultimately embraced. Between 1965 and 1969, production designers Harry Pottle, Wilfred Shingleton, and Robert Jones contributed decisively to the changing ethos of the series, just as predecessors such as Patrick Downing had helped to define *The Avengers* as a stylistically distinctive and "off-the-wall" show during its second and third seasons.[10]

The gradual shift of design idiom in *The Avengers,* from the realist beginnings to the wacky conclusion, would make for an engaging full-length analysis. However, our focus here is mostly on two aspects of design for the series during the years when it was produced by the film company Independent Artists (1964–1969): first, the distinctive costume image created for John Steed, the hero played by Patrick Macnee; second, scenic design during the fourth season (1965–1966).

The fact that such luminaries of the fashion world as Hardy Amies and

FIGURE 2.1. *Patrick Macnee as Steed and Honor Blackman as Catherine Gale in* The Avengers. *Costumes designed by Audrey Liddle.* © *Canal + Image UK Ltd.*

Pierre Cardin designed outfits for Steed has been discussed elsewhere;[11] our concern is much more with Macnee's role in devising and developing his character's wardrobe. No one has hitherto dealt fully with the vicissitudes of the Steed image or with its subtleties. Far less attention has been given to the impact that Steed's appearance had on the character of *The Avengers* as a whole. As we will show, the ramifications of Steed's idiosyncratic style

38
AGENTS EXTRAORDINARY
39

were complex, and its effect upon the overall character of the series cumulative: Steed's dress and manners set the tone for the pointed class values of the program and, even more crucially, provided a nice foil to the radically novel clothing of his female accomplices.

"*Avengers* style" has traditionally been embodied in the mod/trad duality of the clothing worn by Steed and his female companions and the overtones of masquerade and gender-bending in their costumes; this style expressed the tensions that lie at the heart of *The Avengers*. In France, the series was called *Chapeau Melon et Bottes de Cuir (Bowler Hat and Leather Boots)*, acknowledging that Steed's hat and Mrs. Peel's footwear could serve as a distillation of the peculiar identity of the series. Early publicity for the movie version of *The Avengers* (Jeremiah Chechik, 1998) consisted almost entirely of stills that reaffirmed the mod/trad contrast between Steed and Mrs. Peel (as Steed always addressed her, with slyly overstated propriety). In these photographs, the new Steed and Mrs. Peel stand side by side against a neutral background, very much as the originals had done in the opening title sequence of the 1967–1968 season.[12]

Yet even if Steed's bowler and Mrs. Peel's boots—or indeed, as we will argue below, the bowler alone—could represent the stylistic distinctiveness of *The Avengers*, the principal characters' costumes were certainly not the be-all and end-all of the designers' visual originality. Toby Miller has suggested that the wide appeal of the show was based on a "combination of exaggerated civility, casual violence and sexual subtlety, all accomplished on a spectrum of style."[13] The breadth of this spectrum was given visual expression by scenic designers whose work reflected the whole gamut of narrative conventions quoted and parodied in the scripts. The subtlest and most innovative of these designers was Harry Pottle, art director for the fourth season (1965–1966). Pottle created a flexible idiom in which generic conventions as diverse as gothic horror and drawing-room comedy could appear to be natural bedfellows. This synthesis of widely divergent effects was unprecedented not only in *The Avengers* but in British television at large; Pottle's work paved the way for the brashly eccentric settings created by Robert Jones in many episodes of the following two seasons. Pottle's images were also distinguished by the way in which they interacted with the dialogue: some straightforwardly supported the mood, while others counterposed or even contradicted it. In fact, his brand of dry wit, very much like that of principal writers Brian Clemens and Philip Levene, was characterized by provocative and knowing postmodern irony.

The idea that *The Avengers* possessed style or stylishness is central to perceptions of the program. Publicity for the 1998 movie proclaimed that agents John Steed and Emma Peel were "Saving the World in Style."[14] Stylishness is also a recurrent theme in Toby Miller's critical study of *The Avengers*, raised by the author and by the enthusiasts whose views he cites.[15] The principal fan-chronicler of the series, Dave Rogers, observed that "for sheer unabashed style there has never been another program quite like it."[16] Tempting as it is to add more voices to the chorus, we cannot simply celebrate *The Avengers* as preeminently "stylish" without further qualifying the claim.

Stylishness exists only in the eye of the beholder as a rather nebulous value judgment: it defines nothing in itself. This is not to underrate the respect that the idea of stylishness can command in metropolitan society. Fashion is entirely concerned with defining and redefining stylishness, and many choose clothing and furnishings based on a notion of what is stylish.

For the work of costume or scenic designers in television, however, the term "stylish" has little usefulness, even as an accolade. For example, a designer working on a contemporary drama like *EastEnders*, which is set in the depressed inner city locale of Walford, is unlikely to produce imagery that could be called "stylish" in the generally accepted sense of the word. Indeed, few television dramas overtly set out to be stylish, courting praise in those terms alone. Yet there is often what might be termed a stylish approach, a stylish vision, underlying almost any kind of design for screen entertainment. By this reckoning, therefore, the term should not be glibly used to set the visual content of one program above that of another: the ugliest or most apparently unstyled sets and the least striking costumes may, in reality, have been subtly crafted by a very "stylish" designer.

If there is little virtue in describing design work for *The Avengers* as stylish, it does seem genuinely meaningful to claim that the series was *about* stylishness — or rather about preoccupation with notions of high style — in a way that few other television programs or films have been. Of course, the detective-*cum*-counterespionage premise of *The Avengers* did not place fashion and lifestyle in the narrative forefront to the same extent as, say, the Audrey Hepburn vehicles *Funny Face* (Stanley Donen, 1957) and *Sabrina* (Billy Wilder, 1954)[17] or, for that matter, the satirical comedy series *Absolutely Fabulous* (BBC TV, 1992–).

Nevertheless, as Kingsley Amis once nicely observed, there is a palpable sense that Steed and his partner of the moment were "inspired amateurs who knock off a couple of world-wide conspiracies in the intervals of choosing their spring wardrobe"—the latter being an altogether more demanding and significant activity.[18] The emphasis in the series, especially after the arrival of Diana Rigg as Emma Peel, was more on the sangfroid with which the Avengers generally dispatched their opponents than on the narrative thrust of the actual conflicts. The pre-title sequence used in America for the 1965–1966 season clearly establishes the mood of unruffled epicureanism: John Steed and Mrs. Peel, confronted with the corpse of a man in waiter's clothing, take no interest in the body, but concentrate instead on opening and sampling the bottle of champagne that the dead man had been carrying.[19]

If *The Avengers* was focused upon stylishness, then, conversely, stylishness—in mid-1960s Britain, at least—was to no small extent focused upon *The Avengers*. In this respect, the series is without precedent or real successor in the history of television. The "Avengerwear" credited to Frederick Starke, a collection of what might be termed "brutalist" clothing designed for Honor Blackman in her role as Catherine Gale, was given its own press launch in 1963.[20] Two years later, the wardrobe created by John Bates for Emma Peel was marketed by Bates' fashion house, Jean Varon.[21]

The series also influenced the design of other products.[22] Some, like a set of wristwatches based on those worn by Diana Rigg in the series, were specifically created as *Avengers* merchandise.[23] In other cases, props specially made for the series were imitated by unlicensed manufacturers. For example, in "What the Butler Saw" (1966), a set of lamp stands shaped like Minoan bulls were created to adorn the bachelor pad of an amorous air force officer. Within six months of the broadcast, copies of the design had, according to one of Pottle's draftsmen, been marketed by a London department store: the image, or its overtones of virility and eroticism, was evidently considered highly saleable.[24]

However, it is not, of course, simply because of its widespread impact on the contemporary scene that we have chosen to devote a chapter of our study to *The Avengers*, nor, for that matter, because the program is now universally perceived as the epitome of elegance and sophistication. If stylishness was the central concern of *The Avengers*, what made the series outstanding in design terms was its bold and witty use of stylization. In view of the general fetish for naturalism, *The Avengers* maintained a level of studied artifice that was quite extraordinary, given that the series was a mainstream, prime-time drama in both Britain and the United States.[25]

DESIGN AND THE POSTMODERN IN *THE AVENGERS*

At its most provocative, *The Avengers* deliberately undermined the reality of its own diegesis. The most extreme example of this occurs in "Epic" (1967), in which a crazed film director, Z. Z. von Schnerk, forces Emma Peel to take the central role in a film about herself.[26] In the tag scene,[27] she and Steed are seen relaxing in what appears to be her apartment, until she kicks down one of the walls, revealing that it is in fact one of von Schnerk's sets. The humor is double-edged: while exploiting the central conceit of the "play within a play," the sequence also forced viewers to confront the fact that they were watching a contrived dramatic production. In other words, the very essence of escapist entertainment was momentarily compromised.

While the wit embodied in the closing scene of "Epic" is palpably "deconstructive," most of the humor expressed in *The Avengers*' imagery is best described with reference to a related cultural outlook—postmodernism.[28] We will, in fact, use the epithet postmodern a good deal in this chapter. It should therefore be registered at once that the term is highly problematic and needs some elucidation. If the word "stylish" is of questionable value because it is used categorically without actually meaning very much, then "postmodern" is ambiguous for precisely the opposite reason—it is a lexicographer's nightmare, being massively overburdened with irreconcilable meanings. The only wholehearted consensus among scholars and critics who have sought to characterize and define the "postmodern" is the tacit acknowledgment that the existence of such a term is needful. In other words, thinkers seem to be in broad agreement that there is a discernible phenomenon, a "something" that has superseded or transformed modernism, the cultural movement that supposedly held sway as an ideal from, roughly, the first to the sixth decade of the twentieth century.[29]

That the postmodern should have such a tortuous etymology and be so uncertain in its parameters is curiously appropriate, for many of the thinkers who have used the term have related it either to eclecticism in aesthetic taste, or to indecisiveness about goals and trajectories, or to the cancerous multiplication of data, stimuli, and choice in the information age. Insofar as there is intrinsic meaning in postmodernism, therefore, it may be said to be that it describes a culture steeped—not to say bogged down—in plurality.

For all that the term did not enter common usage until the early 1970s, the application of the word "postmodern" to cultural trends of the 1960s is now thoroughly sanctioned by precedent.[30] However, this is not our justification for using the term in relation to *The Avengers*. Nor, for that matter, are we merely taking our cue from Toby Miller, who devoted one whole chapter of his book on *The Avengers* to "The Postmodern" in the series. Our choice is specifically governed by the fact that design in *The Avengers* was characterized by what the architectural historian Charles Jencks has termed the "double-coding" and "multiple-coding" properties of postmodernism.[31] In Jencks' formulation, postmodernism is an attitude of mind that allows for different, often opposing values and meanings to be "encoded" into a single work of art. The important point, however, is that these divergent or contradictory principles are allowed to coexist within the given work without there being any resolution of the tensions between them.[32] This notion of double or multiple coding is extremely apt for the imagery in *The Avengers,* which, for example, constantly juxtaposes the progressive with the conservative, managing to celebrate and mock both of them at once.

Also germane to *The Avengers* is the inherently parodic character that many people have recognized in postmodernism. Because the postmodern outlook is one that delights in juggling and juxtaposing different paradigms, it is almost inevitable that the postmodern mindset should have a strong inclination towards burlesque. In order to play with two or more divergent ideas in an open-ended way, one has to maintain a large measure of detachment from both; and detachment, in turn, is very readily attended by the ironic and parodic. Among commentators on the subject, Umberto Eco has been especially attentive to the particular tenor of postmodern irony. He characterized this irony by the use of a metaphor which, though oft quoted, is worth repeating again here, because it seems so apposite to *The Avengers* that it might almost be extrapolated from one of the show's scripts.

I think of the postmodern attitude as that of a man who loves a very cultivated woman and knows he cannot say to her, "I love you madly," because he knows that she knows (and that she knows that he knows) that these words have already been written by Barbara Cartland. Still, there is a solution. He can say, "As Barbara Cartland would put it, I love you madly." At this point, having avoided false innocence, having said clearly that it is no longer possible to speak innocently, he will nevertheless have said what he wanted to say to the woman: that he loves her, but he loves her in an age of lost innocence. Neither of the two speakers will feel innocent, both will have accepted the challenge of the past, of the already said, which cannot be eliminated; both will consciously and with pleasure play the game of irony.[33]

Steed and his companions personify just this kind of ironic aloofness. Loss of cool, for them, is quite clearly a fate worse than death. Conversational ease and relaxed grace are maintained even in the most dangerous situation and in face of the deadliest opponent. Moreover, in maintaining this studied calm, bordering on ennui, Steed and Mrs. Peel not only convey that they have seen it all before, but seem to acknowledge tacitly that the audience has *also* seen it all before. What Eco describes as "the challenge of the past" was present in *The Avengers* in that the series always embraced cliché, stereotype, and nostalgia as warmly as a bad B movie, but did so with infinite knowing. *The Avengers* was never in any danger of becoming hackneyed in itself, for the simple reason that it dined on platitudes. The conventions of a certain genre might be exploited for all or part of a given script, but at the same time generic clichés would always be adroitly lampooned and deconstructed. No particular genre was ever seriously or consistently espoused in the series. In the context of *The Avengers,* one cannot really speak of the genres of the macabre, the thriller, science fiction, and so on: one has to envisage these terms placed in the inverted commas that denote irony or sarcasm.

Much of what can most obviously be identified as postmodern in *The Avengers* is, of course, incorporated into the scripts. What was exceptional about the series, however, was the extent to which design played an active and independent role in what Eco calls "the game of irony." Designers' activities were not confined to underscoring the parodic elements in the narrative by means of, say, a particular choice of costume for Steed and his partner or by the use of humorous exaggeration in the décor of a set. Design also frequently embodied anomalies, ambivalences, and unexpected juxtapositions not inspired directly by the script, which therefore made their own peculiar kind of mental demand on the viewer.

The best example of this is the blurring of gender boundaries, or at least the upsetting of gender norms, in the clothing of Steed and his first two female partners. Little or no reference was made in the scripts to their singular modes of dress. Yet the costumes suggested some fairly obvious paradoxes. "I was the woman and she was the man," Patrick Macnee once remarked of Honor Blackman's character, Cathy Gale.[34] Indeed, the typical dress of Steed and Mrs. Gale lends some credence to this (see fig. 2.1). Her celebrated leather bodysuits were "butch" in the same measure that Steed's more foppish garb was "pansy." However, even the kinkiness of these images—enhanced, of course, by their juxtaposition—was misleading. For all her physical prowess and scientific detachment, Mrs. Gale was typically feminine in her compassion, while the often harsh and relentless Steed was definitely not as ineffectual and softly effeminate as his clothing might suggest.

THE STEED IMAGE

In the pages that follow, we pursue half of the mod/trad dichotomy by looking at the sartorial image of John Steed, which became enormously influential both on enduring perceptions of *The Avengers* and, rather more remarkably, on the character of the series itself. This last point is of great importance to the overarching arguments of our book, concerned as this study is with the expressive power of design and with the way that its meanings can hive off from the original narrative premise of a television series. The Steed image proves that a design component can establish itself not just as a media icon but also as a prime transforming force within the overall stylistic development of the series itself.

The second aspect of the Steed image that we will explore is its contribution to the studiedly ambivalent sexual identity of the character. We have already mentioned that Steed's playfully dandified sartorial style was strongly at odds with both the "tough" modes affected by his female accomplices and the harsher aspects of his own persona. To understand better the "multiple-coding" of the image, we will examine closely the way in which Steed's suave and individualistic attire related to contemporary trends in men's fashion. His dress provides an interesting reflection (or perhaps it would be more accurate to say "refraction") of the way in which gender norms were being upset by cultural sea changes in the mid-to-late 1960s. Consideration of this issue will lead us, in conclusion, to argue that there is a strongly "postmodern" flavor to the Steed image.

First, a short outline of the internal history of the Steed image—its evolution, its rationale, and its vicissitudes. The story of the emergence of "Steed style" has been oft told in both scholarly and appreciative literature on *The Avengers* and also in the memoirs of Patrick Macnee, who played the character. Macnee was intimately involved in the shaping of Steed's style, but he has acknowledged that designing the costumes was a collaborative effort, in the first instance with wardrobe supervisor Audrey Liddle: "I didn't really design them, of course, I just said how I'd like this, how I'd like that, and the wardrobe people [Liddle and Head of Wardrobe Department at ABC, Ambren Garland] passed my ideas along to the tailor." [35]

The impetus to create the classic Steed image actually came from Sydney Newman, the Head of Drama at ABC TV who devised *The Avengers*. Early in production of the first season, Newman suggested to Patrick Macnee that he abandon the trench coated, gumshoe image that he had so far shared with his costar, Ian Hendry. [36] Newman felt that Steed, the amoral, ruthless, yet charming counterweight to Hendry's hero, should dress in a more flamboyant manner. Macnee, together with Audrey Liddle and his tailors, devised a striking new image that cleverly belied the more inhuman aspects of the character:

I thought of Regency days—the most flamboyant, sartorially, for men—and imagined Steed in waisted jackets and embroidered waistcoats. Steed I was stuck with as a name and it stayed. Underneath he was steel. Outwardly he was charming and vain and representative, I suppose, of the kind of Englishman who is more valued abroad. The point about Steed was that he led a fantasy life—a hero dressed and accoutred like a junior cabinet minister. An Old Etonian whose most lethal weapon was the hallmark of the English gentleman—a furled umbrella. [37]

Over the next four years, working with Liddle (and later with Frances Bolwell and Jackie Jackson) and his cutter at Bailey and Weatherill of Regent Street, Mr. James, Macnee took Steed's foppery to ever greater lengths. [38] He wore trilby hats and curly-brim bowlers; silk shirts, invariably with spread collars; Chelsea boots in patent leather and suede; and an array of ever more distinctive sports jackets and suits. Although the generally close-fitting styles of his clothes were consonant with 1960s fashions, Macnee's outfits had a number of peculiarities that subtly set him apart even from the senior civil servants and wealthy industrialists with whom Steed mixed. All these refinements were redolent of the Regency period from which Macnee took his inspiration. Jackets were rather long and markedly waisted, while vests were almost always straight-cut across the bottom; in each case, the allusion to early-nineteenth-century modes was unmistakable. Other echoes of the period included covered buttons, braiding, elasticated trouser bottoms, and revers on the jacket cuffs (see fig. 2.1).

The distillation of the Steed style was fully accomplished in the first series of *The Avengers* shot on film, production of which began in May 1965. Macnee's subtle variations on conventional gentlemen's attire were also most adventurous during this season. For example, shooting on film meant more location work out of town, and Macnee devised appropriate accoutrements for these excursions, becoming the huntin', shootin', and fishin' man of rural pursuits.[39] Hunting overtones were especially strong in his new country outfit, which consisted of a rust-colored jacket, buff trousers, and a checkered stock. For headgear, Patrick Macnee adopted a unique flat-topped hard felt, apparently of his own design, which hovered in shape between bowler and the top hat still sometimes worn with hunting pinks. A long cane replaced his umbrella.

In his more characteristic guise as the man about town, Steed's formal dress also underwent evolution in the first filmed season of *The Avengers*. This latest development produced what was to become, in effect, the archetypal Steed image. What most obviously distinguished his two new suits was that each had a velvet collar, a feature more usually associated with gentlemen's overcoats and riding coats (fig. 2.2). According to Macnee, at least part of the reason for this was that it contributed to the overall effect of supple contouring:

I like the idea of velvet for the collars, it helps mould and complement the suits. There are no breast pockets and only one button to give the best moulding to the chest. Plus a deliberately low waist, to give the effect of simplicity, but with an individual style.[40]

Overt preoccupation with Steed's clothing within the individual episode narratives reached its height at this time. Steed was often shown finishing dressing or beginning to undress. In "Dial a Deadly Number," for example, Steed receives a female visitor while in the middle of his morning routine: the fact that he has not yet put on his waistcoat allows her to exchange a bomb for his pocket watch. In "The Cybernauts" Steed calls at his flat between two undercover operations because he is going to impersonate a journalist. When Mrs. Peel enters, he is already in the process of changing into an outfit with "a literary sheen." In the tag scene of "The Murder Market," he is seen changing suit and tie in the back of a limousine, this time for no readily discernible reason. The apogee of this dressing-and-grooming

FIGURE 2.2. *Steed style: Patrick Macnee models his new lovat green suit with matching bowler in a publicity shot for the fourth season of* **The Avengers.** *Costume designed by Patrick Macnee.* © *Canal + Image UK Ltd.*

theme occurs in "Two's a Crowd," in which Steed adopts the guise of a shady male model, Gordon Webster, who is in turn called upon by Russian spies to impersonate Steed. The contorted scenario allows for plenty of detailed discussion about the niceties of Steed's personal habits and etiquette.

Even when the main action is not concerned with Steed's grooming, the viewer's attention is often specifically directed to his clothes. In an early scene of "Dial a Deadly Number," a supercilious banker tells Steed that the financial institution he represents still judges creditworthiness by the color of a man's socks. The shot of the two men conversing cuts to a close-up of Steed's lower half, as he gently hitches up one trouser leg to reveal suitably staid black hosiery; the camera then pans up to show his quizzical expression.

In 1966, Steed's tailoring was taken up by the world of haute couture. For the first color series, ABC TV commissioned Pierre Cardin, whose star was in the ascendant throughout Europe at this time, to design the principal items in Macnee's wardrobe.[41] After 1967, suits in the mode popularized by Cardin, with high-fastening, double-breasted jackets and "pencil-line" trousers cut straight from knee to ankle, were promulgated in Britain by Savile Row tailors and department stores alike—and, interestingly, the style was referred to as "Edwardian."[42] Macnee and others had also used this word to describe Steed's style of dress. Macnee, voted one of the Ten Best-Dressed Men in the World in 1963,[43] was now modeling Cardin's clothes in a prime-time series shown in both Britain and America. This can only have helped the designer's growing reputation. For Macnee, on the other hand, it was neither a financial success (he was persuaded not to sign with Cardin for the marketing of a "Steed" line)[44] nor an enhancement of his performance. In fact, Cardin's designs were a travesty of the Steed style and all but undermined the character's credibility.

At best, Cardin paid faint lip service to the established Steed idiom in his designs for Patrick Macnee. A charitable explanation for this, put forward by Anthony Powell, the costume designer on the 1998 *Avengers* movie, is that Cardin, as a Frenchman, could not help but dress Steed in "what the French imagined was the British gentleman's style," the result being, in Powell's view, "totally wrong."[45] A more cynical assessment would be that Cardin's approach was wholly self-serving and that Steed was shaped to the Cardin image, not vice versa.

Although the waisted line of Macnee's lounge coats and the straight-cut vests were retained, most other distinctive features of Steed's earlier outfits were discarded. Cardin's innovations, most notably the introduction of double-breasted jackets, invariably produced an effect that was at odds with what had gone before. Suit fabrics became coarser and more brashly patterned; straight-cut trousers replaced peg tops; and Macnee's neatly geometric Windsor-knotted ties often gave way to showy, bulky ascots. Most discordantly of all, the Steed hallmark of low-fastening jackets, generally with a single button and sans breast pocket, was ignored by Cardin: the new lounge coats and sports jackets were invariably high-cut with three buttons and usually with a breast pocket. In short, Cardin's style was squared-off where Macnee's had been streamlined, and the new outfits had the unfortunate effect of emphasizing the actor's tendency to plumpness.

As if the new outfits themselves were not enough of an insult to Macnee's vision of Steed, the coup de grâce was that, as a Cardin clotheshorse, the actor was now obliged to wear formal garb throughout the whole of each episode, even when Steed was supposedly relaxing in his flat. Steed's sensitivity to the etiquette of dress—a prime element of his old-world gentlemanliness—was overturned at a stroke. In previous seasons, when he was off duty in his apartment, or in circumstances that demanded informality, Steed was typically seen wearing a black polo shirt or turtleneck sweater, sometimes with a chunky cardigan (see fig. 2.16). Now, seated on his scarlet Chesterfield settee wearing a loudly over-checked, brass-buttoned Norfolk jacket, cream shirt, and spotted ascot, the avowedly overweight Macnee looked not merely effete but—to use an expressive piece of British slang "poncey."

The association with Cardin was relatively brief. In what turned out to be the final season of *The Avengers,* broadcast in 1969, Macnee abruptly abandoned the Cardin wardrobe and restored the style that was proper and peculiar to his screen character. Although the series was by this time more distant from day-to-day normality than ever, Macnee even returned to the traditional practice of dressing informally for scenes with a domestic setting—though his new leisure wear was rather brasher and more "youthful" than before.[46] Indeed, for all that it provided a return to the Steed image, the final season ushered in a number of significant changes to the character's status that deprived both him and the series of their subtlety.

If *The Avengers* lost some of its finesse during its last season on the air, it lost none of its playful daring. However, by 1976 when it was resurrected as *The New Avengers,* its ludic quality, which Steed's sartorial image in many ways epitomized, was gone. Even the Steed image itself was briefly threatened, as Macnee met with some difficulties acquiring an appropriate wardrobe for his reprise of the role. His outfitters tried to persuade him to adopt the fashions of the mid-1970s,[47] but since these were diametrically opposed to the established Steed style, the actor stalwartly resisted. As a result, the dapper Macnee was a sartorial anachronism and stood in the strongest possible contrast to one of his costars. Gareth Hunt, who played Steed's youth-

FIGURE 2.3. *Best of three?: Patrick Macnee as Steed, with Joanna Lumley as Purdey and Gareth Hunt as Gambit. Macnee's and Hunt's clothing by Gieves; Lumley's outfit by Catherine Buckley. Publicity photograph for* **The New Avengers** *(IDTV/Avengers, 1976). © Canal + Image UK Ltd.*

ful sidekick, Mike Gambit, wore the loud modes of the moment: broad-shouldered and wide-lapelled jackets, kipper ties, and flared slacks, or safari outfits (fig. 2.3).

The fastidious Steed, however, remained true to form in peg-top trousers and waisted jackets with lapels almost as reticently narrow as those on his 1960s outfits. He also retained his bowler hat and furled umbrella, which placed him in a social minority that was by then verging on extinction: at that date, few men wore hats at all, and only the truest of true-blue traditionalists wore bowlers. Yet by this point, it would have been virtually impossible for Steed to appear without these accoutrements: they had become his "trademark."

Macnee's small victory over a transient fad in the 1970s may seem to be of no more than anecdotal interest, but this is far from the case. The preservation of his image served to emphasize that Steed had become a media icon: he had become "the man in the bowler hat."[48] This was, in fact, the end of a process whereby Steed's style gained ever greater influence over the total character of *The Avengers*.

Even today, John Steed's bowler and brolly constitute one of the best-known and most evocative images ever to emerge from a television series. Not only can these items "stand in" for Steed, but to a great extent they do the same for *The Avengers*. Men's hats and accessories, in fact, have often played what might be termed synecdochic or metonymic roles in the mass media since the end of the nineteenth century. The most obvious example is Sherlock Holmes' deerstalker cap and calabash pipe, which can conjure up the character—and, indeed, the whole genre of British detective fiction—without any other referent; indeed, it is hard to see a deerstalker in any context without thinking of Holmes.

Yet Conan Doyle's detective is not at all the same kind of fictional character as Steed, for the latter was to all intents and purposes created by Patrick Macnee in performance.[49] Consequently, the bowler and brolly have become as much a signifier for Macnee as for Steed. Macnee's case is different again from that of silver-screen stars such as Fred Astaire, Humphrey Bogart, or Frank Sinatra, all of whom can be represented by their headgear—respectively the top hat, the snap-brim, and the trilby. Astaire's topper is certainly not his *prime* signifier, nor the snap brim Bogart's, whereas Macnee's international fame is entirely bound up with his portrayal of a man in a bowler hat. It is noteworthy that while biographers of Bogart, for instance, tend generally to eschew the now-classic publicity still showing him in snap-brim and trench-coat,[50] the cover of Macnee's autobiography has him in his Steed costume, doffing his bowler and toting his umbrella.[51]

To be wholly associated, as Patrick Macnee is, with one's screen alter ego is not in itself unusual. Stars of "Golden Age" Hollywood comedies such as Groucho and Harpo Marx, Buster Keaton, Stan Laurel, and Oliver Hardy, are for most of us identical with their cinematic personae (an association that is encouraged by the fact that these clowns generally retained their real names in performance). The elision of player and character has again become widespread since the television series as a form came into its own, though the phenomenon seems confined to comic or character roles.[52] Tom Baker's autobiography, like Patrick Macnee's, is adorned by a close-up of the actor in costume for the role with which he is principally identified—in this case, the fourth incarnation of Doctor Who.[53]

However, Macnee's is still a special case. Well-known as the images of Baker have undoubtedly become, he did not embody the series in which he starred. The Steed image, on the other hand, even more than Cathy Gale's and Emma Peel's leather boots, became the visual essence of *The Avengers*. Stuart Craig, the production designer on the 1998 *Avengers* movie, indicated not only that the re-creation of the Steed look was a sine qua non for the new film, but that this potent image effectively served as the benchmark for all other design choices in the film, more or less forcing the decision to represent "Avengerland" as a Britain in which the 1960s never ended:

A chap in a Savile Row suit with a rolled umbrella was pretty extraordinary then; and it's even more so now. As a cliché image of England it's kind of okay. If you try and present it as totally contemporary, you'd have trouble, I think, selling that in America. I think you were duty-bound to leave it there in the 1960s.[54]

Yet the importance of the Steed image for *The Avengers* was more than that it transcended the reality of the series: to a great extent, Steed's appearance actually determined that reality. Brian Clemens, who together with Albert Fennell produced the show from 1965 until 1969, has made the following remarkable claim about the way in which he construed and controlled the *Avengers* aesthetic:

I laid down the ground rule that no woman should be killed, no extras should populate the streets. We admitted to only one class . . . and that was the upper. As a fantasy, we would not show a uniformed policeman or a colored man. And you would not see anything so common as blood in The Avengers. *Had we introduced a colored man or a policeman, we would have had the yardstick of social reality and that would have made the whole thing quite ridiculous. Alongside a bus queue of ordinary men-in-the-street, Steed would have become a caricature.*[55]

Clemens' assertion about the tenor of the show was substantially borne out, though all of the conventions described were occasionally overridden during his tenure. Any recreational or commercial institution in *The Avengers* is marked by its exclusivity, be it marriage bureau, country club, or department store. Oxford accents are the norm, except for the odd local yokel, who is usually drawn as either amiably dotty or psychotic. Clemens' fantasy world also kept its color bar to an extent that is retrospectively rather disturbing, with black African characters appearing in only four of the episodes made during his tenure.

In fact, it is easy to expand on Clemens' claim for Steed's centrality in the series' ideological matrix. For example, as Steed is the epitome of unforced good manners, so representatives of "the other side" are usually characterized by their egregious behavior, their pettiness, and, above all, their snobbery. Obsessive-compulsives, embittered has-beens, and Eastern Bloc diplomats trying to affect English manners are implicitly or explicitly ridiculed and effortlessly floored, over and over again.

Clemens emphasized the need to prevent Steed from seeming like a caricature. Many of the scripts for *The Avengers* were set in heartlands of Tory power occupied by ministers and merchant bankers. Here, studied conservatism of dress ensured that the bowler hat, like the morning coat, was not yet an anachronism in the 1960s, and Steed looked perfectly at home (though even in this context, as will be discussed below, his dress remained subtly distinctive).

However, as 1970 approached and the series was more heavily laced with the quirky and the surreal, the process of molding the world of *The Avengers* around Steed underwent exponential growth. The appearance in 1969 of Steed's superior, Mother, a formidable but engaging "old school" complement to Steed himself, signaled the universal gentrification of characters in the show. By the final season, the ranks of the great and the good had embraced such bizarre figures as Bertram Fortescue Winthrop Smythe, the aristocratic chimney sweep in "From Venus with Love" (1967), who went by the name of Bert Smith for the sake of commercial credibility,[56] while business establishments were invariably the *crème de la crème* of their trade. A good example was the Classy Glass Cleaning Co. in "The Super Secret Cypher Snatch" (1969) whose motto was "We're behind all the best windows." Some establishments were even purveyors exclusively to the nobility, like Martin's Toyshop and the Guild of Noble Nannies in "Something Nasty in the Nursery" (1968).

By the end of the series, Steed was not merely one toff among many but one eccentric toff among many. Once distinctive by virtue of his subtle traditionalism, Steed ended up being distinctive chiefly because of his familiarity. By contrast, when the character returned during the mid-1970s in *The New Avengers,* he was visually isolated in a world where bowler hats were the province of undertakers and senior citizens. In this new series, no attempt was made to integrate Steed with his environment. Even the narrative acknowledged his displacement from the contemporary scene, for he had moved from his London dwelling, 3 Stable Mews, to semiretirement in a country house. The very name of this rural home, "Steed's Stud," which (like Stable Mews) puns suggestively on the equestrian overtones of "Steed," invites the inference that the character is now in some degree a racehorse who is out of the running.

In fact, the denial of the Steed-oriented values of the old series went much further in *The New Avengers:* Brian Clemens, once again coproducer, broke his taboo of acknowledging a class other than the upper and did so in a decisive way. Though Steed's new female companion, Purdey, played by Joanna Lumley, was in the well-bred mold of Mrs. Gale and Mrs. Peel, Steed's male colleague, Mike Gambit, played by Gareth Hunt, was unabashedly a member of the lower classes by birth.[57] The only thing that made Steed acceptable in this alien world was his iconic status: The viewer accepted the bowler and brolly because they were sported by Steed; conversely, the character would have seemed more of a hoary anachronism, not less, if stripped of his identifying attributes.

To focus exclusively on its enshrinement as a media icon or its role as an over-determinant for the character of *The Avengers* as a whole would be to bypass much of the expressive subtlety of the Steed image. Our second major theme is the intersection of the "Steed style" with contemporary men's fashion and, more particularly, with the dissolution of normative gender identities in the mid-1960s. We have already noted the brief convergence of costume design for Steed with Parisian haute couture in the "collaboration" between Macnee and Cardin. As we will discuss, the failure of this association, which is palpably attested by the fact that it was so short-lived, was symptomatic of there being limits beyond which the Macnee image had little meaning, or at least, no further currency. Five years after being voted one of the ten best-dressed men in the world, Macnee was in danger of becoming a dinosaur and found himself having to compromise not merely with an individual such as Cardin but in effect with the tumultuous forces of youth culture at the close of the 1960s. Indeed, we will argue that the Steed persona, so long daringly subversive in its distortion of gender norms, was ultimately debased by an attempt to embrace the new machismo of late-1960s "psychedelic" culture.

In shaping the Steed image, Macnee was, of course, not devising a sartorial style for its own sake: he was building up a dramatic character. Because of Steed's status as a media icon, it is easy to forget that the character's mode of dress had, from its inception, a clear role within the diegesis of *The Avengers*. Steed's sartorial narcissism, like his insouciant sense of fun, was one facet of a complex persona and counterpoised less amiable traits such as a rakish attitude to women and an implacable ruthlessness. For example, in "The Town of No Return," one scene finds Steed, dressed up in his most splendidly dandified overcoat (with velvet shawl-collar, enormous mother-of-pearl buttons, and flared sleeves), cavorting with child-like delight on a schoolyard merry-go-round. In the next, he restrains an imposturing enemy with the handle of his umbrella and, in order to extort information, he calmly sets fire to the man's moustache.

Beyond the confines of the narrative, the social significance of Steed's apparel is that it situated Patrick Macnee as the object of the male viewer's acquisitive gaze and by extension placed him in a key position within the discourse of male fashion during the 1960s.[58] Steed's suits, eventually mar-keted to the public at large by Macnee's tailors, Bailey and Weatherill, be-came the openly acknowledged focus of male desire and identification, in effect sexualizing the Steed persona almost as much as the "kinky" leather and stretch-jersey sexualized Cathy Gale and Emma Peel.[59]

Earlier, we quoted Macnee's remarks about the special style of jacket that he devised for Steed (c. 1964) with a single low-placed button and a vel-vet collar. His comments are interesting for two reasons. First, they reflect a changed attitude toward male grooming around this time. Such openly expressed interest in clothing had long been represented by men as unbe-coming their sex.[60] Yet Macnee's musings on the cut of his suits indicate that the cultural climate of the mid-1960s sanctioned, even fostered, male preoccupation with dress.

Macnee's insistence on the desirability of garments "moulded" to the body also gives focus to the problem of defining, or at least interpreting, the sexuality of the Steed image. In contour and silhouette, Steed's suits, while scarcely "butch," were assertively manly. Jackets and waistcoats closely followed the figure, giving particular emphasis, as Macnee clearly wished, to the chest, which is traditionally an important locus of male sexuality.[61] As Stella Bruzzi stressed in her discussion of the "continental look" outfits worn by the gangsters in Quentin Tarantino's *Reservoir Dogs* (1992), close-fitting suits, though "far from overtly sexual," may nevertheless serve as "symbols of virile, active masculinity."[62] The early 1960s saw the heyday of the "continental look,"[63] but even by Italian and French standards of the period, Steed's suits were specially productive of the *bella figura;* indeed, no less than Mrs. Peel's stretch-jersey "Emmapeelers," his clothes fitted him like a second skin.[64]

Yet if Steed's suits enhanced his aura of masculine cool, the associations of his style of dress somewhat complicated his sexual identity. Looking back on the series in 1984, Brian Clemens reflected that the program could not have been made in the United States, because an American television-production company would never have tolerated "an effete-looking hero in a bowler hat carrying an umbrella."[65] Even Macnee himself, writing in the 1990s, referred to Steed as "this rather strange, old-fashioned man who dressed in sort of pansy clothes."[66]

Macnee's and Clemens' implication that the Steed image carried overtones of effeminacy or homosexuality is not without indirect precedent from the years of production. This is not to say that there is a lack of evidence for Steed's being wholeheartedly, if not quite wholesomely, straight. Early in the series, Macnee described Steed as "a wolf with the women,"[67] and his more or less openly lecherous repartee with his professional partners, as well as with numerous incidental female characters, represented a leitmotiv in Steed's behavior.

Nevertheless, the original producer, Leonard White, obviously felt some insecurity about Steed's sexual orientation. In a production memo drawn up six weeks into the first recording block, White describes the character as "a sophisticate but not lacking in virility" and, as if to validate this uneasy claim, goes on (rather repellently) to cite beauty competitions as among Steed's "sports." Immediately thereafter, Steed's sexual tastes and proficiencies are clearly defined: "He has an eye for the beautiful and unusual—be it *objets d'art* or women. He will never be serious with any one woman, however. He is very experienced." White's anxieties are repeated a little later, when he remarks that Steed has "'special' tastes," adding defensively, "Some might think these slightly decadent—but they would be wrong."[68]

If it is reasonable to assume that for White, as later for Clemens, Steed's tailoring—a conspicuous expression of his "special" tastes—potentially denoted effeteness, why should this be the case? After all, as late as 1955, Ronald Searle could represent garb very like Steed's as the epitome of stuffy, late-imperial rectitude, in his cartoon of "the Major" (Steed himself, incidentally, possessed this rank) (fig. 2.4).[69]

However, precedents for Steed's style of dress certainly existed among upper-crust homosexuals as well as other members of the British elite during the first postwar decade. The fashion cultivated in these circles was referred to as the Edwardian revival—and it is no coincidence that, as noted earlier, the epithet "Edwardian" has also frequently been used to describe Steed's costumes.[70] Indeed, Steed's clothing c. 1965 closely resembles the "Edwardianism" of Cecil Beaton's outfit in a photograph of him taken in 1955:[71] Beaton's narrow-brimmed bowler, Chesterfield overcoat with

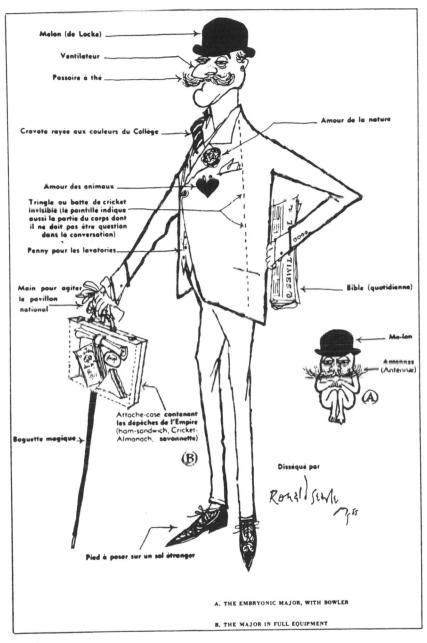

FIGURE 2.4. *Cartoon of "The Major" (1955) by Ronald Searle.*

stitched lower edge and velvet collar, calf-skin gloves, tapering trousers, and spread-collared shirt all seem to foreshadow Steed's costume.[72]

However, there is an important distinction to be made between Steed and his real-life precursors. Cecil Beaton, Oliver Messel, and the young officers of the Guards who, according to Farid Chenoune, cultivated the Edwardian mode as a response to the perceived vulgarity of the "American fashion invasion" clearly took themselves very seriously.[73] Macnee's Steed, on the other hand, twirled his umbrella and tapped his bowler to a jaunty angle with knowing irony. No viewer could really believe that Steed was committed to his traditionalism, far less that he was unaware of his affectation. On the contrary, it is quite clear that in adopting this mannered style, Steed was playing games with those whom he encountered—and, by extension, with the audience. This ironic detachment was conveyed through Macnee's insouciant facial expressions and deftly parodic gestures, but it also had a more concrete manifestation. As noted briefly above, except during the Cardin interlude Steed's "off duty" scenes found him wearing heavy turtleneck sweaters or polo shirts, often with cardigans. These casual garments, though still flattering, were as studiedly neutral and commonplace as the rest of Steed's wardrobe was arresting and idiosyncratic.

Yet, just as television critics seemed unable to grasp that *The Avengers* was not conceived as a "straight" spy series like its contemporary, *Danger Man,* the producers of the show were apparently incapable of recognizing that the overtones of camp in the Steed image were deftly managed and that the whole thing amounted to a "wink at the audience, a joke shared with them."[74] At the time of Diana Rigg's departure from *The Avengers* in 1967, fears that Steed was unmasculine were aired again, this time by ABC chief executive, Howard Thomas. His reservations did not concern Macnee's appearance, but centered on Steed's being portrayed as so absurdly weak that Emma Peel was always needed to rescue him from danger.[75]

Even though his comments were not specifically image-related, it cannot be coincidental that a radical change of look for Steed followed Thomas' diatribe. There were immediate attempts to emphasize Steed's heterosexual virility in the scripts. Much is made of his "Achilles' heel," a susceptibility to women, in the first episode to feature his new partner, Tara King, played by the 20-year-old Linda Thorson.[76] Tara is evidently quite ready to indulge Steed's "weakness": she proffers him her phone number within a few minutes of their first meeting.

Rather more visceral transformations followed for Steed and Tara early in

1968, for both Macnee and Thorson were prescribed amphetamines to help them lose weight. As a result, Thorson's remaining puppy fat disappeared, while Macnee shed thirty pounds. It has been stated that the seams of his *Avenger* suits were taken in to match his slimmer figure.[77] However, it was not the Cardin range that was altered: a few episodes into the new season, the credits began to read "Patrick Macnee's suits designed by Himself," and Steed was back once more in his old clothes.

There were no new departures in the design of Steed's dress after the Cardin interlude: Macnee returned to the suits with velvet-collared, one-button jackets that he had designed to "mould" to his physique. Macnee now had four such velvet-trimmed outfits, all in different shades, and the style came to serve virtually as Steed's uniform. The appeal of these suits for the actor was, surely, twofold: As Macnee's most distinctive designs, they reaffirmed the creative control he had lost to Cardin, and, perhaps more important, they flattered his new physique (reaffirming also Steed's masculinity). Macnee has been candid about his fears of appearing "like Methuselah" beside his ingenue companion, and, interestingly enough, once he had regained a well-toned figure, the actor made his first concession to prevailing youth trends by growing a substantial pair of sideburns.[78] Indeed, though Macnee was by this time nearer fifty than forty, Steed was represented as a more conventionally virile figure than ever before in this era of the student uprisings and the Summer of Love.

The opening title sequence for the Linda Thorson episodes of *The Avengers* displays an unprecedented clarity of gender roles. Steed is shown first brandishing a lion-emblazoned buckler and then playfully decapitating a suit of armor, which "bleeds" carnations. Light-hearted though it may be, this little mime clearly places Steed in a tradition of chivalric derring-do, remote from the languid opening of a champagne bottle that had been his principal activity in the pre-credit sequences for earlier series. Tara King's clothes also help to underscore Steed's manliness by means of antithesis. Rather than the yellow space-age bodysuit worn by the boyish Emma Peel in the previous title sequence, Tara appears first in a décolleté black evening gown and a pearl necklace and then, after a magic transformation, in a burgundy vest and slacks worn over a balloon-sleeved, florally patterned blouse. Steed, by contrast, wears a close-fitting dove-gray suit, only his tie providing a flash of color to answer the vivid hues of Tara's billowing shirt: masculine simplicity complements feminine frivolity.

If the removal of any equivocation about Steed's sexuality had always been desirable for anxious producers, it was actually a cultural sea change that led Steed, rather improbably, to metamorphose into the latter-day knight of the Tara King title-sequence. In the later 1960s, the Sixties of popular myth, when the ultra-fashion-conscious preferred historically inspired Biba to functionalist Quant, *The Avengers* was edging toward psychedelia-drenched neo-Romanticism.[79] Kooky and kinky the series remained, but its studied ambivalence was gone. Linda Thorson spoke of Tara's using her sexuality to defeat the opposition rather than relying on martial arts like her androgynous predecessors.[80] Similarly, though Steed's old-world charm remained, the inner "steel" upon which Macnee had once insisted,[81] which had made the character captivating and unpredictable, was well and truly melted. Indeed, Macnee has recently admitted that he tried to make Steed more human as the plots of the screenplays became more bizarre.[82]

The simplification of Steed's character for what proved to be the final season of *The Avengers* also reflects his changed position within the discourse of men's fashion. In 1968, the "Edwardian" suit, which Macnee had helped to make popular, was standard fare in the shops. Steed was no longer in any sense avant-garde, and upcoming trends were, in fact, veering sharply away from the constraints of Edwardianism. By 1970, when *The Avengers* had discontinued production, long hair had ceased to be a sign of effeminacy for men, notwithstanding the derision of reactionaries; nor did bright clothes with exaggerated silhouettes and plush textures any longer indicate a "queer."[83] Two of the most popular heroes in early-1970s British television were Jon Pertwee's incarnation of *Doctor Who* and Peter Wyngarde's Jason King in *Department S* (ITC/ATV, 1969–1970). Both were considered sex symbols among straight viewers, and though Jason King was presented as wholly nonaggressive, his prowess in the bedroom was flaunted. Wyngarde and Pertwee affected a style of dress and grooming that would have been unthinkable a decade before for the portrayal of red-blooded virility. Shaggy manes of hair, thick sideburns, scarves, foulard ties, tight-fitting shirts with huge collars, jabots, frilly cuffs, velvets, and silks in a variety of bright colors and patterns—all these extravagances were products of the Peacock Revolution.[84]

Steed occupied a curious position in relation to this "revolution," and to the television heroes who flourished in its wake. Whereas Pertwee's Doctor Who and Wyngarde's Jason King could not be called direct heirs of Steed, the longstanding popularity of Macnee's witty fop surely helped to make these flamboyant figures acceptable. Yet the model of masculinity purveyed through Peacock fashions, which in effect harked back to the Cavalier styles of the Jacobean and Caroline ages, was not Steed's. The differing behavior of Steed and his successors confirms this. Like the fictional figure upon whom Patrick Macnee in part based his screen character, the wily Scarlet Pimpernel,[85] Steed typically achieved his ends by deviousness, dissimulation, and seductive charm, traditionally considered feminine wiles. Jon Pertwee's Doctor, on the other hand, keeping a straight bat and maintaining an earnest machismo worthy of Errol Flynn, swashbuckled his way through his adventures, prostrating his enemies with "Venusian aikido" or overwhelming them with the help of his (decidedly phallic) sonic screwdriver. Pertwee avowedly sought to present the Doctor as "someone who would always box by the Queensberry rules,"[86] whereas Macnee's Steed, at his scintillating best, would stoop cheerfully to immobilize opponents with the heel of a patent-leather dancing pump.[87]

The cancellation of *The Avengers* after the Tara King season was due to a ratings failure in the U.S.[88] However, *The Avengers* could probably not have survived much longer, even under more favorable conditions, for in its last two seasons the series had gradually been divested of its nuances. From Cathy Gale's advent to Emma Peel's departure, *The Avengers* had thrived on the unresolved sexual tensions between the main protagonists and also, as we have noted, on the polysexuality of these characters. As metafeminists, Mrs. Peel and Mrs. Gale often dressed like boys and intellectually outshone both Steed and their male adversaries—but they were at the same time alluring and quite capable of projecting a powerful femininity.

A nice example of what might be called gender layering in the persona of Mrs. Peel is provided by "The Cybernauts" (1965). In this episode, she seeks admission to a karate school; for an entrance test, she must overcome the star pupil. Her peerless proficiency at the martial art does not have to be proven to the audience, and her swift victory is entirely predictable. However, the encounter with her opponent is given a neat twist in that Emma does not, on this occasion, wear the uninhibiting black leather bodysuit usually reserved for action sequences—though this is the outfit that she actually sports for much of the rest of the episode. She is dressed in a close-fitting wool jacket and matching short, straight-cut skirt, with kid gloves, stiletto heels, and a patent-leather handbag. She carefully sets aside the stilettos, gloves, and bag during the brief struggle (fig. 2.5), and once

FIGURE 2.5. *The over-the-shoulder look: Emma Peel (Diana Rigg) floors Oyuka (Katherine Schofield) in "The Cybernauts" (1965). Diana Rigg's costume by Jan Rowell. Courtesy of BFI Stills, Posters and Designs.*

welcomed as a member of the school, she bows to the karate master and leaves in stocking feet, twirling her shoes coquettishly over one shoulder. Her vanquished opponent is chided by the instructor for underestimating Mrs. Peel, who, he observes, thinks not like a woman but like a man.

Steed, too, was epicene; to borrow the memorable phrase used by one member of the production team, "you were never quite sure whether he was AC or DC."[89] Expressions of Steed's "real" personality were at best evanescent—and generally hidden. What makes the character fascinating is the sense that his demeanor and dress constitute a subtly woven tissue of masquerade. If we want to give Steed's fugitive persona a label, then the most secure is that he was a sort of "practicing postmodernist." Toby Miller, in his book on *The Avengers,* has nicely characterized the postmodern as "a jokey troping that breaks up identity, certainty and knowledge,"[90] and further as "a sophistication that is determined to avoid looking surprised."[91] By this reckoning, indeed, Steed is the very incarnation of postmodernism.

The knife-edge balance that Macnee achieved in the portrayal of Steed was first seriously upset when Pierre Cardin's designs pushed the Steed image from foppery into camp. It would, of course, be a crass mistake to attribute this misjudgment to the fact that Cardin was gay: the relative ostentation of his outfits for Steed reflected his professional stake in the developing Peacock aesthetic for men—an idiom that simply could not be integrated with Steed's muted elegance. With the arrival of Tara King and the encroachment of a neo-Romantic sensibility, Steed was in a sense emasculated, for he lost his subversive edge.

Before, *The Avengers* had been an ongoing saturnalia, where the values of conventional melodrama were constantly upturned and where Macnee's character was the ultrarefined Lord of Misrule. Having to serve tea with milk rather than lemon could evince a frown from Steed,[92] whereas diabolical masterminds were invariably confronted with negligent calm and laconic wit. In the Tara King season, Macnee's performance was virtually the only element that was not overstated, and the problem was, perhaps, that another kind of inversion had taken place. Steed was by then one eccentric among many, for "Avengerland," very much like Macnee's suits, was molded around him. So while Steed's image was a signifier for *The Avengers*, it could be said that *The Avengers* finally became little more than a signifier for Steed. Bowler and brolly and "Edwardian" clothes could no longer be invested with the same dry, mocking, and self-mocking humor, for the ludic had been supplanted by the ludicrous.

QUITE, QUITE FANTASTIC: HARRY POTTLE AND "POLYGENERIC" DESIGN

Until Honor Blackman's departure at the end of the third season, the only consistently way-out elements in *The Avengers* were the sartorial styles of the two main characters. However, in Diana Rigg's first season (1965–1966), the series as a whole became suffused with Steed's élan, eccentricity, and gently teasing wit. The 1965–1966 season was arguably the high-water mark of overall achievement in *The Avengers;* it certainly showed the greatest subtlety in design imagery. Harry Pottle, scenic designer for the entire season,[93] paved the way for the wacky creations seen in the last years of the series, but at the same time maintained a poised and restrained precision that his successors did not attempt to emulate. What makes his designs of particular interest for our purposes is that they engaged the viewer at a number of different levels and in unusual ways.

Harry Pottle trained in the art department of Alexander Korda's vast production company, London Films, and by 1960 he had established himself as an art director in the movies. As a film designer, his entry into television was in many ways fortuitous. In the early 1960s, television companies occasionally farmed out successful series shot on film so that they could be marketed overseas (taped programs could not then be converted for transmission via non–UK broadcast systems).[94] Independent Artists had taken on one film-for-TV venture, the psychological drama series *The Human Jungle,* in 1962, and in 1964 the company was entrusted with *The Avengers,* which was being groomed for U.S. sales. As the resident designer for Independent Artists, Harry Pottle was automatically assigned to *The Avengers,* as he had been to *The Human Jungle.*

Pottle's experience on *The Human Jungle* and before that on a number of "three-weekers" (sixty-five-minute, second-feature films produced rapidly and cheaply) prepared him at a practical level for the exigencies of working on *The Avengers.*[95] Here he was expected to devise eight to ten sets for each episode, and an episode was shot every two weeks. Pottle recalled that this tight schedule was complicated by the slow delivery of screenplays: he often had to produce drawings based on notes taken from an oral description. He cited a design from "The Master Minds" (1965) as an example (see frontispiece):

I'd be on the phone to Brian Clemens [script editor] at the weekend. He'd say: "There's a stockbroker who lives in Surrey in a ranch-style house—you go in and there's a lounge with a bar in it and a view over the garden, a corridor, a bedroom at the end . . ." and so on. They'd be writing the scripts over the weekend and I'd have to have the sets designed by Monday![96]

However, the liberating aesthetic of the show ameliorated many difficulties:

For the first time, there was an opportunity to do something tongue-in-cheek, something stylized. One could send it up a bit. The good thing was that if the script said, for example, you need an umbrella shop, you could set up a counter with a few umbrellas and really stylize it, put some strange spiral staircase in the background. You could tell the cameraman to forget the background. . . .

Where we were lucky was that we could do odd things purely for effect. In the video series, Steed would leave a room and the camera would track into the clock. This wasn't just to be clever. It was because they had to get him from one set to another, possibly with a costume change on the way.[97]

Pottle made full use of the opportunity for essays into pure whimsy, enlivening minor or commonplace environments with motifs that would stretch credulity in a serious drama, and even in most sitcoms. Thus, a baby-carriage manufacturer in "How to Succeed at Murder" (1966) does not have a liquor cabinet in his office, but instead keeps the bottles in one of his own perambulators, which he wheels out for guests; a Turkish bath in "Honey for the Prince" (1966) is illuminated by a fanlight—at floor level; and so on.

While it is generally true that scenic design, moving in lockstep with narrative, embodied more and more elements of zany in episodes produced after the midseason break in filming, Pottle in fact adopted a fluid, heterogeneous idiom—or, rather, carefully orchestrated idiomatic variety—from the outset. The range of devices and approaches he used will be sketched below. However, before going into minutiae it is important to make a general statement about the expressive scope of design in *The Avengers* under his aegis.

The essence of Pottle's achievement was that he produced discursive rather than descriptive imagery. He created a visual correlative to the "layered" scripts that were being written for *The Avengers* at this time, in which immanent meanings, subtexts, and double entendres were given great prominence and obviously intended to furnish much of the watcher's enjoyment. The quibble-drenched exchanges between Steed and Mrs. Peel; the parodic allusions to film, popular fiction, and other television series; trenchant vignettes of the rituals and recreations of the British ruling classes, and so on were at least as rich in entertainment value as the suspense plots that were the *raison d'être* of the series. The inherently suggestive nature of design was well suited to optimizing such pleasures. However, Pottle pushed the expressive role of his art still further. Many of his bolder set pieces served neither simply to denote a particular physical and psychological situation nor to encourage particular emotional responses: like the heavily satirical scripts, they invited a more cerebral mode of appreciation. In other words, rather than deepening the viewer's sense of involvement, as design for screen drama is typically supposed to do, some of Pottle's *Avengers* imagery actively promoted detachment.

Pottle achieved this distancing effect by creating sets that invited acknowledgment of their own artifice—their status as designed objects—rather than belying their manufacture. His permissive approach was justified, indeed made desirable, by the outré attire of the main protagonists. It would have been almost impossible to overwhelm the visual impact of Steed and Mrs. Peel, and all too easy, as Brian Clemens acknowledged, to create a world in which these singular superheroes seemed absurd.

In *The Avengers,* as in any other drama, it was important that the main characters' domiciles reflected their personae. However, because Steed and Mrs. Peel were so much larger than life and because the series was shot

FIGURE 2.6. *Steed's shadow catches Emma's spy eye in "The Town of No Return" (1966). Set and prop designed by Harry Pottle.* © *Canal + Image UK Ltd.*

through with paradox and ambivalence, Pottle was able to play games with audience expectation even in these sets. This is especially evident in the décor of Emma Peel's flat.

The female heroes in *The Avengers* were invariably representatives of modernity, and Pottle's design for Emma's apartment fully acknowledged this: her quarters embodied avant-garde cool, just as Steed's exuded Georgian warmth. Yet Emma's brand of progressiveness was remote from that of her predecessor, Cathy Gale, as expressed in Douglas James' design for that character's flat. Mrs. Gale's décor and furnishings were a brutalist variation on Japanese interior design, with low-line, backless settees, sliding doors, and shutters of burnished steel dividing up the interior space. The effect of embattled inhospitability was increased by the presence of a closed-circuit television that allowed Mrs. Gale to see who was at her door. Although striking, the set was barely plausible as a living environment: it created the impression that Cathy was not only mannishly tough but also inhuman.

Mrs. Peel, too, had a security device at the door of her flat: but it could not have been more unlike her predecessor's. Emma's "spy eye" was quite literally that—a lone, large, long-lashed female eye molded in plastic—the lids of which part to allow Mrs. Peel to survey her visitors through a lens in the pupil (fig. 2.6).

As a conceit, this spy eye typifies Pottle's puckish approach to designing for *The Avengers:* the motif is intriguing, riddling, and slightly discomfiting. Whereas Cathy Gale's aggressive machine-aesthetic implied lack of humor and denial of femininity, the spy eye seemed to announce someone of uninhibited levity with a detached enjoyment of her own womanhood. If Mrs. Peel was superficially "making eyes" at her most frequent visitor, Steed (who often addressed sparring remarks to the eye before being let into the flat), it could equally well be said that she was returning and reversing the male gaze.[98] The unflinching stare of the cyclopean eye offered no submissive encouragement to Steed—or by extension to the male viewer. On the contrary, it emphasized Mrs. Peel's empowerment, not least by virtue of its colossal scale. Amusing as this practical prop undoubtedly was at one level, it was also slightly threatening, as Steed's mock-combative attitude seemed to imply: the hairy organ carried vague overtones of the *vagina dentata.* At yet another level, Mrs. Peel's spyglass could be taken as a humorous manifestation of the All-Seeing Eye proper to the goddess of truth and judgment.[99] Mrs. Peel was, after all, goddess-like in her omniscience and omnicompetence, and Steed beat a path to the portal of her sanctuary whenever he wished to draw on her scientific wisdom and powers of logical reasoning.

Since we claimed in the previous chapter that meanings for design imagery cannot be definitively pinned down, it should be made clear that the foregoing is *not* intended to stand as a serious explanation of the metaphorical significance of Emma's spy eye. We have, rather, indulged in an interpretative game, and in suggesting some "meanings" that occur to us, we are responding in kind to the playfulness that informs the motif of the spy eye itself. Another important point to make, since we have so far considered the eye in isolation, is that the conceit derives some of its potency from its relationship with the interior of Mrs. Peel's apartment. Given that her front door is the first thing seen in Diana Rigg's debut episode, "The Town of No Return" (1965), the viewer might be forgiven for expecting what lay behind to be as funky as the spy eye. However, while he says that he looked upon the character of Mrs. Peel as "way out" (referring in large part to her style of clothing),[100] Harry Pottle did not opt for wall-to-wall kookiness in the décor of her apartment. Inside Mrs. Peel's living room, all is serenity and restraint (fig. 2.7)—a condition that we are allowed ample opportunity to relish in "The Town of No Return" (fig. 2.8).

In their opening scene, Steed and Mrs. Peel fight a mock duel around the room, allowing the camera to pan after them as they fence. The overall effect created by sliding, fabric-covered doors and the built-in seating

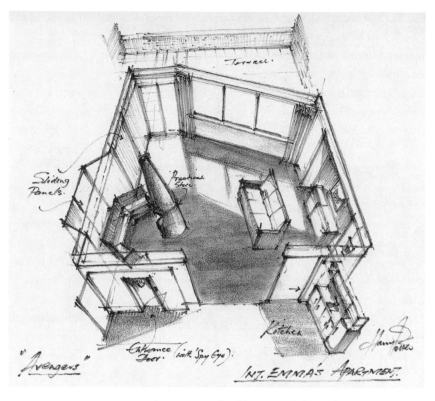

FIGURE 2.7. *Reconstruction by Harry Pottle of his original design for Emma Peel's flat in* The Avengers *(1965). Courtesy of Denise Pottle.*

around the sleek central stove is of a commodious, feminized modernism, and this is tempered by a scattering of *objets d'art,* which range from Meissen figurines on the backs of the built-in seats (lifted out of harm's way by Steed with ostentatious care during the fencing match) to a semiabstract painting over the liquor cabinet.

How can the splendidly vulgar Pop artifact on Mrs. Peel's front door be reconciled with the chaste, Eamesian elegance within her flat? Whether one responds by drawing back from the narrative and merely enjoying the absurdity of the visual joke, or whether one tries hard to accept the eye motif as representing, in diegetical terms, a particular facet of Emma's personality, the real point is that the image demands some kind of response. Mrs. Gale's modernist fortress had required no such imaginative participation by the viewer: the set served a straightforward, confirmatory role, underscoring her status as a futuristic superwoman. The tensions within Mrs. Peel's décor, on the other hand, create a *disconfirmatory* effect, threatening to fragment identity and multiplying possible meanings.

Few of Pottle's sets used ambivalence to the same extent as that for Mrs. Peel's flat, but then few had to withstand and repay sustained scrutiny in the same way. Incidental settings, even where they were heavily used in a given episode, were boldly conceived for immediate effect rather than being laden with nuances that were meant to be savored over repeated viewings. The devices that Pottle used most consistently to surprise and amuse the viewer were kitsch and stylization; the two were, in fact, often united. In the context of this bitingly satirical program, there could, of course, be no danger of mistaking Pottle's kitsch for ingenuous bad taste on the part of the program-makers; as we will argue, the invocation of kitsch generally announced a very specific intent: the exposure of dissimulation. Stylized imagery, too, was generally calculated to complement and emphasize a satirical message.

Assertive and unusual forms of design were freely mixed with more standard imagery in Pottle's work for *The Avengers.* Many of his sets were conventionally reticent, while others, following well-established cinematic traditions, used expressionistic effects to engage the viewer at an emotional (rather than cerebral) level. Pottle made a virtuoso demonstration out of mixing up different idiomatic tendencies, varying his approach from episode to episode. This flexibility is nicely exemplified by contrasting "The Town of No Return" with the previous episode to be filmed, "The Hour That Never Was" (broadcast in 1966).

FIGURE 2.8. *Steed and Mrs. Peel trade barbs in her flat in "The Town of No Return." Patrick Macnee's costume by Audrey Liddle, Diana Rigg's costume by John Bates. © Canal + Image UK Ltd.*

In "The Town of No Return," the interiors for "The Inebriated Gremlin," the village inn where Steed and Mrs. Peel stay, are manifestly created for emotional impact: as an environment, the pub is palpably hostile and almost viscerally nauseating. The lounge bar is thoroughly dilapidated and heavily cobwebbed, with a transistor radio perched on an old sofa cushion in lieu of a jukebox. Steed's bedroom is an even more powerful study in insalubrity. Chipped enamel basin, tarnished metal bedstead, tattered curtains and towels, a lumpy, ill-made bed, and a flypaper choked with its victims all proclaim the fact that visitors are not welcome. Pottle manipulated the very space of the set so as to ensure that it is unsettling: the strongly inclined coving of the ceiling creates an oppressive atmosphere, which resonates with Steed's discovery that the windows are boarded up on the outside.

The teleplay for "The Hour That Never Was" demanded a far less flamboyant approach. This episode was conceived as a straightforward psychological thriller, drawing on the *Mary Celeste* scenario: the personnel of an air base (aptly named RAF Hamelin) have all mysteriously disappeared when Steed and Mrs. Peel visit for the closing-down party. By contrast, Clemens' script for "The Town of No Return" works on more than one level. The explicit narrative concerns the wholesale takeover of a secluded coastal village by fifth columnists, but underlying the story is a near-the-bone exposé of parochial insularity and xenophobia in rural Norfolk. Pottle provided the context for Clemens' black humor with a series of intentionally stereotypical "rustic village" images—as well as the inhospitable hostelry there is a starkly silhouetted gothic church and a soot-darkened smithy—and the clichés are all knowingly writ large.

Pottle's technique in "The Town of No Return" could be called the visual equivalent of hyperbole. In "The Hour That Never Was," on the other hand, the designer opted for a corresponding "meiosis," creating an effect not simply of diurnal normality but of deliberate neutrality. Except for the tinsel- and streamer-strewn officers' mess, abandoned in mid-festivities, every set was made as blank and devoid of humanizing features as possible in order to enhance the eerie quality of the story, which is largely a two-hander between the bemused Steed and Mrs. Peel. The introduction of anything visually remarkable or eccentric would have disturbed the atmosphere of unnatural quiet. In the "Gremlin" bedroom, and many other sets for "The Town of No Return," every excuse was taken to break up wall-contour and create an interesting play of light and shade. In "The Hour That Never Was,"

Pottle suppressed surface variety to facilitate the bland, even illumination of the episode.

Toward the latter end of the season, he sometimes used a range of idiomatic approaches within a single episode. That such multiform experiments could work is partly testimony to his judgment and finesse. However, it is also due to the fact that the audience were acclimatized to the studiedly polygeneric nature of *The Avengers,* which by this time was conducive to such variety. Indeed, episodes such as "Quick-Quick Slow Death," with their multiple comic vignettes, evoke the loose assemblage of sketches proper to variety shows.

The designer's ludic approach invited correspondingly ludic responses from directors, cameramen, and actors.[101] Pottle conceived some sets with specific (unscripted) sight gags in mind,[102] and others were playrooms in which ideas for comic business or one-liners naturally presented themselves. This process of inventive interplay is neatly exemplified by the comic use of a prop from "The Man Eater of Surrey Green." For the entrance hall of a mansion belonging to a crazed millionaire botanist, Pottle not only used a virulently foliage-patterned Morris/Liberty wallpaper, but also ranged creeper-covered nude mannequins around the walls (instead of the suits of armor one might expect in a stately home). In one scene, Steed, momentarily left alone in the hall, approaches one of the mannequins and, after glancing down at its "clothing," dryly remarks, "Come the autumn, I hope to see more of you." Whether the line was an ad lib by Macnee or a late addition by the scriptwriter, Philip Levene, is unimportant: the point is that this exemplifies the consonance of Pottle's conceits with the spirit of *Avengers* humor.

Pottle's use of kitsch and stylization, which served both to consolidate and to underscore ideas in the narrative, and his use of "generic collage," which was meant to create more complex refractions of narrative subject matter, must obviously be given separate treatment through independent case studies. The first episodes considered here, "The Murder Market" and "Dial a Deadly Number," were among the very earliest in the production schedule, while the third, "Quick-Quick Slow Death," was made much later, after the midseason break in filming. The early episodes typify Pottle's initial practice, which was to make only localized and limited use of strongly offbeat designs; these isolated images stood out from a norm of more commonplace, realist imagery. "Quick-Quick Slow Death," on the

FIGURE 2.9. *Wearing its heart on its sleeve: The set for the Togetherness marriage bureau in "The Murder Market." Set designed by Harry Pottle. © Canal + Image UK Ltd.*

other hand, was one of several later episodes in which he made extremely free use of different effects; though it should be added that our chosen example is perhaps the most "advanced" in this respect.

"The Murder Market" was only the second episode of *The Avengers* on which Pottle worked, but already he had identified ways in which design could be made to complement the narrative humor.[103] Pottle selectively extrapolated ideas from the script, creating sets that were, in effect, mute commentaries on the story. Design will always inflect narrative, but not always in predictable ways: as we and other commentators have already noted, there is no guarantee that viewers will pick up on the preferred reading. Pottle maximized the chances of stable evocation by refining and focusing the range of visual signifiers that he offered to audiences. In other words, he restricted possible interpretations by bombarding the spectator with multiple, intensive expressions of a single thematic motif.

Central to "The Murder Market" is the composite set that makes up the offices of Togetherness, the exclusive marriage bureau around which the action revolves. The décor of the reception area is heavily stylized and overwhelmingly "themed," the germ idea for the whole being wedding-cake ornament. The design reeks of nuptial clichés: the receptionist's desk is shaped like a giant, tiered cake; there is a plethora of frills and doilies, a veritable squadron of flying gilt cherubs, and other Rococo gewgaws; and even the doors are stenciled with little hearts (fig. 2.9).

The inescapable nature of the wedding-cake motif presses home the comic aims of the script. First, there is a blackly humorous paradox at the heart of the story: the marriage bureau also functions as an assassination agency for selected clients. No opportunity for milking the perverse juxtaposition of murder and marriage is missed. For example, Steed, as a client—and also, in the eyes of the executive director, Lovejoy, a potential assassin—is invited to a wedding-cake tasting. Here, the possibility of Steed's becoming a paid murderer is placidly introduced between genteel sips and nibbles, and Lovejoy's remarks on the quality of the wedding-breakfast fare become an implicit commentary on Steed's eligibility as a spouse and a killer.

"The Murder Market" also acts as an extended satirical comment on the British middle- and upper class penchant for evasion and denial. The far-fetched plot is, in a sense, just an excuse for this commentary. It is at the satirical level that the manifest artifice of Pottle's design comes into its own in expressive terms. The extreme emphasis on Barbie-doll sweetness, and the corresponding occlusion of anything else, reciprocates the script's exposé of the English genius for verbal equivocation. The avoidance of disagreeable truths is at its height in the cake-tasting scene, where Lovejoy displaces his concerns about Steed's marriageability onto remarks about the comestibles, while Steed characterizes the disadvantages of being hanged for murder with super-cool understatement: "I've always preferred soft collars—and besides, the idea of getting up at *eight o'clock in the morning!*"

The Togetherness set is a prime example of Harry Pottle's use of kitsch. A German word denoting something that exhibits bad taste, often with overtones of sentimentality, kitsch is a term often used by critics from the 1930s onwards to describe what they perceived as mass-produced pseudo art.[104] Latterly, the word has come to connote not just the vulgarized but also the pretentious, and it is generally as a function of the latter than the idiom is manifest in Pottle's designs. Pretentiousness is, in fact, the most frequent target of satire in *The Avengers,* and almost invariably goes hand in hand with pretence of some kind. This dissimulation can range from the perniciously calculating, as in the case of Togetherness, to the relatively innocent, and the extent and nature of the kitsch in the settings is correspondingly varied.

Part of the interest of *The Avengers* resides in the fact that it straddles the usual definitions of drama and light entertainment by virtue of its strong element of burlesque. As a function of the sardonic humor in the series, the visual hyperbole and unabashed kitsch were easily sustainable. Pottle, however, was bold enough to extend the use of these devices beyond their overtly comic applications. In "Dial a Deadly Number," an episode that deals with suspicious deaths among top financiers in the City of London, the director, Don Leaver, paid close attention to artifacts in the episode's photography, perhaps stimulated by Pottle's exceptionally dense set-dressing. For example, a scene in a broker's office finds Steed making deliberately provocative use of the expression "quite a killing" (ostensibly, of course, in relation to speculative success on the stock market). A head-and-shoulders image of Steed cuts to a staccato series of shots that show, in increasing close-up, a display case which contains a stuffed pike in the middle of devouring its prey.

Expressive integration of decorative details into the narrative is taken even further in a dinner-party scene set in the penthouse of banker Henry Boardman. Pottle's décor for this apartment is among the most thematically intensive that he produced. Here, kitsch is rife, but it is far from a cue for amusement. Here, the distancing effect of the stylized imagery encourages dispassionate recognition of the irony in the situation. Boardman is trebly pathetic in that he is a dupe, a cuckold, and the head of a failing bank. His flat is decorated with an artiness that tries just a little too hard to affirm his prosperity. (When they leave, Steed and Emma comment on the lack of *objets d'art* in the flat and the fact that the banker no longer owns a country house—both reflections of his "going down in the world.") The motif for the decorative scheme is, appropriately enough, money. Framed collections of coins hang on the walls in the sitting room; bank notes in different currencies are mounted on the lower sections of tall glass screens that surround the sitting area; while the upper sections of these screens are etched with large medallic images (fig. 2.10). Even the table in the dining room is decorated to look like a huge coin—the most monstrous example of Boardman's hollow self-congratulation.

The key elements of the Boardman apartment's décor are not only interesting in terms of their content but also in the way that they are used. Our first view of the dining room is an overhead shot looking down on the coin-like table, which is spotlit to maximize its impact (fig. 2.11). When Boardman comments that his broker has not turned up for the meal—he has been murdered—the camera zooms in on the empty place with its undisturbed cutlery. Similarly, in the preceding scene, the décor of the sitting room is made the focus of the characters' attention—and thus also the viewer's. Steed and Mrs. Peel, invited separately to the dinner and, to deceive their suspects, pretending not to know each another, engage in verbal sparring designed to put the hosts on edge. To underscore his feigned indifference to Mrs. Peel, Steed looks at the images etched on the glass screens rather than

FIGURE 2.10. *To coin a frieze: Henry Boardman (Clifford Evans), Ruth Boardman (Jan Holden), Steed, John Harvey (Peter Bowles), and Emma amidst the bills and coins decorating the Boardmans' flat in "Dial a Deadly Number" (1965). Set designed by Harry Pottle. Patrick Macnee's costume designed by Audrey Liddle, Diana Rigg's costume by John Bates, other costumes by Jackie Jackson. Courtesy of BFI Stills, Posters and Designs.*

at her (incidentally allowing the cameraman to film him through the translucent surface). Here, then, the décor is implicated in *Steed's* dissimulation. What remains constant throughout these two sequences is that the audience is encouraged to view the design imagery in terms of specific occurrences or information in the narrative.

Where, in later episodes, there was fragmentation of narrative into a series of "sketches," Pottle took this as a cue for experiment. He used design not to unify and confirm the reality of the diegesis but, in effect, to drive a stronger wedge between scenes, making each situation more idiosyncratic and memorable. Pottle played with expectations and conventions even in the slightest of vignettes and occasionally used disjunction of styles for shock value. Single-conceit imagery of the kind we have been discussing was selectively deployed, with the real space of the set often being effectively dissolved in an accretion of emblematic objects. Interspersed with such stuffed spaces, Pottle might use sets that incorporated little or no dressing, and therefore appeared disorientatingly empty. Similarly, low-key

FIGURE 2.11. *The Boardmans at the board: The numismatic dining table in "Dial a Deadly Number." Prop designed by Harry Pottle.* © Canal + Image UK Ltd.

naturalism might give way abruptly to blatant kitsch, and kitsch in turn to surrealism.

"Quick-Quick Slow Death" embraces the full panoply of design modes in its seven sets. As the title indicates, the script concerns murders in a dancing school (the work, as so often, of fifth columnists), and the key set, therefore, is the school itself—a composite of four rooms. The studio's name, Terpsichorean Training Techniques, is in itself the acme of kitsch, and Pottle created an environment of piquant vulgarity. However, in many ways he went beyond kitsch with the dance-school set, straying once again over the frontiers of surrealism. One especially curious feature is that the floor of the foyer is patterned with footprints, looking as though they had escaped from the pages of a ballroom-dancing manual (Pottle's source was a primer by Victor Sylvester).[105] These footprints stray from the realm of affected gaucherie into that of the plain bizarre when they mount the wall (fig. 2.12). This feature led to an unscripted piece of business by Patrick Macnee: Left alone in the foyer, Steed dances along the sequence of footmarks, until their ascent of the wall halts his progress.

Stylized though it is, the set for the dance school is rich in visual incident. By stark contrast, two of the other sets for "Quick-Quick Slow Death," Lichen's gentlemen's outfitters and a shoe boutique, Piedi's, are bereft of ornamental detail, their function being denoted solely by displays of wares; and in Piedi's case (somewhat kinkily) also by plaster casts of his clients' feet. In both sets, variation in texture is restricted and the palette confined to mid-tones, whereas contrasts of values and surface abound at Terpsichorean Training Techniques: there is a profusion of drapes, fluted columns, sprigged wallpaper, photographic blow-up displays, and, of course, the white foot-prints picked out on the otherwise slick, dark surface of the floor.

Minimalism and surreal stylization are both deployed as a function of satire or parody in "Quick-Quick Slow Death." However, there is also a vignette of less barbed, more situation-based comedy in the episode, and for this Pottle's chosen idiom was an almost straightforward realism. Following a lead in her investigations, Emma visits the workshop of an endearingly garrulous tattooist, a character who is as homely and uninhibited as the members of staff at the dance school are insincere and repressed. His cramped room contains a plethora of suggestive details, all suitably distressed so as to appear cheerfully dowdy. The accretion of professional paraphernalia in the tattooist's is exaggerated for humorous effect, but there is no hint of stylization here. The tattooist's shop is as seemingly undesigned

FIGURE 2.12. *Steed enrolls for dancing lessons with Lucille Banks (Eunice Gayson), proprietor of Terpsichorean Training Techniques in "Quick-Quick Slow Death" (1966). Set designed by Harry Pottle. Courtesy of BFI Stills, Posters and Designs.*

as Terpsichorean Training Techniques is studiedly artificial, and the contrast between them is therefore overtly conceptual as well as dramatic.

While many sets, in different ways, contribute to the humor of the episode, one was conceived by Pottle specifically to provide for a visual joke. Seeking information at a bank, Steed attempts to interview one of the tellers, who proves elusive. The bank is actually a one-wall set, articulated by three grills, and the teller shifts from one to another of these positions throughout his conversation with Steed, who tries to keep up with his unpredictable movements—as does the camera, tracking frantically from side to side. Pottle was here making a deliberate nod to a famous scene from the Will Hay film *Oh, Mr. Porter!* (1937), where the irascible stationmaster performed a similarly bewildering "cup and bean" routine in his ticket office.

The bank, though conceived primarily for humor, was an essentially realistic set. For the next scene (after a brief location establishing shot), Pottle made an essay into a refined form of expressionism. Following up a clue he was given at the bank, Steed visits the ninth-floor offices of Purbright & Co., which proves to be a dummy organization. When Steed forces the office door, he finds that there is not only no company but also no office—only a sheer drop to the street below. Pottle set the scene for this moment of quasi-surreal horror. The corridor leading to the office door, though superficially drab and dull, is cleverly designed to promote unease in the viewer. The walls are relieved vertically by pilasters and door surrounds every few feet, and horizontally by a continuous stringcourse; in the raking light used for the scene, these strips create a grid of harsh, sinister shadows. Furthermore, light shining obliquely through a window at back of the set casts a sharp, crooked silhouette of the glazing bars onto the rear wall. Although the set is naturalistic, its disquieting fragmentation of light is reminiscent of that in *Das Kabinett des Doktor Caligari* (Robert Weiner, 1920).[106] The *coup de grâce* is that this starkly simplified set gives way (literally) to one conceived in a spirit of meticulous naturalism. The assemblage of girders against a partly rendered brick wall that lie behind Purbright & Co.'s office door, shockingly revealed as Steed narrowly avoids falling to his death, is entirely lifelike in effect, even though the conceit of the sheer drop is absurd.

For the interrogation room that serves as Steed's and Mrs. Peel's base of operations, Pottle offered a demonstration of postmodern archness par excellence. The wit in this set actually lies more in what is absent than what is present. The interrogation room is a subversive design, which mocks a

FIGURE 2.13. *Harry Pottle's design drawing for the Interrogation Room in "Quick-Quick Slow Death." Courtesy of Denise Pottle.*

particular convention of the espionage genre by representing its antithesis. In 1960s Cold War melodramas like *The Ipcress File* (1965) and *Goldfinger* (1964)—and, of course, *The Prisoner*—debriefing and interrogation were central: psychotropic drugs, electric shocks, brain surgery, and lasers were variously used to implant instructions or wring out information. These nightmares of mental rapine were invariably played out, with morbid fascination, in enclosed, fascistic environments, usually bristling with shiny electronic gizmos, spotlights, hypodermics, and electrodes.

In stark contrast to these mechanistic fantasies, Harry Pottle's *Avengers* interrogation room is exaggerated in its mundanity (figs. 2.13 and 2.14). Nor is it even the kind of claustrophobic interview room so often seen in police dramas and in slightly later espionage programs such as *Callan* (ABC/Thames TV, 1967–1972). The chamber is almost agoraphobically large and empty, except for the high kitchen chair on which the prisoner sits and an enamel bath surmounted by a small water boiler. The humorous incongruity of the bath, a motif that Pottle introduced quite late in the design process (see fig. 2.14), is self-evident. Much less obvious, however, is the subtle way in which he gave an off-kilter inflection to the whole design by

FIGURE 2.14. *We have ways of making you . . . bathe?: Captain Noble (John Woodnutt) attempts to debrief the taciturn Eastern Bloc agent Willi Fehr (Michael Peake) in the Interrogation Room in "Quick-Quick Slow Death." Set designed by Harry Pottle.
© Canal + Image UK Ltd.*

his articulation of the walls. The splendid baroque fireplace, though quite appropriate to such a large chamber, is at odds with the bath and radiators on the contiguous wall; more delightfully illogical still is the picture rail, which is manifestly far too bulky and far too low to serve its purpose. For the sake of perversity, Pottle deliberately gave this feature the massive proportions of a cornice, not a rail, and the effect is enhanced by virtue of the fact that, thanks to its low placement, this bulky feature is jammed against the window architraves. In many ways, then, Pottle's interrogation room is as disconcerting as any futuristic chamber of horrors, but wittily understated rather than emphatically arresting.[107]

Pottle's willingness to trip up the viewer, to introduce subtle elements of paradox, is epitomized by his design for Steed's apartment (figs. 2.15 and 2.16). This was a particularly important design, as it was the most oft seen in the season and shot from every manageable angle. Yet Pottle was not afraid to build in a number of anomalies, some of which reside in the structure as well as the décor. The spatial configuration of the interior is exceedingly odd: the room is unmistakably trapezoidal, narrowing sharply to the French windows at the rear,[108] and even the broadest part is interrupted on one side by a short flight of steps to the landing that serves as the entrance lobby to the flat.

The unconventional arrangement of space is echoed in the architectural details. Although the paneling and wrought ironwork clearly evoke the Georgian era, Pottle did not simply settle for the conventional "classical" idiom of the period. Instead, he adopted the Georgians' most self-consciously playful style, the "Gothick": the French doors and even the little window over Steed's escritoire have lancet-shaped upper lights, while the deep window embrasure is divided from the rest of the room by a Tudor arch.[109] One especially curious feature is the slender, velvet-clad column beside Steed's Knole settee. A structural justification for this pole could be found, but to seek one would be pedantic. The real point, surely, is that this feature is meant to be relished for its mild perversity. Perhaps it is meant to be understood as a reflection of Macnee/Steed's impishness. An analogous perversity is apparent in the treatment of one of the room's most conspicuous movable furnishings. A gilded carriage lamp, the mace-like splendor of which seems to demand that it be given pride of place among the various light fixtures, is in fact lashed casually to the stair rail whence it leans tipsily into the main part of the room (see fig. 2.16).

Kingsley Amis wrote that the audience of *The Avengers* "must have the mental agility to appreciate the odd satirical nudge while still believing in the story as a thriller."[110] Steed's apartment attests that Pottle believed in viewers' capacity to be detached and credulous at the same time. Steed's drawing room, though eccentrically shaped, could still conceivably belong to the real world. The place is also believable as Steed's domicile: the furnishings can, as Pottle intended, suggest "the elegant, suave, ex-military gentleman," and reflect "'club'-style comfort and good taste."[111] On the other hand, the playful elements, though refined, are profuse and promi-

FIGURE 2.15. *The sitting room in Steed's flat, from the fireplace wall. Set designed by Harry Pottle. Composite image courtesy of David K. Smith.* © Canal + Image UK Ltd.

FIGURE 2.16. *Where there's mock, there's brass: Steed and Emma practicing (respectively) golf and the tuba in Steed's sitting room. Note that Steed is in his "civvies": turtleneck sweater and cardigan. Patrick Macnee's costume designed by himself; Diana Rigg's costume designed by Jan Rowell. © Canal + Image UK Ltd.*

nent enough to create an overall effect, if not actually of antinaturalism, then certainly ironic hyperrealism. "Good taste" is both shown and derided: design-magazine preciosity is lampooned by the velvet-covered pole and the listing carriage lamp.

To return to our point of departure in this chapter, neither Steed's nor Mrs. Peel's apartment can simply be called stylish: they are about style and stylishness. The Gothick overtones of Steed's apartment are, from this perspective, peculiarly resonant of the *Avengers* ethos. The eighteenth-century Gothick style, unlike the work of the impassioned Gothic Revivalists of the nineteenth century, was a wry pastiche of medieval modes. The Georgians plundered the architectural forms of the Middle Ages merely for the sake of having another stylistic string to their bow, another pleasing reminder of the past; they remained almost entirely uninterested in the cultural ideals that those forms had originally served.[112] Similarly, though Macnee/Steed adopted the dandified style and manners of the neo-Edwardian (or Regency Buck) and affected the traditional tastes of the ex-military clubman, he subverted all this ultraconservatism with his veiled impudence and playfulness.

BIZARRE: SCENIC DESIGN IN THE LATER *AVENGERS*

Earlier we spoke of a decadence in *The Avengers* during its last two seasons, a coarsening of both narrative content and imagery. Design for the show was deprived of its subversive edge by the rapid expansion of full-fledged surrealism, which was the corollary of increasingly wacky scripts. The very last story in the series was actually entitled "Bizarre." This might have served equally well for any of the previous forty or so episodes.

Yet, even this relatively one-dimensional final phase produced some undeniably striking scenic-design imagery. The shift of direction was accomplished by Robert Jones, who was production designer for most of the last two seasons. After Harry Pottle's departure, design for the series had briefly languished in the doldrums, with some outstandingly unimaginative designs by Wilfred Shingleton: he was responsible, for example, for Steed's new pine-clad apartment interior, a monument to banal vulgarity. Robert Jones' arrival after a few episodes gave production design for the series a palpable shot in the arm.

Jones' designs were much more straightforward than Pottle's and made no conceptual demands on the viewer; gone were the laconic touches and witty manipulations of stereotype. However, Jones' sensibility was assertive, and he often contrived sets that were radically abstracted from reality. The offices of Classy Glass Cleaning Co., for example, seen in "The Super Secret Cypher Snatch" (1969), consisted of nothing but a large chamber with windowless walls that were painted alternately blue and gray. Against this neutral background there was a peculiar assortment of furnishings. On the one hand there were the trappings of prestige—a large gilded Louis Quinze desk and matching chairs for the company director, a chandelier, and gilt coats of arms (presumably indicating the social caliber of the firm's clientele) adorning the walls. Juxtaposed with these rococo elements were a cluster of glass sheets in elevated gold frames upon which apprentices, dressed in white overalls and hats and standing on gold-painted stepladders, practiced their trade.

At the headquarters of another company, Jig Creations, the self-proclaimed "center of the jigsaw universe" seen briefly in "Game" (1969), the inner partition walls took the form of huge jigsaw pieces. Similarly, an admiral's office in "A Funny Thing Happened on the Way to the Station" (1967) was shaped like the captain's cabin on a sailing ship—and so on.

If a label were sought to describe the heavily stylized imagery produced for *The Avengers* by Robert Jones, one could do worse than "Pop"—a term which, unlike "postmodern," enjoyed considerable currency in the 1960s. Pop art was an established and saleable phenomenon in Britain and the States by the middle of the decade.[113] Moreover, British exponents who had first sought in the late 1950s and early 1960s to introduce elements of popular mass culture into their "fine" art, were, so to speak, repaying the compliment: in 1967 Peter Blake devised the cover for *Sergeant Pepper's Lonely Hearts Club Band,* while in the following year Richard Hamilton created the sleeve for The Beatles' "White Album",[114] It was Hamilton who, in 1957, had produced an "inventory" of the characteristics of Pop art—although, as he later pointed out, his use of the term at this point referred "solely to art manufactured for a mass audience," since at the time "there was no such thing as 'Pop Art' as we now know it."[115] Hamilton's list runs as follows:

> *Pop Art is:*
> *Popular (designed for a mass audience)*
> *Transient (short-term solution)*
> *Expendable (easily forgotten)*
> *Low cost*
> *Mass produced*
> *Young (aimed at youth)*
> *Witty*
> *Sexy*
> *Gimmicky*
> *Glamorous*
> *Big business*[116]

Most of these apply to *The Avengers.* Of course, all television programs are transient, mass-produced, and expendable. Some of Hamilton's other descriptors were more particularly applicable to *The Avengers:* the series had been glamorous, witty, and sexy since the first appearance of Honor Blackman, and from the advent of Diana Rigg, it had certainly become big business. In the last two seasons of *The Avengers,* especially after the arrival of Tara King and Mother, two other elements of Pop came into their own—the young and the gimmicky.

Robert Jones' set for Jig Creations could certainly be said to epitomize the gimmicky, but a love of this quality was expressed above all in the many sight gags involving Mother. For all that he was confined to a wheelchair, which was pushed around by a silent, blond amazon called Rhonda, Mother proved to be a remarkably elusive figure: his base of operations was never in the same place twice. He might be found seated on one side of a set of jockey's scales among a gaggle of huge photographic blow-ups (fig. 2.17); amid indoor cricket nets (where he sat, in his wheelchair, fitted with pads

FIGURE 2.17. *In the balance: "Mother" (Patrick Newell) maintains the status quo of British security from one side of a set of jockey scales, assisted by Steed and Rhonda (Rhonda Parker) in "Wish You Were Here" (1969).* © Canal + Image UK Ltd.

and brandishing a bat); on the top deck of a London bus; or on a tennis umpire's high chair in the middle of a swimming pool. Alternatively, he might be in his convertible Bentley Continental, which could be parked anywhere from a flowering meadow to a pink-walled underground chamber filled with an assortment of scale-model trucks. The gimmicks might be taken further still: in "The Rotters," Mother's office was entirely composed of and furnished with the kind of translucent vinyl that was so trendy at the time. Mother himself was seated in an inflatable chair, which Rhonda continually blew up throughout the episode.

The imagery built around Mother had its pleasures, but—in true Pop style—these pleasures were transient and without nuance or resonance, especially compared to those from earlier seasons. In the 1965–1966 episodes, for example, Mrs. Peel and Steed drove away from the camera at the end of each show in a different mode of transport. These vehicles had often been relevant to the content of the script: a story with Chinese associations ended with Steed leading Mrs. Peel off in a rickshaw, while a story concerning an Arabian prince saw the couple departing on a "magic carpet," which was actually being carried on the roof of a van. In Mother's case, the gimmicks were dissociated from anything except precedent: the only question each week was how the previous week's conceit could be capped. Certainly there was no attempt at integration with other ideas in the scripts, far less the kind of sly twist embodied in the "magic" carpet.

With the advent of Linda Thorson as Tara King, *The Avengers* also became more overtly "young," in Richard Hamilton's sense of being "aimed at youth." As noted, Thorson was much more of an ingenue than either

Honor Blackman or Diana Rigg had been when they took up their roles in the series, and this youthfulness was fully exploited in visual terms. John Bates' designs for Rigg's clothing had been deliberately conceived so as not to date too quickly: Alun Hughes' and Harvey Gould's outfits for Thorson, by contrast, were unmistakably of the moment, and her predecessors' austerity and classicism were thrown to the winds.

Furnishing and decorating Tara King's apartment was also taken as an opportunity for excessive frivolity. Set designer Kenneth Tait, who created the interior, pushed late-1960s fads to an extreme. The taste for primary colors, and more particularly for psychedelic mixtures of bright shades, was fully expressed in Miss King's apartment, as was the contemporary nostalgia boom. The fabric used for the curtains, sofa, and ottoman had a big, bold pattern of sunflowers in yellow, orange, green, and white, which shouted in competition with the throw pillows, the bright pink carpet (later modified to red), and the wall panels in a variety of hues from yellow to mauve. The apartment also contained so many knickknacks and bibelots that it looked more like an overstocked curiosity shop than a home. Tara had more than ten antique telephones, and there was a weird assortment of objects from storefronts and pubs, including a giant model of a mortar and pestle from a pharmacy and an equally huge pair of spectacles from an optometrist's. The apartment had two levels, and even the means of communication between the floors were old-fashioned and quaint: a white, Victorian cast-iron staircase was complemented by a fireman's pole. In many ways, this was as implausible a living environment as Mrs. Gale's mechanistic flat; but plausibility was beside the point. Tara King's apartment served as a showcase—almost a showroom—for ideas on what was hip in décor, ideas that could be spread among the well-to-do, fashion-conscious youth epitomized by London's Primrose Hill set (Miss King's address, tellingly enough, was No. 9 Primrose Crescent).

To charge Kenneth Tait with overdesigning Tara King's flat would be to misunderstand the visual ethos that prevailed during Robert Jones' years as production designer on *The Avengers*—and the slogan for this ethos, it might well be said, was that nothing succeeds like excess. The seeds of Jones' colorful stylization had been present in Harry Pottle's work—and to some extent in even earlier episodes—but under Pottle's masterful hand the stylized was just one element in a web of imaginatively interwoven design modes.

Because *The Avengers* so quickly became polygeneric, boundaries and therefore restraints ceased to exist. Although naturalism remained a rough "mean" from which designers could work, there were no concrete rules to hinder the imagery of the program from becoming tendentious in one way and another; and this is what ultimately happened. Novelty was still guaranteed from week to week in Robert Jones' designs, but innovation of the finely turned kind practiced by Harry Pottle had been almost entirely lost along the way. Nevertheless, it is only fair to say that the spirit of inventiveness had become overripe rather than stale: imagery in *The Avengers* remained distinctive and daring to the last.

RETRO FAILURE—*THE AVENGERS* MOVIE

The visual distinctiveness and daring of *The Avengers* were never fully developed in television in the years after the demise of the program. In fact, approaches to television production have become increasingly conservative and cautious since 1969. Nor have attempts to resuscitate *The Avengers* itself produced anything comparable to the original series. As already noted, *The New Avengers,* produced in the mid-1970s by Brian Clemens and Albert Fennell, bore little resemblance to its progenitor except by virtue of its name and the presence of Patrick Macnee as Steed. The visual style of the new show, like that of Clemens' and Fennell's crime-*cum*-espionage series, *The Professionals* (LWT/AMI, 1977–1983)—for which *The New Avengers* retrospectively seemed like a rather lame dry run—was dully naturalistic, despite a modicum of inventiveness in some of the teleplays. *The New Avengers* enjoyed modest success with audiences for two seasons. The next revival of *The Avengers* was not so fortunate.

During the 1980s and 1990s, when films based on 1960s television series were staple Hollywood fare, there was almost continual talk of bringing *The Avengers* to the silver screen. In August 1998, after more than ten years of gestation, an *Avengers* movie was released by Warner Brothers. Notwithstanding its all-star cast, led by Sean Connery, Ralph Fiennes, and Uma Thurman, the film was a commercial and critical washout. Fiona Sturges of *The Independent* accounted for its failure with nice concision: the film's "principal downfall is its attempt at a postmodern perspective," and "it is so pleased with its arch script and retro-kitsch aesthetics that the basic tension you would expect from any spy thriller is absent."[117] The implications that design as well as dialogue was heavy-handed and (more particularly) that the visual imagery was too strongly backward-looking are worth considering briefly for the interesting light they cast on aspects of the original *Avengers*.

The makers of *The Avengers* movie faced a problem common to all those who produce feature films based on television series: the incompatibility of the two forms. However committed and able the stylists of the *Avengers* movie, many of the nuances of the original were bound to be lost. Part of the delight of the television adventures of Steed and Mrs. Peel was the leisurely, week-by-week exploration of the various clichés of British culture—the English butler, the hunt, golfing, and so on. Although an *Avengers* "house style" can be extrapolated from the series, full appreciation of the incidental wit, whether in Philip Levene's scripts or Harry Pottle's set designs, depended on familiarity with the unique idiomatic character of the program. In a feature film, the whole business of introducing the audience to the protagonists and their frame of reference precludes this kind of refined enjoyment. Larger-than-life characters and situations demand latitude in order to be relished: where the spectator's experience is highly concentrated, stylization, however deft in conception, can easily seem crass.

A more specifically visual challenge, which the makers of the *Avengers* movie failed to overcome, was posed by the sheer potency of images from the original series. For most people it would be as unthinkable to present Steed without a bowler or Peel without a bodysuit as to portray Sherlock Holmes without pipe and deerstalker. Yet a bowler in 1998 was a total anachronism in a way that it was not in 1965; and the bodysuit is the very essence of mid-1960s space-age style. Retaining the main characters' images, therefore, meant that the decision to set the movie in a 1999 "where the sixties have never ended" was almost unavoidable.[118] Yet in conceding the power of the original imagery in this manner, the producers were making a rod for their designers' backs. In the first place, odious comparisons with the television program became inevitable, and in the second, *The Avengers* was effectively reduced to a period piece, a glorified pastiche.

The "retro-kitsch" of the movie distances it from the television series and produces an effect that is cloying in proportion to the piquancy of the original. *The Avengers* of mid-1960s vintage maintained a dynamic balance between the conservative and the progressive. The main characters expressed this balance: sexually liberated scientist and ex-industrialist Emma Peel represented the technological "white heat" that Harold Wilson believed he saw in mid-1960s Britain, while Steed represented the legacy of amiable Macmillanite conservatism, as yet undisturbed by the rise of a "New

Right" that was red in tooth and claw.[119] Incidental characters, too, were drawn evenhandedly from the ranks of the forward-looking and the reactionary. The ruling classes of 1960s Britain repeatedly came under scrutiny and under fire in the series—but this did not simply mean the old-fashioned Tory establishment, for the new wave of plutocrats and technocrats were just as often targets of satire. The technological avant-garde was teased for its smug self-satisfaction, and the moribund ex-imperial elite was mocked for the grotesque emptiness of its forms and rituals. In the *Avengers* movie, this balance was undermined. Visually, the imbalance is most apparent in the look of the new Mrs. Peel. The heavy 1960s accent of Anthony Powell's designs makes her look almost as anachronistic as Steed. Diana Rigg had literally embodied the futuristic when wearing John Bates' vinyl flying suit and Alun Hughes' "Emmapeelers"; Uma Thurman's Mrs. Peel is just another retro chick.

The nostalgic treatment of *The Avengers* in the Warner Brothers movie was in line with the prevailing aesthetic of the late 1990s. Period style had little distinct meaning in the retro-oriented fashion climate, which persists today. Pastiche no longer represents a pejorative value judgment in the postmodern visual arts. Above all, modernity no longer necessarily means modernism. With all this in mind, it might seem pointless to chide the designers of the film for not taking their courage in their hands and establishing a visual idiom that was new and original, as both Harry Pottle and John Bates once did. After all, in a postmodern world, the very notion of originality is old-hat.[120] Yet even if it echoed contemporary aesthetic trends, the movie did not provoke a more virulent outbreak of retro-fever, as its makers might have hoped. On the contrary, the baggage that the film brought from the 1960s was more than audiences would patiently bear. The wallowing in "retro-kitsch," which seemed so self-congratulatory to Sturges, was an inevitable consequence of the wholesale cannibalism of the original series by the film.

The Avengers was a film about a mythical Britain made by and for Americans. It might therefore be averred that the movie, with its incessant harping on those alleged British obsessions, tea and the weather, proved definitively that Americans never really understood the innovative brilliancy of the original series, and that they are incapable of comparable sophistication themselves. Yet, insofar as the intelligent and experimental use of the visual pioneered by *The Avengers* has been echoed at all in television of the 1990s, it is in North America that this has happened. *The X Files* (Fox/Ten-

Thirteen, 1993–2002) is not directly comparable with *The Avengers,* since its paranormal subject matter made the maintenance of realism essential. Like all horror, *The X Files* had the potential to disintegrate into bathos and farce unless plausibility was maintained. Yet as its following increased, *The X Files* toyed more and more archly with its own visual conventions, which were those of the documentary. One way the "news report" character was sustained was by the regular appearance of typescript at the bottom left of the screen announcing the location of the action. In "Bad Blood" (1998), which, with delicious postmodern irony, revolves around a real vampire obsessed with Bela Lugosi's Dracula movies, the story is told twice, from the points of view of the two heroes, FBI Agents Mulder and Scully (David Duchovny and Gillian Anderson). Narration is another documentary device, but here it is the speakers' subjectivity rather than objectivity that is stressed. Scully and Mulder correct each other as they go along, and a squabble over the name of a motel results in the mandatory typescript deleting itself and then reappearing with the corrected information.

In another episode, "Postmodern Prometheus" (1997), documentary veracity is entirely overridden in what proves to be a facetious homage to James Whale's *Frankenstein* (1931). The episode is shot in monochrome and oozes intertextuality in every scene. In each case, the way in which diegetical "reality" is disrupted recalls the archness of *The Avengers,* and on both occasions it is the visual rather than the verbal that is used to explode the viewers' faith in the narrative coherence and "factuality" of the series.

In "Hollywood A.D." (2000), *The X-Files* confronted its own artifice very much as *The Avengers* had done in the episode "Epic," albeit in a more sustained fashion. Given the broad audience approval of the series in the late 1990s, this was a daring departure from the ironclad realism of most contemporary escapist television drama. The agents travel to Los Angeles to visit the set of a movie being made about their latest case. Corey Kaplan's graveyard set is a wonderful cross between the moody and oppressive cemeteries seen in earlier episodes and the famously stagy graveyard from Ed Wood's quintessentially awful B movie *Plan 9 from Outer Space* (1959) — a film that Mulder watches in the course of the story. The "play within a play" stars David Duchovny's off-screen wife, Tea Leoni, as Scully and is shot at the 20th Century Fox studios where the program itself was being made. Again, visual cues and jokes furnish the principal means by which the diegetical stability of the series is undermined.

Another American television series of the 1990s deserves to be mentioned in relation to the use of surrealism by *The Avengers*. *Ally McBeal* (ABC/Fox, 1998–2002) is a comedy of manners and sexual mores that rises well above the commonplace both narratively, by its inclusion of disquieting insights into its protagonists' personalities, and visually, by repeatedly disrupting the naturalism of the drama. The lead character's mental responses to social encounters play out for the audience as objective occurrences: she turns to ice and cracks into shards when embarrassed; she is suddenly swimming underwater through her office when pressures at work become too much; she develops a chameleon-like tongue to lick a man she is attracted to; and whenever a boyfriend breaks off his relationship with her, she is catapulted out of an industrial trash can into a dump truck. The tone of all this resembles the calculated anomalies in Harry Pottle's set designs for *The Avengers*, though the vehicle is different. Despite Ally's transformations being computer-generated and animated, the community of spirit between the series is worth stressing.

Ally McBeal represented a call for the mainstream to experiment with the kind of antinaturalism pioneered in *The Avengers*. Whether an art director undertakes such experimentation at a drawing board or in front of a screen is, in a sense, irrelevant. That computer technology is now used to stimulate rather than supplant the imagination helps affirm that *The Avengers* was not a cultural fluke but a cultural trailblazer.

C
H
A
P
T
E
YOUR R **VILLAGE**
T
H
R
E
E

THE WATCHER AND THE WATCHED

The Avengers must be reckoned a highly successful television series on two counts: first, it ran for a whole decade, enjoying international acclaim; second, the program has had a legacy. Its offbeat whimsy and satire resurfaced in later shows, from the knowing detective spoofs *Remington Steele* (NBC/MTM, 1982–1987) and *Moonlighting* (ABC/Picturemaker, 1985–1989) in the 1980s to the fanciful tragicomedies *Ally McBeal* and *Buffy the Vampire Slayer* in the 1990s. In other words, the program fulfilled the two main criteria by which the commercial and artistic success of a series can be judged: longevity and ongoing influence.

Doctor Who, while it has not really produced imitators or influenced the tone of other shows, was a commercial success: it remained in production for nearly thirty years and continues even now to be a cash cow for the BBC through merchandising. Both *The Avengers* and *Doctor Who* possessed what the British television mogul Lew Grade termed a "winning formula."

Ironically, *The Prisoner,* which Grade produced, enjoyed neither commercial success nor far-reaching artistic influence—though this is no reflection on its artistic merit. The formula in this case was not so much weak as characterized by belligerent perversity. The series in effect had built-in obsolescence. Drama series are typically conceived as open-ended narratives; *The Prisoner* was not. It was a biting critique of the series form and the pappy commercialism associated with most escapist television drama (including, arguably, *The Avengers* and *Doctor Who*) in the mid-1960s.

Comparing the early critical and commercial fortunes of *The Avengers* and *The Prisoner* reveals the limits of the viewing public's tolerance for stylized imagery. The context rather than the degree of stylization qualifies this tolerance. The likeness of *The Avengers* to revue and satire was undisguised, and its wacky designs were correspondingly easy to accept. The difficulty for most first-time viewers of *The Prisoner* arose from the clash between its imagery (and the character of the show sustained by that imagery) and its guise as a suspense drama.

Suspense works for only a limited time without a climax—or at least, without increasingly clever deferrals of a climax. *The Prisoner* took little account of this. Its opening episode posed broad narrative questions that, within a couple of weeks, were shown to be irrelevant to its truly anarchic concerns. More important, the strident antinaturalism of the scenic and costume imagery undermined the suspense plot from the outset.

Unlike *The Avengers* and *Doctor Who*, *The Prisoner* offers no opportunity for investigating the changing role of design during the development of a series. Its importance for the present study rests on the stylized imagery that was integral to the program-makers' conception. The power of design within the cumulative narrative of *The Prisoner* is therefore quite different from the power of the Steed image, for example, or that of Honor Blackman's leather fighting gear, which became such a cultural icon.

The uncompromisingly antinatural design idiom of *The Prisoner* was intended to do more than satirize both an entire genre and some aspects of society, as did much of the stylization in *The Avengers*. The target here was more specific: the authenticity of the television image itself was under attack.

In the 1960s, television was still a relatively new form of mass entertainment. Although it had become a force in its own right rather than a country cousin of film and theater, the medium had not yet become self-reflexive, i.e., few, if any, programs addressed the nature and effects of television itself.

FIGURE 3.1. *The drugged and kidnapped agent (Patrick McGoohan) comes groggily to his window . . .*

In many ways *The Prisoner,* which began airing in 1967 and was curtailed early the following year after only seventeen episodes, was the first television series to be about television. Not only did it explore the technical and expressive possibilities of the medium, but it also probed the viewer's status as watcher.

Each episode of *The Prisoner* begins with a mute replay of the basic premise: a man resigns angrily from his job and is spirited away, unconscious, from his home to a strange place known only as "the Village." He awakens, disoriented but still apparently in his own house, lifts his blinds, and gazes through his window (fig. 3.1). When he is confronted with a scene of picture-perfect rustic charm rather than the expected London skyscrapers, we receive a clear hint that the program will be about perception and viewing—looking at things, looking through things, and being looked at (fig. 3.2).

At the beginning of every episode, the vista out of the Prisoner's window becomes both the canvas on which the story title is painted and an extension of the viewer's act of watching. The television set, so often metaphorically compared to a window, brings other worlds into the home. In the story, the window in the Prisoner's sitting room also opens onto an "other" world.

Other images of watching are plentiful in the series. In one episode, the chief administrator of the Village, Number 2, appears on the Prisoner's television set and converses with him in a kind of video conference. Furthermore, viewers frequently observe Number 2 and his lackeys while they observe the Prisoner's activities on large "movie screens" in their headquarters;

the protagonist is thus doubly a spectacle (fig. 3.3).[1] There are also slyer and more rarefied allusions to television and viewing. In one episode, we learn that the Prisoner keeps his safe behind a television set in his London home; in another, a group of Villagers sit around a glowing white sphere, staring at its nothingness in a parody of the near-catatonic state of the television junkie.

A critique of enthusiasm for television is particularly clear in an episode called "The General." The story centers around "speedlearn," a way to educate people subliminally through television images—a process the Prisoner regards as at best the soulless transfer of information, at worst brainwashing.[2] The Village inhabitants tune in to lectures—actually strobing images that last only a few seconds—and then repeat by rote the facts instilled into them. When the Prisoner discovers the shallowness of knowledge gained so passively, he breaks into the Village Projection Room in an attempt to substitute his own dissident transmission for the evening's history class. This reflects the program-makers' attempts to use television against itself by slipping their inflammatory messages into an ostensibly diverting espionage melodrama. Commenting on the collective oblivion of the Villagers, Patrick McGoohan, the star and prime mover of the series, said, "Their souls have been brainwashed out of them. Watching too many commercials is what happened to them."[3]

True to the makers' subversive intent, *The Prisoner* is not easy to watch. Although in certain respects remorselessly repetitive, the cumulative narrative is full of elliptical references and imponderables. Indeed, *The Pris-*

FIGURE 3.2. . . . *to find that he is in the Village. Note episode title caption.*
The Prisoner *(ITC, 1967–8).* © *Carlton International Media Limited.*

FIGURE 3.3. *Image within image: Number 2 (Leo McKern) watches the Prisoner in "Once Upon a Time" (1968).* © Carlton International Media Limited.

oner ends without conventional closure, which provoked vociferous outrage from the original viewing audience.[4] McGoohan has said that *The Prisoner* was meant to be "an allegorical conundrum,"[5] and it succeeded in being one in all respects. We noted in relation to Harry Pottle's work for *The Avengers* that design can work at cross-purposes with the supposed frame of reference for the show. This same tendency is evident in *The Prisoner,* with its conspicuous irregularities and its questioning of the normal illusionism of screen drama.

It should be noted here that, insofar as the record permits a reconstruction of the way that *The Prisoner* was shaped and made, Patrick McGoohan —an actor, sometime writer and director, and executive producer of the series—does emerge as the dictator, or at least the éminence grise, of most aspects, including design.[6] To a great extent, therefore, the difficult nature of *The Prisoner* can be attributed to the influence of McGoohan's own ideas and worldview.

Two overarching points about the role of design in *The Prisoner* must be made before examining the program in detail. First, it is a fact of great importance that the visual imagery for *The Prisoner* was conceived concurrently with the narrative premise. When McGoohan, who was to be executive producer, approached the television mogul Lew Grade with a proposal for the project, he went armed with designs (some by scenic designer Jack Shampan[7] and perhaps also some by costume designer Masada Wilmot), and he already had the idea for the idiosyncratic principal location in mind.[8] We must assume that these images added to the cogency of McGoohan's pitch—or at least that he believed that they would do. For a television series, such early emphasis on the visual, as an integral part of the initial concept, is highly unusual.

The second general point about design in *The Prisoner* ties in with the first, but is, for our purposes, more significant. Not only were narrative and design given parity in the conceptual process, but the storytelling of the series, as realized, was highly unusual in that it behaved, so to speak, like design. Design, as we have argued, has the innate tendency to proliferate associations, none of which is necessarily confirmed by any external referent. In many episodes of *The Prisoner,* there are evocative scenes and exchanges that are suggestive in their own right but do little to clarify any aspect of the overall narrative thrust.

For example, in "Dance of the Dead," the Prisoner attends a Village costume ball that is suddenly transformed into a tribunal, at which he is accused of dangerously independent and antisocial behavior. The language used by all the participants at the hearing, including the Prisoner himself, is a mixture of clipped aphorisms and hieratic, pseudolegal floridity. The whole affair seems impromptu and is certainly arbitrary. It dissolves into a sequence that is both comic and horrific, with the costumed Villagers pursuing the Prisoner like a lynch mob through a maze of corridors and chambers until he finds safety in a secret room with Number 2. This disturbing sequence teases the viewer with things that seem significant: for example, the members of the tribunal are decked out as Nero, Napoleon, and Elizabeth I. Two of the judges had been seen earlier in the episode: "Napoleon" is the quietly psychotic doctor who administers the drugs meant to break the Village inmates, and "Elizabeth" is the Prisoner's pert and provocative maid.

It is easy to suggest wider meanings for the various aspects of the ball/ trial.[9] The invocation of autocrats from the past might reflect the latent intolerance in democratic society; the chase seems to point to the proximity of community to mob; the baroque rhetoric of the trial suggests the cumbersome arcana of the legal system; and so on. However, as soon as we begin to speculate along these lines, we become deflected from the narrative premise of the series—the battle of wits between the Prisoner and his captors. In other words, this philosophizing splinters the outward narrative, deliberately exploding the wholeness of the diegesis.

The refractory narrative of *The Prisoner* was superficially at odds with the simplicity and coherence of its design aesthetic. The visual imagery of the program was essentially a closed system: there were very few deviations from the limited repertory of images seen in the first episode. Furthermore, while the imagery of *The Prisoner* was certainly aesthetically cogent, it had no obvious "meanings." Although Jack Shampan's sets were more stylized than anything seen in *The Avengers,* his aim was apparently not to clarify narrative intent by concentrating on significant motifs, as Harry Pottle had done. Shampan presumably wanted to emphasize the fact that the program was a conundrum: design, like the challenging narrative, was conceived so as to make the viewer think.

Because we do not propose to offer any cut-and-dried solution to McGoohan's puzzle, there is little alternative but to concentrate on the several means whereby significance in design for *The Prisoner* is deliberately and pointedly withheld. We will also include some observations on consistent formal properties of design within the series, which seem to be keyed into the makers' overall approach to manipulating the series form.

Because it was ostensibly conceived as a successor to (arguably even a continuation of) Patrick McGoohan's previous star vehicle, the espionage series *Danger Man* (U.S. title: *Secret Agent*), which ran intermittently from 1960 to 1966, *The Prisoner* must be considered in relation to its precursor.[10] Both series must initially be considered in relation to the term "cool." *Danger Man* was calculated to be cool in the popular sense, for McGoohan's secret agent, John Drake, was nothing if not snazzy and up-to-the-minute.[11] *The Prisoner,* on the other hand, was cool in the more rarefied sense of the term used by Marshall McLuhan; in other words, the program made heavy demands on viewers' willingness to participate imaginatively in what they were watching, rather than offering a complete package that could be passively consumed.

The appeal of *Danger Man,* very much like that of the James Bond novels and films whose influence it reflects, was based on contemporary fascination with technology, a cosmopolitan lifestyle, and the sexual tensions (in this case unresolved) between the handsome hero and a range of beautiful women. As well as restricting the protagonist's freedom of movement, *The Prisoner* differed vastly from *Danger Man* in that its hero was an out-and-out misogynist—notwithstanding that his deadliest opponents were women—and the portrayal of technology in the new series was anything but attractive and consumer-oriented.[12]

Something should at once be said about *The Prisoner* in relation to its historical context. For some, the defiant attitude of *The Prisoner* to the pleasures of consumerism may make the series seem more truly representative of the Sixties than *The Avengers*. After all, the decade has been historicized as a period in which a range of countercultural trends, from civil rights, feminism, and free-speech movements to beatnik and hippie culture, had unprecedented potency within European and American society.[13] As the British viewing public's outraged response to its denouement proved, *The Prisoner* was certainly perceived as unacceptably radical. Without question, it was more politically challenging than the other two series considered in this book, for all that they are not without their strongly unconventional aspects. After all, the "revolutionary" use of antinatural design in *The Avengers* hardly constitutes a tilt at normative values within society. Nor were the jibes at the ruling classes in any real way countercultural, for social satire, in Britain at least, is a venerable and culturally legitimated mode of expression. In a similar way, *Doctor Who*, though visually even more outré than *The Avengers*, was in many ways conservative, as we will demonstrate in the next chapter.

It is in the nature of counterculture that it may run not only against some established precedent — or, to put it more simply, against the "Establishment" — but also against other forms of counterculture. The Sixties was not a period in which all revolutionary and progressive forces were allied with one another, nor even a period when all counterculture was in any real sense progressive and revolutionary.[14] The values inscribed into *The Prisoner* were certainly not those that are most commonly associated with the Sixties. The puritanical McGoohan was, for example, outspokenly averse to sexual prodigality and promiscuity, and in both his star roles on television he firmly refused to project an image like that of the bed-hopping James Bond.[15] However, the ethos of *The Prisoner* did have certain important things clearly in common with the mood of the times. Appearing as it did at a moment when America and increasingly also Britain were being affected by the advent of hippie culture,[16] *The Prisoner*, like hippiedom, embodied a heartfelt condemnation of technology-oriented Western materialism.[17]

Yet the true radicalism of the series lay not in any particular "agenda" for criticism, but in the fact that as a whole the programs were calculated to make audiences reflect. *The Prisoner* did not preach or moralize; it was no mere allegory of or commentary upon the dangers of this or that aspect of modern life, and conventional moral referents, such as the "democratic" emphasis on the value of individualism, were absent. Individualism was, in fact, treated as a double-edged sword. The ostensibly heroic Prisoner was in certain respects as objectionable as his captors: he embodied the dangers as well as the ideal of "doing your own thing."[18] The essential purpose of *The Prisoner* was to raise questions about the relationship between self and society in the technocracy of the global village.[19]

THE COOL WAR

In the introduction to the second edition of his seminal volume *Understanding Media,* Marshall McLuhan pointed out that the terms "hot" and "cool," which he uses in a specialized way, had successively enjoyed widespread usage as accolades during the twentieth century.[20] As McLuhan implied, the popular, acclamatory usages of "hot" and "cool" are, perversely enough, more or less cognate with one another: to use another vernacular term, they both denote the "hip."

McLuhan's use of the hot/cool polarity, on the other hand, was expressive of an opposition (as one might logically expect) and precise in its parameters. From one point of view, it is perhaps unfortunate that, as with "postmodern" in the last chapter, we are obliged to use terms that are fraught with conflicting meanings. However, there is no avoiding the dichotomous word "cool," since it is preeminently applicable in one sense (the popular) to *Danger Man* and in the other sense (the theoretical) to *The Prisoner.*

It is impossible to overstate the degree in which McLuhan's definition of "cool" is pertinent to *The Prisoner.* In the first chapter, we noted that television is described by McLuhan as a cool medium in comparison with film because it demands a greater degree of involvement on the part of the spectator. This need for active involvement stems in part from the fact that, on commercial channels, programs are interrupted regularly by advertisements, which create what McLuhan calls the "mosaic" effect.[21] The low definition of the television image also calls upon the viewer to supply what is missing in the image. Going beyond McLuhan's definition, we have further suggested that the series, as a form, is inherently "cooler" than other kinds of drama because it requires that the viewer imaginatively fill in lacunae in the piecemeal, partial narrative.[22]

The Prisoner took coolness further still, for it was certainly not a program that could be casually watched, and as we have already indicated, its narratives were in many cases calculatedly disjointed. At an overt level, the individual episodes consistently withheld important information from the viewer in order, apparently, to sustain the suspense plot of the cumulative narrative of the series.

Thus, the first episode, "Arrival," reveals that the Prisoner is a British ex-spy whose sudden resignation is taken for a defection, but nothing else concrete is disclosed about him or his captors throughout the entire seventeen-episode run. The Prisoner's name is never given: he is only ever referred to as Number 6.[23] The basis for his incarceration is also concealed. Is he being imprisoned and debriefed by his own people, anxious to protect their own interests and secrets? Or is the Village actually, as suggested in the episode "The Chimes of Big Ben," within the Eastern Bloc? Or is it run by an unknown third party and located somewhere off the Spanish peninsula? Red herrings abound. Above all, intriguing mystery surrounds the identity of the ultimate power in the Village, Number 1, who is never seen, but works solely through his deputies, the ever-changing succession of men and women designated as Number 2. Until the final episode, the only visible sign of Number 1's controlling presence is the large red cordless telephone with which he keeps in touch with Number 2.

But a more substantial intellectual contribution is demanded of viewers than speculating about missing pieces in the plot. As the ball/trial from "Dance of the Dead" showed, the audience is called upon to recognize the hollowness of the suspense narrative. Viewers are asked to understand that, as McGoohan has expressed it, the series was "an allegorical conundrum for people to interpret for themselves."[24]

In fact, most episodes of *The Prisoner* pay only lip service to the central spy story, which is overridden by a variety of discourses on ethical, ideological, or societal problems. "The General," as noted, raises questions about not only the ethics of subliminal mental stimulation but also the nature of what is categorized as learning in an information-obsessed society. "Free for All" finds Number 6 apparently in a position to stand for election to the post held by Number 2—but his campaign assistant turns out to be the incoming governor, and the election a ruse to break him. Here, the power of the electorate and the elected to effect change in a purported democracy is called into question: in the course of his apparently victorious run, Number 6's subversive campaign speeches evaporate and are replaced, after his brainwashing, by empty political cant in support of the reactionary policies in the Village. The implicit rejection of the spy genre in *The Prisoner* is driven home by a biting indictment of the immorality of the secret service in the penultimate episode, "Once Upon a Time," while in the last episode,

"Fall Out," the espionage narrative is exploded. Prior to making good his final escape from the Village, Number 6 at last unmasks Number 1, only to reveal his own face, laughing maniacally.

In light of the studied lack of plot development in *The Prisoner* from episode to episode, and, more important, its failure to provide neat explanations for the main questions raised at the outset, it is entirely unsurprising that audiences were so hostile in their response. McGoohan later claimed that he was actively courting this hullabaloo, and on balance there seems no real reason to disbelieve him.[25] What is particularly indicative of an intent to wrong-foot the viewer is the way that *The Prisoner* traded strongly off *Danger Man,* laying false scents that would lead the unwary into vain expectations about the new series. Foremost among these teasing deceptions is the intimation that Number 6 is, in fact, John Drake—an inference encouraged not only by the elementary fact that McGoohan was again portraying a spy, but also by palpable factors such as his dress (a matter to which we will return). In short, viewers of *The Prisoner* were led to expect one kind of cool and were in fact given another.

Danger Man was also less than straightforward. Drake was always an elusive character and became increasingly so as the plots began to deal with the ruthlessness and dissimulation necessary to the secret agent's profession. This contrasted sharply with James Bond, for example. Fleming's novels contain a surfeit of descriptive information. Bond's personal tastes and attitudes were patently a reflection of the author's, and Fleming lavished as much detail on the agent's choice of shirts or shampoo as on his many amorous conquests and other undercover activities. Bond was a gambler and gourmet, and his car, significantly, was the grandest of British-made coupés, the Bentley Continental R convertible. Drake, by contrast, though well dressed, was not portrayed as a bon vivant, his only vice being a predilection for the occasional Havana cigar. McGoohan also insisted that Drake should drive a Mini-Cooper. This car, one of Britain's acknowledged triumphs of industrial design in the late Fifties, performed nippily in car chases but was unpretentious—in contrast to what McGoohan called the "fantastic engines of adolescent wish-fulfillment" used by Bond.[26]

McGoohan's preference for the Mini was not a rejection of the hip and cool—it was merely the espousal of a different kind of cool from Bond's. The Mini was a real style icon by the mid-1960s,[27] and his lack of conspicuous consumption certainly did not make John Drake a square. In fact, the consumer orientation of *Danger Man,* especially regarding dress, was more "happening" than that in either the Bond books or the "James Bond 007" films starring Sean Connery. Nor was the series reticent about its modishness. The producers of *Danger Man* were among the first to furnish their lead player with a stylish wardrobe through an arrangement with a fashion designer or manufacturer; McGoohan's outfits were devised, from the second series on, by "The Fashion House Group of London."

McGoohan exuded cosmopolitan cool. The actor's lean frame and austere charisma lent themselves to a style of dress that was distinctive without being implausibly obtrusive. Hats became the most distinctive part of the Drake image: During the first season he sported a range of modish, narrow-brimmed trilby hats, most notably one in hound's-tooth that complemented a similarly checked overcoat. With the second season, the hats became more daring—a porkpie in dark straw, a trilby in black vinyl, and a selection of cloth caps (fig. 3.4).

However, this headgear was the only remotely showy element in Drake's wardrobe. For the most part, his outfits were characterized by their practicality; when not in heavy disguise, the agent was always dapper, but never a Savile Row clotheshorse. His clothes were by no means uninteresting: stylish checked sports jackets, striped blazers, fleecy reefers or pea coats, and suede bomber jackets were donned and doffed as the climate and circumstances demanded. Yet Drake's wardrobe was generally at the casual end of the sartorial spectrum, and in this respect, too, he was very much a man of the moment.

Superb and sharply styled though Sean Connery's tailoring indubitably was in the "James Bond 007" movies, the city suiting that was Bond's normal attire made him appear to be a relatively conservative figure, an exquisite who represented the elegantly fading empire. Significantly, *Danger Man* eschewed the showy evening wear that became a cliché of the Bond movies. After the first season, the thoroughly modern Drake attended formal occasions in one of his dark two-piece suits, upgraded by a dress shirt and bow tie.

The cool of the Bond films and *Danger Man* converged in the deployment of cute technology: each episode of *Danger Man* and each new Bond movie were replete with "toys for boys." These mostly took the form of electronic gadgets for personal defense or surveillance, and in *Danger Man* in particular the spy's equipment was generally miniaturized and disguised. Once the precedent for ingenuity had been set, as it was early in the first season, the writers, crew, and McGoohan himself racked their brains try-

FIGURE 3.4. *Special Agent John Drake (Patrick McGoohan)—elegant but unostentatious. Publicity photograph for **Danger Man** (ITC, 1964). Costume by "The Fashion House Group of London." © Carlton International Media Limited.*

ing to think of new ways of turning the commonplace into the remarkable.[28] These dinky appliances fascinated audiences because of prevailing excitement over domestic technology and the trend toward the compact and handheld.[29] Drake's gadgets pointed the way, however indirectly, to forthcoming attractions in the shops.

Danger Man set the tone for cool that was to endure in British action series for the next decade. Gadgetry became ever more prominent in the Bond movies, and in the early 1970s *Doctor Who* was steered by its star, the self-confessed "machine-mad maniac," Jon Pertwee, toward exactly the same kind of exploitation of technology.[30] The preoccupation with travel in *Danger Man* also laid the groundwork for things to come. *The Persuaders* (ITC/Tribune, 1970–1971), which concerned the international exploits of two playboys played by Roger Moore and Tony Curtis, not only made use of cleverly conceived sets representing foreign locales (much like those created by Frank White, Jack Shampan, and Albert Whitterick for *Danger Man*) but also incorporated a great deal of location filming actually undertaken on the continent. Although little more than establishing shots of the heroes driving around in their cars, this footage flaunted travel on the Riviera and other European beauty spots as a commodity, the "purchase" of which was to be desired. The conspicuous consumption of travel was more ostentatious than in *Danger Man*, but the debt to the earlier series is unmistakable. The emphasis on foreign locales—shared also with such series as *Paul Temple* (BBC TV, 1969–1971) and *The Protectors* (ITC/Group 3, 1972–1973)—suggests that an attempt to explain the popularity of *Danger Man* must take account of this. Irrespective of its quiet probity and willingness to address moral dilemmas, *Danger Man* probably attracted the bulk of its viewers because it provided vicarious wish fulfillment in the form of armchair travel.

THE GLOBAL VILLAGE

Danger Man represented the aspiration to realism in television design at its most developed. When creating a set or overseeing the choice and dressing of a location in the British Isles, the scenic designer's aim was to help persuade viewers that they were looking at events taking place in foreign locales. Drake's technological gadgets, too, had to seem to work; in nearly every case they were conspicuously practical props, shot in close-up for the viewer to appreciate fully. All this meant that design as design had no place in *Danger Man*.

The Prisoner, in aggressive contrast, made great play of visual artifice and potently stylized design. In the introductory episode, the viewer, like the newly interned Number 6, is bombarded with the full panoply of Village imagery, much of which is remote from day-to-day experience: the picture-book architecture, the myriad candy-striped signs and awnings with their distinctive Albertus script, and the grimly metallic, subterranean interiors. Most bizarre and puzzling of all is Rover, the corpuscle-like, giant sentient white balloon that acts as Village "guardian," chasing our hero along the beach and rendering him unconscious by suffocation (fig. 3.5).

FIGURE 3.5.
Watchdog: The Prisoner approached by Rover with Atlas and the Green Dome in the background in "Free for All" (1967). Prop designed by Jack Shampan, costumes by Masada Wilmot.

This glut of visual imagery was intentional. McGoohan stressed the primacy of the visual in *The Prisoner:* "The style was clearly laid out and the designs of the sets, those were all clearly laid out from the inception of it. There was no accident in that area."[31] The creative team on the show was already familiar with his approach and interests, almost all of them having worked on *Danger Man:* art director Jack Shampan had been responsible for most of the second season of that series; Masada Wilmot had been a long-time costume supervisor; Brendan J. Stafford had been director of photography; and Lee Doig had frequently acted as editor.[32] Stafford's photography and Doig's crisp editing were particularly important in establishing design as central to the overall impact of the first episode.

The choice and use of location epitomize the way in which McGoohan's conception of the series ran contrary to that of *Danger Man*. This was the folly village of Portmeirion in North Wales, designed by the architect Clough Williams-Ellis (fig. 3.6). Because some of its buildings were believably Italianate, Portmeirion had been used in early episodes of *Danger Man* to simulate continental locations.[33] For *The Prisoner,* this kind of illusionistic device was thrown aside: Ellis' creation was revealed as what it was, an eclectic architectural curio. In the context of *The Prisoner,* the toy-town cheerfulness of Portmeirion was not so much exotic as sinister by association with the tyrannical regime of the Village.

A place of enforced order, an oppressively perfect microcosm, the quaint little utopia seemed to deride its dejected inmates through its relentless cheeriness. Some of Ellis' architectural eccentricities were even used specifically to evoke entrapment. For example, the coastal setting of the Village should have suggested the possibility of freedom and maritime adventure—and indeed, most of the Prisoner's jailbreaks were made by sea rather than land. Yet the fruitlessness of trying to escape from the Village was mockingly underscored by one of the most curious landmarks in Ellis' sprawling folly, a small ship that appears to be moored to the quay but is actually a monumental stone "dummy" built into it.[34]

Although Portmeirion contains quite a number of buildings inspired by Mediterranean architecture, the Village of *The Prisoner* is the quintessence of Englishness. Ostensibly an international community, this social microcosm is never shown to be, as is asserted in the first episode, "very cosmopolitan." Apart from the Japanese girl who utters this claim, and a few other exceptions such as the Eastern Bloc agent Nadia in "The Chimes of Big Ben," and the Haitian supervisor in "The Schizoid Man," there is no ethnic or racial diversity in the Village. On the contrary, the populace is rife with British stereotypes that belie the claim for internationalism, such as the gruff General in "The Chimes of Big Ben" and the Town Crier in "Dance of the Dead." Nor, in fact, are the Italianate features of the architecture, when taken en masse, especially redolent of the Mediterranean: with its double-hung sash windows and slate roofs, Portmeirion is unmistakably in a Georgian vein

FIGURE 3.6. *"Your Village": A view of the picturesque prison, Clough Williams-Ellis' Portmeirion. Photograph courtesy of Keith Barker.*

FIGURE 3.7. *The terror beneath: Number 6 struggles to negotiate the corridors of power beneath the Village in "Free For All" (1967). Set designed by Jack Shampan. © Carlton International Media Limited.*

rather than a southern European "classical" tradition. Furthermore, most of the surface-level interiors that we see are equally redolent of Georgian styles, sporting the kind of color and fussy detail that is emphatically missing from the "deeper" chambers of the Village, where the real power lies.

On the surface, the Village has a picturesque topography, but the saccharine whimsicality of its architecture, with its dome and towers, its rustic cottages, gazebos, and fountains, is emphatically at odds with what lies physically and psychologically beneath. Jack Shampan conceived the corridors of power in the Village as a subterranean warren of chambers and tunnels, threateningly fascistic in their scale and character (fig. 3.7).

They recall the disturbing side of technology in that they carry a strong air of the bunker or bomb-shelter. Where slate roofs, weatherboarding, sash windows, and gaily painted stucco prevail on the surface, within the control centers of the Village—including the interiors of such institutions as the Town Hall, the Labor Exchange, and the Hospital—the architectural vocabulary is an especially stark version of the International Style, with exposed metal and sheer, windowless walls either in shades of gray or primary colors. Ellis' Portmeirion, with its attractively informal clustering of built structures, rockeries, and foliage is easy on the eye, if not altogether easy to take in. Shampan's futuristic interiors, by contrast, are readily assimilated by virtue of the use of repeated forms, but nevertheless have a profoundly disorienting effect. Most of the interiors look alike, and there is no clear indication of how the labyrinth of control chambers relate to one another.

The new/old duality in the Village is impossible to miss, as is the fact that the impingement of technology and a modernist architectural vocabulary increases below ground level. Because they are linked in this way, the up/down, old/new pairings reinforce one another. However, there is also a dichotomy in the design imagery that goes beyond matters of contrasting style, gnawing at the fabric of the diegesis. The viewer cannot help but become aware that many of the interiors are spatially irreconcilable with their architectural shells; outwardly the Village is obviously an architectural miniature, while the spaces supposedly within and beneath are exaggeratedly monumental. Number 2's house, for example, is identified with one of the most prominent landmarks in Portmeirion, the lead-domed rotunda — the "the Green Dome" (see fig. 3.6). Yet within, the main chamber clearly has little to do with the structure in Portmeirion, except that inside, as outside, there is a dome. In Shampan's interior, there is no airy drum, punctuated with lofty windows, to support the dome. Like Buckminster Fuller's geodesic structures, the inner dome rises directly from the ground, a metal frame encased in an unrelieved mauve screen.[35] More notable still is the undisguised discrepancy between the rambling interior and tiny exterior of Number 6's residence: the minuscule, round-walled cottage in Portmeirion might just about be believed to accommodate the Prisoner's living room, but there is also a kitchenette and, behind a sliding panel, a generously proportioned bedroom (see fig. 3.17) [36] Although it may affect the viewer at only a subliminal level, this visual dissonance inevitably adds to the disconcerting effect of the drama as a whole.

So far, we have emphasized the strongly marked divergence between seeming and being in the design of the Village — between the old-fashioned surface appearance and the futuristic, subterranean reality. From another point of view, these contrasted elements are merely obverse and reverse of the same coin — and such a view becomes inescapable if one acknowledges *The Prisoner* as an allegory rather than trying to see it simply as a weird sci-fi/spy drama. Jack Shampan juxtaposed his specially devised sets with the imagery of the Portmeirion location to form an integrated artistic whole. The Village, as conceived by Shampan and his colleagues, is a little world that is riven with contrasts in just the same way as world society at large, for the simple reason that it is (however one interprets the fine details) a microcosm of the great global village itself.[37]

The global overtones are given inescapable visual expression in Shampan's repeated use of the circle and sphere.[38] Clough Williams-Ellis fortuitously supplied one such image: the statue of Atlas bearing the world that stands in the main square (fig. 3.8). However, this is complemented with nu-

FIGURE 3.8. *The weight of the world: Number 6 regards the statue of Atlas in "Arrival." © Carlton International Media Limited.*

merous specially created or selected examples of the circle or sphere motif. Primary among these is the penny-farthing bicycle that is used as a suitably archaic mode of transport in the Village. One of these old bicycles stands as a kind of objet trouvé sculpture in Number 2's residence. The penny-farthing is also represented as a graphic on the number badges worn by each Villager (except the defiant Number 6). The circle form is also seen prominently in the "keyhole" doorway between Number 6's living room and bedroom, and other Village portals.

The globe manifests in several of the most oft-seen images in the series, including Number 2's revolving Aarnio-designed "ball chair" and the surveillance "eye" that is suspended from the round ceiling panel of the Village Control Room. The globe motif reaches saturation level in the climactic scene of the final episode, "Fall Out." Number 6's confrontation with his alter ego, Number 1, takes place inside a rocket, which is, of course, circular in cross-section. The hooded figure is seated behind a circular table entirely covered by terrestrial globes, and as he turns to greet Number 6, he holds out a crystal ball, which the Prisoner smashes to the ground.

The most abstract of the spherical forms in *The Prisoner,* the balloon-like Village Guardian, Rover, is also the most distinctive and threatening (fig. 3.5). This oddity is hardly acceptable as a real thing, either organic or robotic. It derives its menace largely from the fact that its strangeness functions so powerfully at an oneiric level: Rover is the stuff of irrational nightmare. Its horror is further increased by the fact that it is most commonly seen not in the modernistic underground spaces of the Village, with which it is most stylistically consonant, but in the picturesque setting of the rustic "upper" world.

The globe motif is given its most powerful and widespread expression in the domed structure of all the major Village interiors, including Number 2's residence, the Surveillance Control Room, the Labor Exchange, the Gymnasium, the Assembly Room, and the Town Hall Council Chamber. All of these spaces are three-quarter spheres in section, strongly implying a full globe rather than a mere hemisphere. The reuse and re-dressing of sets is common in television, for reasons of expense, but here Shampan made it a conspicuous aesthetic virtue. The basic set, which Shampan referred to as "the Living Space," consisted of a cyclorama encircling a domical metal grid and a floor ornamented with a bull's-eye pattern of concentric circles.[39] The various domed rooms created from this set were differentiated by their furnishings and the color of lighting on the cyclorama. The interior of No. 2's house, the simplest variant, is the first and most frequently encountered (fig. 3.9).

The main feature of this room is the Aarnio "globe" chair, placed on a circular podium in the center of the room with a control desk before it, shaped to correspond with the arc of the next concentric circle on the ground. In some scenes, circular sections of the floor slide back, allowing further seats and circular tables to rise from beneath. The principal means of illumination is a large flat suspended disc containing recessed circular lamps. The only angular element in the set, apart from the vast surveillance screen, is

FIGURE 3.9. *Behind the Green Dome: Number 2's residence in "Arrival." Set designed by Jack Shampan.* © *Carlton International Media Limited.*

FIGURE 3.10. *The eyes have it: The Control Room in "Arrival." Set designed by Jack Shampan. © Carlton International Media Limited.*

the studded and polished metal sliding door, rendered doubly stark by its clash with the overall scheme.

In the Control Room, the global overtones of the set are enhanced by the fact that the steel grid of the dome, already suggestive of lines of longitude and latitude, is backed by maps of earth and skies (fig. 3.10). In other respects, the room has something of the character of a minimalist installation. No complex contour is used where a simple one will do, and every element relates in formal terms either to the circular shape of the room or the rectilinear skeleton that defines its domical volume. The only complex shape is the rotating seesaw in the center on which are seated two "observers," who peer into camera-like surveillance machines. This curious object introduces an element of what appears to be pure symbolism. There is no deducible reason for the incessant revolutions or the rising and falling of its two occupants; instead, these movements provide a strong visual metaphor for the perpetual, all-embracing watchfulness of the masters of the Village. In purely formal terms, like the Aarnio chair, the seesaw also makes a striking centerpiece to the set.

Photography, editing, and narrative events all emphasize the circle/sphere motif. In "Arrival," Number 6's first tour of the Village incorporates a high-viewpoint shot of the new inmate from between the arms of the Atlas sculpture, his globe filling the upper part of the frame. Moments later, Rover makes its first appearance, riding the jet of water from the fountain in the center of the square and then settling on the top of a garden loggia. More striking and sinister is the "Russian doll" effect at the beginning of "Once Upon a Time." Here Number 2 rises on one of the circular lifts in the floor of his hemispherical chamber and finds, much to his chagrin, that the spherical Aarnio chair is occupied—entirely filled, in fact—by the spherical Rover (fig. 3.11). If McGoohan and his colleagues did not intend viewers to attribute emotional and philosophical import to the device of the globe, their campaign of misdirection was masterly.

In fact, circular imagery is not solely the province of design in the series: there are clearly defined cyclical aspects to the narrative. As we have suggested, most television series are cyclical in that they endlessly repeat a successful formula; this characteristic is deliberately exaggerated in *The Prisoner*. Each episode emphatically begins and ends the same way: at the outset there is the long sequence showing Number 6's abduction, and at the conclusion the animated image of his face advancing toward the camera over a caption slide of the Village—only to be "trapped" behind animated bars. No effort is made to conceal the fact that every episode, like the ballads of Robin Hood and the Sheriff of Nottingham, is at certain levels a reworking of every previous one: at the climax of the long opening sequence, Number 6 "converses," in a kind of ritualized exchange, with "the new Number 2," who utters exactly the same words of threat as his or her predecessor. Furthermore, there is no clear evidence of chronology within the series. On the contrary, there are lacunae and contradictions that defy any attempt to come up with a convincing sequence. For example, in the eighth broadcast episode ("Dance of the Dead"), parts of the dialogue suggest that Number 6 is a new arrival. Nor, again, is there any character development in the series, any more than in the Ballads of Robin Hood: everyone plays his or

FIGURE 3.11. *Spheres within spheres: Number 2 is displaced by Rover in "Once Upon a Time" (1968).* © *Carlton International Media Limited.*

FIGURE 3.12. *Circling the triangle: The Village Council Chamber in "Free For All." Set designed by Jack Shampan. © Carlton International Media Limited.*

her part according to type. In short, then, the episodes do not really relate to one another syntactically; rather, they are linked *syntagmatically,* each one rearranging the different ideas implicit in the basic premise.

Another motivic dichotomy in design for *The Prisoner* is less obvious than those of above/below and old/new, but still striking: this is the opposition between circles and straight lines. This juxtaposition is particularly prominent in the design for one of the domed rooms, the Town Hall Council Chamber, seen in "Free for All" (fig. 3.12). Here, the concentric circles on the floor are overlaid by a pattern of radiating triangles, and this form appears on every other furnishing in the room except the long flight of stairs leading down from a door high in the dome. The councilors' lecterns, ranged around the room, are made of interlocking triangles, as is the dais at the rear where Number 2 sits in front of a kind of altar (fig. 3.13). The altar itself bears an empty, stylized throne, again composed of triangular forms. An eye, redolent of Masonic imagery (though now most familiar from the one dollar bill), flashes down from the top of this throne structure, which takes the form of a kind of exploded pyramid. So insistent is the jagged triangular motif that the human body seems out of place—an untidy irregularity. The chamber embodies design operating boldly at the margins of pure abstraction, and this is integral to the disturbing character of *The Prisoner.*

The frantic scene played out in the Council Chamber, where an orderly "vote of thanks" to Number 6 is transformed suddenly into the first stage of a psychedelic brainwashing procedure, would lose much of its impact in a less shockingly alien, hostile environment. In a similar way, the pervasive mood of menace in *The Prisoner* at large would be less sustainable without the leitmotiv of the scenes in the Control Room, with its sinister seesaw. These are not diverting sets, mere embellishments to the narrative: they are visually arresting and confusing in the same measure that the staccato, anomaly-ridden scripts are conceptually challenging.

All in all, then, design in *The Prisoner,* while providing the program with visual unity of a sort, emphasizes and often amplifies the intangibility of the complex and many-layered discursive structure of the saga. Visual coherence is certainly far from being a device that offers reassurance to the viewer, since the very familiarity of the furnishings of the Village and rainbow-clad populace becomes, after an episode or so, stifling rather than comfortable. Although the kind of images seen may in a sense be constant, the visual parameters of the series are not absolutely stable. In two of the later episodes, for example, the Village set-up seems to have been entirely abandoned. One of these episodes finds the main character inexplicably transposed to Harmony, a small town in the American West, while the next shows him apparently a free agent once again, pitted against a diabolical villain in a spy spoof worthy of *The Avengers*.[40] In the end, both these dream-like scenarios turn out to be manifestations of the psychological war between prisoner and captors. What is significant for our study is that these interludes serve to emphasize that visual as well as narrative elements could be used to upset the viewer's expectations.

In fact, the last five episodes of *The Prisoner* increasingly disrupt the visual integrity of the series. "Living in Harmony" presents an American township

FIGURE 3.13. *Number 2 (Eric Portman) and his lackeys confront Number 6 from behind their ultrastylized desks in the Council Chamber in "Free For All." Set and props designed by Jack Shampan. © Carlton International Media Limited.*

FIGURE 3.14. *Behind bars: The self-contained living space from "Once Upon a Time" (1968). Set designed by Jack Shampan. © Carlton International Media Limited.*

rather than the Village as the microcosm. The iconic status of the western in screen entertainment helps stress that *The Prisoner* is exploring universal themes, not just one secret agent's problems with his employers. The episode is also the one that most forcibly reminds viewers that *The Prisoner* is a dramatic construct. Events in the ironically named town are a collection of western-movie clichés: mob rule, lynching, the conflict between the honest lawman and the corrupt judge, and so on. At the end of the episode, Number 6 wakes up to discover that his experiences in Harmony have been a hallucinogen-induced illusion. He runs from the "town" to the nearest hill, only to see the Village in the vale just beyond. Harmony is revealed to be a literal back lot filled with literal cardboard characters. The analogy with the artifice of *The Prisoner* as a whole, and of the drama series as a form per se, could hardly be writ larger for viewers.

The last two stories, "Once Upon a Time" and "Fall Out," are set back in the Village, but in previously unseen parts of the complex. The main sets for both these episodes break radically with the established tradition of Village interiors. Gone are the domed chambers. Instead, the Embryo Room in "Once Upon a Time" is a black space of unclear dimensions, a kind of playroom furnished with a variety of objects used by Number 2 to lead the Prisoner through a reenactment of his life up to his fateful resignation from the service. Theatricality, and more particularly the spirit of improvisatory theatre, is undisguised.[41] At one end of the Embryo Room is a discrete living space, actually a kind of mobile home, behind bars—the first to be seen in the whole series, apart from the animated shutters that close each episode.[42] Whereas most Village interiors contain some element of curvature, this barred mobile home is emphatically rectilinear (fig. 3.14).

The Cavern in which most of the action of "Fall Out" takes place is also surrounded by impenetrable darkness and theatrically composed (fig. 3.15). While the set represents a departure from established architectural forms, "Fall Out" also draws together familiar visual motifs and familiar faces. Most of the recurring characters are present: Number 6, Number 2's butler, the bespectacled Control Room Supervisor, and the most formidable of the Number 2s, with whom Number 6 had been vying in "Once Upon a Time." Two actors seen in the immediately foregoing episodes appear again in new guises, and using recognizable performers to play new characters contributes strongly to the tangible sense of artifice: any attempt by viewers to go on doggedly suspending their disbelief is seriously undermined. Alexis Kanner, who played the psychotic "Kid" in "Living in Harmony" returns as the

FIGURE 3.15. *It all comes together in the end: The Cavern in "Fall Out" (1968). Set designed by Jack Shampan, costumes by Dora Lloyd.* © *Carlton International Media Limited.*

FIGURE 3.16.
*Ploughshares into
swords: The seesaw
refitted in "Fall Out."
Prop designed by Jack
Shampan. © Carlton
International Media
Limited.*

Hippie, Number 48, and Kenneth Griffith, who played the bumbling mega-
lomaniac "Schnipps" in "The Girl Who Was Death," appears as the pompous
but sinister figure of "the President."

Many of the key props and furnishings in the Cavern obviously come
from earlier episodes. For example, the mobile home from the Embryo
Room in "Once Upon a Time" appears again, now mounted on what proves
to be the trailer of a flatbed truck. Some returning features are doctored,
most notably the revolving seesaw from the Control Room, which now has
machine guns mounted in place of the cameras (fig. 3.16). Here, implied in-
vasiveness has finally become overt threat. Several new props are also seen
in the Cavern. A dais bearing a throne for Number 6, to whom ultimate
power is supposedly being given, is faced by a pulpit and benches that are
occupied, respectively, by the judge-like President and a group of bizarrely
robed and masked "delegates." These linear furnishings have supplanted the
circular elements that had previously dominated Village interiors.

This shift to predominantly rectangular forms seems to denote a move
away from "global" symbolism to a preoccupation with the framed images
of theatre and television. When the truck-mounted mobile home is driven
up the highway by the Butler, the suggestion of a stage behind a prosce-
nium arch becomes especially clear. Behind the bars are Number 6 and his
fellow escapees, Numbers 2 and 48, whirling in a manic dance that might
almost be a kind of moving street-performance, enacted for the benefit of
motorists in the inside lane. Ironically, the appalled reaction of the staid
bowler-hatted gent who observes the fugitives from his car prefigures the
outraged audience-response to the episode.

Other elements of scenes in the Cavern suggest that the program-makers were upping the stakes in the hermeneutic game for "Fall Out." As the Prisoner leads a violent break-out, firing bullets into the crowd of white-hooded delegates, the surrounding jukeboxes play the Beatles' "All You Need Is Love." Likewise, as the Prisoner enters the cave at the beginning of the episode, he passes through a metal door bearing a sign with the word "WELL" over the word "COME." This curious split-word sign seems to demand interpretation, but presents very little in the way of clues. It is a far cry from the sententious village epigrams of earlier episodes (such as the spine-chilling variant on wartime caveats—"Questions are a burden to others; answers, a prison for oneself"). The title of the episode itself, "Fall Out," implies or recalls several different things—nuclear war, argument, the verbal order to disband a military parade, and perhaps Timothy Leary's famous acid axiom "Tune in, turn on, drop out."

"Fall Out" destabilizes the "givens" in the series and alerts anyone trying to unravel the meaning of *The Prisoner* that the rules are changing. Having denied any absolute value for visual and verbal motifs in the series, this terminal episode of *The Prisoner* finally sends the viewer back to square one, with the repetition of the opening shot. In a way, some fundamental questions are answered: we find out, for example, who Number 1 is. Yet the viewer cannot but be left with a nagging sense that these purely narrative issues are unimportant in the face of larger questions of personal identity and freedom posed by McGoohan and his colleagues.

The malcontents who inundated ITC with complaints in the wake of "Fall Out" failed to recognize that the disappointment of their expectations was part and parcel of the challenge of *The Prisoner* to contemporary culture. In spite of his having been obliged to lie low at the time of the furor,[43] McGoohan subsequently claimed that the public response was very much what he had sought:

I wanted to have controversy, argument, fights, discussions, people in anger waving fists in my face saying, "How dare you? Why don't you do more 'Secret Agents' that we can understand?" I was delighted with the reaction. I think it's a very good one. That was the intention of the exercise.[44]

The cause célèbre provoked by "Fall Out" indicates that, for the dissatisfied viewers at least, a television series, no matter how disturbing it may be during its run, should ultimately be reassuring. The only answers that the final installment of *The Prisoner* furnishes are uncomfortable ones that no one wants to hear: there is no absolute freedom; there are no final victories over oppression; and we are all, ultimately, our own worst enemies.

THE MAN IN GRAY

The dichotomies in set design for *The Prisoner* are not echoed in the costumes for the Villagers. For the most part, their outfits simply underscore the bogus atmosphere of seaside holiday-making; men and women wear colorfully striped jerseys, deck shoes, summer-weight slacks, and sometimes short, brightly striped capes fastened with tassels, the men's garb being topped off by straw boaters and the women's by soft sun hats or yachting caps. There are also strong overtones of holiday camps, so popular as resorts in Britain during the postwar decades. The uniform of the "redcoat" staff in Butlin's holiday camps is closely echoed in the piped blazers sported by some (mostly senior) male figures in the Village.[45]

Everyone in the Village, including Number 2, wears a large badge bearing the pervasive penny-farthing motif and his or her number in red. These badges suggest another arena of enforced good humor, the conference or the corporate Christmas party, where one is obliged to don a button or tag saying "Hello, my name is ____." There is also the clear connection with the numbering and bar-coding of products that was only in its infancy in the 1960s.

Just as Clough Williams-Ellis' Portmeirion is dressed and filmed to create an impression of quaint "Englishness," so the costume design for certain, specific characters functions as caricature. For example, the proprietor of the General Store wears a blue-and-white-striped apron and straw hat, and an ex-admiral tops off his attire with a large moustache and a cap befitting his rank. The female staff who clean the prisoners' houses and serve in the café all dress in dark blue frocks with white pinafores that were, in the 1960s, still conventional (though no longer universal) for maids (fig. 3.17).

Although a gender stereotype is upheld in the maids' costumes, the rank-and-file Villagers wear styles that are virtually unisex (to invoke a term that was first enjoying currency at this time[46]), and traditionally distinguishing garments of the sexes, such as neckties for men and skirts for women, are not seen at all. The asexuality of women is particularly marked—and all the more arresting, therefore, are the few examples of deviation from this neu-

tral, neutered norm. If the maids' uniform is part of an ironic distillation of English cliché, the use of frocks for two other prominent female characters has an importance that warrants more detailed consideration.

In "A Change of Mind," Number 86, an attractive young surgeon who performs a mock lobotomy on Number 6, subsequently becomes his constant companion in order to administer the drug that convinces him that he is a changed man. Her donning of a dress is explicitly a means of engaging Number 6's interest. Yet when Number 6 turns the tables, drugging and hypnotizing Number 86, her change of attire suggests something else. As a surgeon, she was an authority figure who literally "wore the trousers." Number 6's ruse repositions her as weak: her miniskirted dress reduces her to a sex object, and in her drugged state she becomes kittenish and flirtatious.

In "Many Happy Returns," the Prisoner escapes to London, where he encounters an attractive older woman who befriends him—only to be revealed at the end as the latest Number 2. In her London guise as "Mrs. Butterworth," she wears tweed pants and jacket, but when she reappears in the Village as Number 2 after the Prisoner's return, she is wearing a simple but flattering dress. Here, the frock becomes an instrument of mockery: From being the slightly tomboyish pal who helped the escaped Prisoner on his way, "Mrs. Butterworth" is now the embodiment of cool, controlled, and unavailable female sexuality. She even carries a cake to wish him, with irony, "many happy returns," and the dress emphasizes how far from motherly domesticity this particular femme fatale is.

It is also worth noting that the Number 2 in the next episode, "Dance of the Dead," is another attractive older woman. She eschews feminine modes, taking Village androgyny a stage further at the costume ball by coming as Peter Pan. Yet of all the female characters in the series, she is the most openly flirtatious in her banter with Number 6. Here again, though, clothes are used as a distancing device: her male attire subtly underscores the fact that she is as sexually unavailable and sexually dominant as her predecessor.[47]

Apart from gender differentiation, certain obvious (though not clearly meaningful) sartorial distinctions among the populace support the allegorical role of the Village as social microcosm. Those who are on the various administrative committees wear top hats, black frock coats and gloves, sometimes with the additional sinister, gangsterish touch of dark glasses. The "observers" who operate the surveillance equipment in the Control Room are visually striking by virtue of their drabness: they wear plain black turtlenecks and trousers. Number 2's immediate assistants usually sport a light blazer with dark piping, while successive managers of the Labor Exchange are accoutered in gray morning suits, and so on. Every detail seems meant to be noticed and, by extension, seems to invite explanation.

This is especially true of the costume for the male Number 2s. These chief administrators have a standard uniform: up-market black blazer, usually double-breasted and without piping, pearl-gray sweater, striped varsity scarf, and shooting stick (fig. 3.18).[48] How much can safely be read into this image? There is a marked suggestion of quasi-aristocratic superiority in the details of the Number 2s' uniform: the outfit possesses a dignity that is denied to ordinary Villagers, with their gaudy stripes, silly hats, and fussy braids. Yet it is also tempting to believe that the continuity of dress from one Number 2 to the next has a satirical function, implying that representatives of authority, be they governors or governments, are really all alike.

The urge to subject dress design in *The Prisoner* to a pat exegesis must be tempered by McGoohan's caveat that "explanation lessens what the piece was supposed to be: an allegorical conundrum for people to interpret for

FIGURE 3.18. *Men in uniform: The Butler, Number 6, and Number 2 (Leo McKern) in "The Chimes of Big Ben" (1967). Set designed by Jack Shampan, costumes by Masada Wilmot © Carlton International Media Limited.*

themselves."[49] If McGoohan's remark is taken at face value, no explanation can be reckoned conclusive, even where a particular costume seems to have an unequivocal emblematic import within the scripted narrative.

The prime example is the dark gray suit that Number 6 is wearing when he arrives in the Village, which is soon taken from him but which reappears at significant moments in the series. The suit already had established associations. The seasoned and attentive *Danger Man* viewer might have recognized it, for McGoohan had worn it during the last full season of the series, once with the same black polo shirt that the Prisoner sports when he arrives in his new home.

Whenever he imagines or dreams of escape, or is temporarily allowed to leave the Village, the Prisoner appears in his gray suit (see fig. 3.17). Furthermore, this clothing is part of the cat-and-mouse game that his oppressors try to play with him, and it periodically becomes a topic of overt discussion in the scripts. At a costume ball the suit is briefly returned to the Prisoner, and it is restored once again in the final episode, in each case, according to the dialogue, so that he can be "himself."[50] The outfit might, therefore, be taken as an emblem of human individualism in face of the pressure to conform.

Yet his stark and forbidding attire could equally well be said to reinforce uneasy concerns about the central character in *The Prisoner.* For the suit to serve as an uncomplicated symbol of heroism, the Prisoner himself would have to be uncomplicatedly heroic—which he is not. A desperate, volatile figure who quickly learns to mistrust all those around him, the Prisoner first responds to his incarceration by smashing the incessantly chattering radio in his cottage and beating up a whole gang of warders who try to prevent his escape. True, he quickly proves to have his own clear moral code and stands by principles of justice that are certainly not practiced by the masters of the Village; but he is also often harsh, cold, withdrawn, and antisocial. While one may admire his unflinching pertinacity, it is not altogether easy to like Number 6. McGoohan has clearly asserted that the character's antiheroic qualities were not accidental:

The series was conceived to make it appear *that our hero was striving to be "completely free," "utterly himself." Too much of that and society would be overrun by rampant extremists and there would be anarchy. The intention was satirical. Be as free as possible within our situation, but the war is with Number One.*[51]

After all, the Prisoner's oppressor turns out to be his own alter ego.

The Prisoner's dark suit seems to resonate in many ways with his misanthropic brand of rebelliousness. Although not completely black, his outfit is shadowy (all the more when set against the brummagem absurdities of Village-wear) and readily calls to mind associations of all-black clothing—menace, melancholy, and monkishness. Yet, as more than one writer on the history and "language" of dress has observed, black is a color with multiple associations, its symbolic significance more unstable than that of any other hue.[52] Any interpretation is necessarily personal: where one sees gloom, others may well see only cool sophistication or a kind of quasi-holy purity or sober respectability, and so on. As with all the carefully orchestrated design components in *The Prisoner,* the powerful image of the suit raises questions. "Orchestration" is perhaps the best metaphor in this context, for to ask what the Prisoner's suit means within the overall framework of the series is ultimately as fruitless as asking what the bassoon or French horn part in a Mozart symphony means. The more telling, honest, and ultimately taxing question is "What does this mean to me?"

"POP" GOES THE WEASEL

It is now something of a cliché to say that *The Prisoner* was ahead of its time,[53] but this is a notion not fully supported by its subsequent fortunes. It may be said that the series was received favorably when it was repeated in the 1970s.[54] Yet echoes of *The Prisoner* proved to be conspicuous by their absence. Within a short time, the still, small voice of the series was drowned out by a raucous succession of action-adventure programs epitomizing all that McGoohan had turned against.

One series that emerged from the ITC stable at about the same time as *The Prisoner* was in certain ways the heir to *Danger Man* that *The Prisoner* had deceptively seemed to be. *Man in a Suitcase* (ITC/ATC, 1967–1968) concerned a former secret agent who led an itinerant lifestyle as a mercenary troubleshooter. This career was evidently the consequence of a problematic resignation from the service. Broad narrative connections aside, nothing could have been further from the provocative fireworks of *The Prisoner*. The lusterless hero's adventures in *Man In A Suitcase* were seedy in a way that *Danger Man* had never been, even at its most formulaic. The artifice of the simulated non-British locations was more evident than in *Danger Man*, partly because the new series was shot in color rather than black and white, but travel-guide naturalism was still the aim. For all its tawdriness, *Man In A Suitcase* was a popular success in a way that *The Prisoner* emphatically was not, as were the several other flashy crime-*cum*-espionage series from the years around 1970, such as *Department S* and *The Persuaders*. None of them even paid lip service to the narrative intensity or visual daring of *The Prisoner*. McGoohan's series might as well never have happened; its innovations were ignored, its challenges bypassed.

The Prisoner may have been ahead of its time, but it has yet to produce any progeny. There is little need to enumerate the list of adventure and thriller series made during the last quarter of the twentieth century that failed to embrace any aspect of contentious antinaturalism. Indeed, the expectation of descendants may be unfair. After all, McGoohan achieved his cultural coup d'état because he had the ear of Lew Grade, whose confidence in the actor's bankability and willingness to indulge his protégé must have been considerable.[55] McGoohan's sympathetic or compliant collaborators, producer David Tomblin and designers Jack Shampan and Masada Wilmot, assisted the realization of his subversive vision. Without these favorable circumstances, such a violent disruption of the undemanding adventure genre would probably never have taken place.

Age has, to some extent, not only mellowed but emasculated *The Prisoner,* and this is in large measure due to the character of its design. This is not to say that the ideas inscribed into the design imagery have lost their relevance. The whole sharply defined dichotomy between historicism and ultramodernism in Shampan's total design framework for the Village reflects characteristics of first-world culture that have become still more marked in Britain since the late 1960s. For one thing, progress and history have both been made ever more concrete in commodities: Those who hanker after the latest in automobile technology, domestic appliances, sound and vision systems, and computers are quite likely to hanker in equal measure after the trappings of upper-crust or (heavily sanitized) rustic life in a bygone era, as the boom in "period interiors" magazines seems to attest.[56] Furthermore, if it is true that there is a duality in many domestic environments between simulations of the past and the technology of the present, then there is a corollary point to be made. In the real world, as in the Village, the more sinister, nondomestic manifestations of technology, such as the many tools of oppression and exploitation that the last hundred years have produced, are occluded from the general view, or, at least, excluded from the all-powerful, beguiling sign systems of consumerism.

If the debates embodied in design for *The Prisoner* remain live, the imagery itself now has a "period" character, a fact that has led to various different kinds of misunderstandings of the program-makers' aim. In a discussion of the series written in the early 1990s, David Buxton suggested that the setting was "too facile" to allow the ideological issues of the series "to be treated with the necessary complexity."[57] One can only assume that he would have found the series more satisfactory if it had been set in the contemporary metropolitan scene whose properties the Village emblematically represents. The counterargument is that Shampan's and McGoohan's stylized miniature world offered a far more effective vehicle for the allegorical representation of society than a naturalistic setting would have done. In the Village, all distractions are pared away: the trappings of daily reality are distilled into some of the most starkly simplified designs ever used in television outside the realm of light entertainment. Buxton, who counts *The Prisoner* as a Pop series, has evidently mistaken means for ends.

Having said that, it must be admitted that it is hard to approach *The Prisoner* without running up against the idea, or rather ideas, of Pop.[58] The term does not seem inappropriate, if by "Pop" we mean the movement in figural art that flourished in Britain and America during the 1960s and 1970s. The bold use of line and hue in Shampan's and Wilmot's designs seems to breathe the same air as paintings by Roy Lichtenstein and Tom Wesselmann and sculptures by Claes Oldenburg.

Nevertheless, an attempt like Buxton's to treat *The Prisoner* as a Pop phenomenon is highly questionable. Insofar as the series appropriated the imagery of Pop design—if by "Pop" we now mean the way-out, disposable, and space-age furniture from the 1960s—it did so in a far from complimentary manner. In the same way that technology was shown in an unflattering light in *The Prisoner*, "funky" features such as the Aarnio "Globe" chair and lava lamps were, so to speak, tarred with the fascist brush since they were furnishings in Number 2's residence.[59] Moreover, the lava lamp was implicitly linked with horror: the image of rising globules was part of the oft-seen sequence that showed the underwater birth of a Rover being sent in pursuit of a dissident or a would-be escapee.

The Prisoner certainly did not court pop culture of the kind embodied in pop music. Most of the incidental scores for the show consisted of curious instrumental versions of nursery rhymes—most notably "Pop Goes the Weasel." For the most part, the title of this nonsense song was as close as the score for the show got to pop. The one striking use of contemporary rock music, already mentioned, was the appearance of the Beatles' "All You Need Is Love" in the final episode of the series. At that time this was not the invocation of a classic tune. Because the song now has classic status, it remains a preeminent signifier for the Sixties. As a result, *The Prisoner* seems to be keyed into Sixties Pop to a much greater extent than it actually was.

Apart from the obvious, grotesquely contradictory application of the Beatles' number to a gun battle, its use strikingly contributed to the establishment of discontinuity in the episode. Like the redefinition of visual imagery (e.g., the seesaw fitted with guns rather than surveillance equipment) and of character roles (e.g., Number 2's unexpectedly becoming one of Number 6's fellow rebels), this emphatically modern sound was a strident, confusing departure. The irony, of course, is comparable to that of the nursery rhymes matching the external architecture but contradicting the underlying function of the Village. However, the tone and pitch of the black humor is rather different.

The increase in the apparent Pop quotient of the series is partly due to the vast retro appeal of what was a small segment of Sixties culture. In our own age, which likes its culture to be "themed," the coherence and quotability of design imagery in *The Prisoner* has surely played a large part in making it an icon of nostalgia.[60] *The Prisoner* represents one of the most striking design packages in the history of screen entertainment. It contained a host of arresting individual images that are now powerfully associated with Sixties cool—the Mini Moke taxis, the unisex clothes, the colored, cordless phones, the balloon-like guard, the Prisoner's Lotus car, and so on. More important, the series had a vivid and attractive overall aesthetic. With its primary colors and candy stripes, its architectural potpourri of space-age modernism and picture-postcard prettiness, and even the Albertus graphics used both in the settings and for the title sequences, the crisp character of the aesthetic is in some ways delightful. In short, *The Prisoner* represents a prime example of the way that the meanings of a design can be lost, or rather changed, in face of enthusiasm for the nature of the design itself.

Probably the most bizarre expression of this embalming attitude toward *Prisoner* imagery is the periodic transformation of Portmeirion into a sort of Disneyland for fans of the series. Their gatherings, featuring reenactments of colorful set pieces, such as the human chess match from "Checkmate" and the election parade from "Free for All," lead one to wonder whether these aficionados understand the questioning tone of *The Prisoner*. The enthusiasts seem, in their own way, just as ensnared in McGoohan's semiotic trap as the original audience, since they have apparently mistaken the Village jail for a place of escape.[61] Unsurprisingly, it is the calculatedly over-sweet English quaintness that the fans reproduce at Portmeirion, not the disturbing haunts of the Village Hospital or Council Chamber. Nothing could be further from the stated aim of Patrick McGoohan, who sought to encourage debate, not devotion.

*Originality and
Conservatism in
the Imagery of
Doctor Who*

C
H
A
P
T
E
R
R

WORLDS APART

F
O
U
R

INTRODUCTION: RELATIVE DIMENSIONS IN SPACE

The design history of *Doctor Who* (BBC TV, 1963–1989; Fox/BBC TV, 1996) is much more complex and unwieldy than those of our other two subject dramas. As a result of the longevity of the series, the expressive function of design changed a number of times, in tune with larger shifts in the overall discursive matrix of the program. These often extreme alterations in the role of design, some of which are worth examining in detail, make *Doctor Who* distinctively different not only from *The Prisoner* but also from *The Avengers*. *The Prisoner*, as we have stressed, was not only short-lived, but in design terms tightly coherent. Although the character of design in *The Avengers* certainly *did* mutate during the course of its decade-long run, change followed a single trajectory: the *Avengers* aesthetic developed systematically from the diurnal neutrality of early adventures in the London underworld to the flamboyant sets and costumes of the ultra-English "Avengerland" seen in the final two seasons. The evolution of design in *Doctor Who* was not nearly so tidy: the experimental and the hackneyed alternated with each other in irregular bursts.

Unlike the design in *The Avengers* and *The Prisoner,* the design in *Doctor Who* was not an indispensable part of the narrative structure of the series. The program was loose-knit at a discursive level, and for the most part the work of the designer was correspondingly free-floating. This is not to say that we are dismissing design imagery for *Doctor Who* as being purely "decorative," far less as being "meaningless." On the contrary, design could be used to provocative, even subversive ends in relation to the underlying ideological assumptions of the series. What may be said, then, is that the significance of design within *Doctor Who* was not furnished, and certainly not guaranteed, by the ethos of the program. Whereas *The Avengers* and *The Prisoner* were seldom narratively banal, *Doctor Who* generally was, and the work of the designer often represented a triumph of the visually expressed idea over the verbally expressed cliché.

The other major distinction between *Doctor Who* and our other subject series is one of quality, or at least perceived quality. Although vilified during its original run by what James Chapman has nicely described as the "middlebrow" tendency in journalistic criticism, *The Avengers* has now been enshrined as a television classic.[1] Critical plaudits were even quicker in coming to *The Prisoner,* whose "difficulty" and uncompromising critique of mainstream entertainment makes it still seem gratifyingly avant-garde today.

Doctor Who, by contrast, remains beyond the critical pale: scholarly treatments such as John Tulloch's and Henry Jenkins' study of audience responses to *Doctor Who* and *Star Trek* belong to that class of book that are the target of journalists' ongoing scorn of cultural studies as a discipline.[2] *Doctor Who* can make no sustainable claims to possessing intellectual respectability. While the delicate, knowing humor in *The Avengers* can be called postmodern, as we and other authors have done, and while *The Prisoner* can be recognized as a masterpiece of deconstruction, there is no convenient philosophical tag that can be plausibly applied to *Doctor Who.* Except for a few dozen episodes produced in the mid-to-late 1970s, *Doctor Who* was inescapably the televisual equivalent of pulp fiction, recycling familiar narrative devices *ad nauseam.* The program seldom tapped deeply into the possibilities inherent in its original, quirkily brilliant premise, and as a result, the whole never really equaled the sum of its parts.

As should now be clear, this chapter is neither an apology for *Doctor Who* nor an attempt to exalt it to the status of high art. We do hope to refute the tediously resilient fallacy that design in *Doctor Who* was cheap and cheerful, its quaint aesthetic defined by cardboard sets and unconvincing rubber monsters. While it has been eclipsed in virtually all areas of special and visual effects, *Doctor Who* was graced by some of the most inventive scenic and costume design work ever contributed to television or film drama, much of which has never been surpassed. In many cases the designer's conceptions were realized with tremendous aplomb and frequently with a high degree of finesse. However, the celebration of design excellence in *Doctor Who* is incidental to our main concerns here, which are much more to do with the politics of design in the broadest sense.

Because it was in production for a quarter of a century, *Doctor Who* offers the chance to study long-term development and change. The vicissitudes of design imagery in *Doctor Who* overwhelmingly demonstrate not just the mutability of the series as a form, but also conversely, the way in which ossification can set in. Certain aspects of the show grew steadily more conservative. The treatment of women, for example, became frankly reactionary. In other respects, too, novelty was stifled and fantasy circumscribed: lore became law, and the series became ensnared in its own internal traditions.

For much of its long run, however, *Doctor Who* was not without its radical edge. Because it largely ignored contemporary social change, *Doctor Who* derived its subtlety in part from being out of touch with the changing realities of life in postimperial Britain. Although it went through moralizing phases—the usual targets for criticism being, ironically, xenophobia, colonialism, and racial intolerance—*Doctor Who* did not pretend to offer a sustained critique of society, as *The Avengers* and *The Prisoner* had both done in their different ways.[3] The reality of *Doctor Who* was not oriented to the reality of its viewers; what the series potentially offered was an unconstricted flight of fancy. Nor did the program always display internal logic and credibility—though many members of its cult following clearly wanted it to.[4]

Doctor Who was founded on a premise that was essentially magical, for all that it was given pseudoscientific window dressing.[5] The Doctor, an extraterrestrial whose civilization had built machines capable of traveling through time as well as space, journeyed to Earth's past, to alien worlds, and to futures in which humans had colonized the stars. His travel machine was bigger on the inside than the outside—a self-contained world entered through what appeared to be a police lock-up box (an oversized telephone booth used by police in early twentieth-century Britain for temporarily detaining suspects).[6] After three years of adventures, the elderly Doctor underwent a remarkable metamorphosis, his body being rejuvenated and his personality altered.[7] This shape-shifting ability manifested on six further occasions, with each Doctor emerging more flamboyant and eccentric than his predecessor.

With his magic cabinet and his ability to change his appearance, the Doctor was analogous to a god from ancient myth or a benign wizard from a fairy tale—a true denizen of the world of the imagination. At its most inventive, *Doctor Who* pursued fanciful epistemological games that transcended usual escapist fare, teasing the watcher with unexpected juxtapositions and clever inversions of the conventional. For visual imagery, the series offered virtual carte blanche to its designers. After all, in a magical world where a police box is a gateway to other dimensions, there is no reason why these other dimensions should look like ours. Never before had the premise of a drama series offered the designer such an invitation to stylize.

It is no exaggeration to say that the long-term success of the show was based on two virtuosically stylized designs. Both almost verged on abstraction, if we follow Richard Levin's definition of the latter as "original design" that is "not in any way related to reality" but is rather "a synthesis of shapes which in themselves may carry an evocative or symbolic thought,"[8] and both appeared very early in the show's run. First came the interior of the Doctor's ship, TARDIS, a spectacle unlike any seen hitherto on television (figs. 4.1a and 4.1b). Even more popular were the fell inhabitants of a metal city on the planet Skaro, which the Doctor visited in the fifth episode: the Daleks (fig. 4.2). Though the Daleks and the TARDIS interior established the benchmark for spectacle in the series, the precedent that they set for quasi-abstraction was often ignored. As a fantasy, *Doctor Who* could not entirely eschew stylization, in Levin's sense of "derived design," but there were times when it came close to doing so. Often, stylization was nothing more than leaven in the loaf of naturalism.

It would be impossible to explore here all points of the *Doctor Who* aesthetic, but its broad trends can be mapped. During the first three seasons, boldly stylized imagery in the science fiction narratives, which gave them their epic quality, alternated with naturalistic imagery in the historical adventures. Designers were called upon to simulate past human cultures, from Kublai Khan's court to Revolutionary France. Flights of fancy and historical simulacra coexisted on paths that did not cross.

After three years, a new producer, Innes Lloyd, made drastic changes

FIGURES 4.1A AND 4.1B. *The honeycomb: The TARDIS and its original crew—the Doctor (William Hartnell) and his passengers, left to right (in fig. 4.1a), Jacqueline Hill, William Russell, and Carole Ann Ford in "An Unearthly Child" (1963). Set designed by Peter Brachacki, costumes by Maureen Heneghan/Daphne Dare. © BBC Worldwide.*

to *Doctor Who*—including the first imposition of a new lead actor as the Doctor.[9] Historical adventures were swept aside, and a much stronger element of horror was introduced into the series.[10] Monsters became a constant presence and an ever-greater number of episodes were set on present-day Earth to heighten the frisson of the Doctor's encounters with his inhuman opponents. The function and character of design changed to serve this new mood. Horror and the macabre depend for their impact on seeming naturalism, and the role of the designer in this more frightening *Doctor Who* was to create images that were not just surprising but believable.

In this horror-oriented phase, adversaries tended, unlike the Daleks, to be anthropomorphic and were designed with attention to such palpable details as scaly hides and matted fur. Where the Daleks and other robotic menaces seen in the early seasons had appeared alien by virtue of the radical

FIGURE 4.2. *The Daleks in their isomorphically designed and scaled living space (none of the actors playing human roles could stand up straight in the Dalek city) in "The Survivors" (1963). Set and Dalek props designed by Raymond P. Cusick. Photograph courtesy of Raymond P. Cusick.*

purity of their design, these mostly biological entities were the viscerally loathsome stuff of nightmares. Several of the most striking and enduringly popular Doctor Who monsters, such as the Yeti and "Ice Warriors," were devised during these years by the costume designer Martin Baugh, who enthusiastically embraced the possibilities inherent in fiberglass and other new materials.[11]

Sets, on the other hand, were generally more neutral; indeed, many were studiedly so. Although lighting became expressionistic (as much as the limitations of video recording, with its requirement of strong light—exacerbated by the need to cater for multiple shots—would permit), the locales themselves were generally much more humdrum: oil refineries, airports, factories, sewers, and even the tunnels of the London Underground. The rationale for this was neatly expressed by Jon Pertwee, who took over the role of the Doctor at a time when this use of scenic naturalism was at its height, "What could be more frightening than finding a Yeti on your looseat?"[12] Unsurprisingly, the image that had epitomized antinaturalism in the series, the TARDIS, disappeared almost entirely from *Doctor Who* at this time; in the early 1970s, the Doctor was based on contemporary Earth.

A new element entered design for *Doctor Who* around 1973. The overtones of pawky humor in the show, and its clear willingness to pay sly homage to the icons (and platitudes) of the horror and sci-fi genres, greatly increased. Design became an instrument of parody, much as it had done almost a decade before in *The Avengers*. The references and allusions in *Doctor Who* were clearly calculated to entertain at more than one level.[13] During the mid-1970s, the series was at its most polished, and consistently clever design imagery contributed to its strength.

The epic quality of design for the science fiction episodes in the first few years, with their rich vein of strikingly simplified imagery, reasserted itself briefly in the eighteenth season, which began airing in 1980. The program was at its most conceptually ambitious at this time, and the producer strongly encouraged the development of a distinctive visual sensibility. This new aesthetic impetus led to some of the most exciting and hauntingly beautiful design images devised for the show. In many ways, *Doctor Who* was at the apogee of its visual inventiveness.

The attainment of zenith was followed by a rapid slide to nadir. An executive decision was taken to begin recycling monsters from past episodes, and designers were suddenly confronted with previously unknown restrictions on creativity. Eventually the series became so stale and self-referential that it was largely unintelligible to the casual watcher. This deterioration was accelerated by competition from overpowering rivals in the form of big-budget Hollywood science fiction. By the 1980s, sci-fi had established itself as a mainstream genre in the cinema (and later also television), and *Doctor Who* had to live up to new standards of hyperrealism. Attempts to attain some semblance of filmic production values led to a watering-down of invention and a loss of distinctiveness. Sets and costumes occasionally managed to look expensive, but conceptually they were often trite and aesthetically they became more and more tawdry.

Too late, its makers seem to have recognized that *Doctor Who* could not compete on equal terms with the veritable tsunami of sci-fi blockbusters sweeping in from the United States and attempted to diversify the tone of the show. In its final two seasons (1988–1989), naturalism was occasionally elbowed aside in favor of an aggressive stylization—most notably in "The Happiness Patrol" (1988). This satirical critique of Thatcherite Britain featured blatantly nonnaturalistic settings and a killer android called the Kandy Man, who looked very much like "Bertie Bassett," the commercial emblem of the British candy manufacturer Bassett's. By this time, however, neither radicalism nor nostalgia could help. *Doctor Who* was axed by the BBC in 1990, reappearing once, in 1996, for an unlikely swan song. This was a Canadian made-for-TV movie, cofunded by the BBC and Fox, whose design perfectly epitomized the slick, expensive, and ultimately unadventurous sci-fi that had become staple fare in American film and television by the early 1990s.[14]

THE OUTER LIMITS: SCI-FI/FANTASY AS A PERMISSIVE GENRE

The visual "center of gravity" of a drama series is, in effect, determined by its genre. The weird and varied imagery of *Doctor Who* is a function of its being a sci-fi/fantasy program rather than "serious" drama.

Designers working on a sci-fi/fantasy drama generally enjoy unusual, though not unlimited, freedom in relation to the scripted narrative. Even stylized design is, as Richard Levin has it, derived from phenomena in the real world.[15] Indeed, the designer Roger Murray-Leach has insisted upon the necessity of incorporating recognizable elements even into an extraterrestrial environment such as the alien jungle he created for the *Doctor Who* episode "Planet of Evil" (1975).

> *To create a hostile environment, however "alien" that landscape is intended to appear, it's paramount to strike a chord of recognition within the mind of the viewer. A world consisting of only geometric shapes, say, might be less effective in touching the psyche of an audience than one that contained elements they might find frightening or threatening in their own lives—whether real or imagined.*
>
> *What I set out to do therefore was to design a jungle that, while being obviously "different," contained enough elements to make it instantly recognizable as a dangerous place, somewhere to anticipate the unexpected. To achieve this, instead of radically changing the shape of things—other than surface treatment, the shape of the plants, and so on, I changed the colors. Most prominent were reds, which are particularly oppressive, with the occasional bright blue and bottle green touches amongst the trees—almost like open wounds—while the water was dyed shades of yellow.*
>
> *Bearing in mind that the needs of those watching in black and white had still to be considered then, plants were designed to be physically different enough to be recognized as alien but to still retain a true jungle feel while the colors chosen gave the whole a negative feel in monochrome.*[16]

Although Murray-Leach's point is well made, the fact remains that the script for a sci-fi/fantasy program is unlikely to contain many immutable points of reference for the designer to work around. Blue-streaked trees and yellow water would be unconvincing in a set representing a real tropical jungle on Earth, but in an alien setting, suspension of disbelief comes into play to a much greater extent. There are, in other words, few visual conceits that will seem inappropriate per se, for the simple reason that there is no benchmark for judging the "authenticity" of futuristic imagery.

The designer enjoys even more freedom in a sci-fi/fantasy series than in a film belonging to the same genre. As noted in *The Avengers*, the design ethos of a television series can be altered over time; and as *The Prisoner* demonstrated, abrupt changes of visual aesthetic for the sake of effect are also sustainable. The room for maneuvering is greater still in a sci-fi/fantasy series. Because *The Avengers* had one foot in the real world, John Steed's sartorial style, once it had been established, could not be significantly altered without undermining the integrity of the character. Even a change in the décor of his flat from Chippendalian gentility to Corbusian severity would probably have struck the viewer as wrong. Internal rules cannot be generated in the same way in a fantastical drama series, where there is no stable associative index for making judgments about the appropriateness of any given image.

A good example of the mutability of design in the sci-fi/fantasy series is provided by the sometime stablemate of *Doctor Who*, the space opera *Blake's 7* (BBC TV, 1978–1981). Even though it had strong narrative continuity, with story arcs sometimes occupying half a season, *Blake's 7* allowed its design imagery to be, in effect, free-floating. The aesthetic, especially for costumes, was transformed at the beginning of the second season, with both regulars and incidental characters for the first time dressed in a flamboyant style, calculatedly unlike the drab anoraks that dominated the first season.[17] Another shift, this time toward minimalist chic, took place at the end of the season,[18] only to be overturned midway through the next by an abrupt switch to soaring high camp.[19] The orientation and character of the narratives never changed at all: it was simply the "look" that altered. Viewers must have registered this, at least at a subliminal level. However, without a concrete contemporary or historical referent, there was no basis for assessing the value of these changes except personal taste.

In *Doctor Who*, the ineffectuality of the scripted narrative in providing a blueprint for design can be demonstrated through a plethora of examples; we will focus on two. The first shows a designer improvising freely with relatively slight information from a script. This was not a radical show of independence, but an enhancement of the normal inventive process. In the second case, design was used to redefine the expressive parameters of a narrative.

The script for "The Brain of Morbius" (1976) was written at the height of Doctor Who's ironic engagement with generic precedent, and drew openly on a range of macabre tales and staples of schlock horror in the movies, most notably *Frankenstein*.[20] The brain of the title is preserved by a mad surgeon, Mehendri Solon, in a bizarre dwelling on the storm-blasted world of Karn. The scientist's workplace is not a deserted hilltop watchtower, as in James Whale's landmark film of *Frankenstein* (1931), but a deserted cliff-top "hydrogen plant."

The supposedly functional role of this building is belied by the prodigality of decoration in Barry Newbery's designs, which includes carved sphinxes flanking a stairway in the grand entrance hall, elaborate window tracery and arcading, and doors decorated with calligraphic figures. The overtones of the futuristic in the name "hydrogen plant" are entirely (and deliberately) overlooked in the design. Newbery's real purpose was not to support this kind of narrative specificity, but to stress its horror-movie lineage. The cliff-top dwelling is referred to in the script as "Solon's castle," and Newbery devised an appropriately ominous, medievalizing structure, albeit elaborating his ideas well beyond the confines of generic precedent.

When you're designing for an ordinary drama, you have to put on what is probable, not just what is possible; whereas with a science fiction program like Doctor Who, *you use what is possible, not just what is probable. This works, because the audience doesn't have preconceived ideas—in fact, there's an expectation of seeing something unusual. If an idea is uncommon, you can use it on* Doctor Who: *if it's common, then you try to find another way.*

In the case of Karn, I imagined a planet very much like Earth which had originally had a human civilization, except that I decided that the human beings there had developed in a way unlike us. Their answers to permanent problems had not been the same as ours. So I began to think about how, architecturally, things might have been different—and my starting point was European Gothic architecture. Traditionally, with our Gothic churches, we put buttresses on the outside. You're always going to need them, because with tall, straight walls the roof presses down and wants to push the walls out. So I thought, "We'll have our buttresses on the inside, because in buildings on Karn the walls are made to lean in."

Another of my ideas was that I wanted to give the impression that the building could move if necessary—not around and about, but that the walls and roof could slightly change position. So when I put cylindrical, column-shaped flying buttresses in on either side of the main entrance doors in the hall, I had a hemisphere attached to the bottom of each column [figs. 4.3a and 4.3b]. . . . The idea was that each of these cylinders could roll slightly on the ball, whenever the planet's storm-winds got really bad and put pressure on the outer walls.[21]

For the viewer, the coherence of Newbery's architectonic logic was no more important than the texturing of component parts of the set, and probably a good deal less so. Details rise to prominence on the television screen, while the overall conception of a set is difficult to take in, even where long shots are possible, because of the poor resolution of the video image. Newbery therefore extended his alien architectural principles into individual elements of the design, and these were brought out by the sensitive, topical illumination contrived by lighting director Peter Catlett. A clear sense of formal coherence was achieved by the repeated use of parabolas, in the shapes of the windows and in the numerous lopsided arches, the latter also suggesting the idea of internal buttressing. In tune with their gothic antecedents, Newbery's windows had elaborate tracery, yet the "organic" irregularity of the lights represented a striking departure from the symmetry of medieval norms. Textures, too, were made to look unusual; for example, stock, vacuum-formed panels representing coursed rubblestone or knapped-flint walling were given a dull metallic sheen, which, under the subtle lighting, lent them an unearthly quality.[22]

If its architectural forms and textures provide a glimpse of the lost civilization of Karn, then the dressing of the sets for Solon's castle more directly proclaim him a mad scientist. Both his study, which serves as his operating theater, and the cellar where he keeps the disembodied brain are cluttered with surgical equipment, chemicals, and machinery. Even these purely denotative elements have a strong evocative charge. At one stage, Solon complains about his primitive working conditions and the makeshift nature of his machinery and surgical equipment, but notions of the primitive and makeshift in a culture accustomed to time travel would be unlikely to correspond with ours. Yet many of his contraptions look clumsy and out-of-date by 1970s standards, strengthening the connection with classic 1930s

FIGURES 4.3A AND 4.3B. *Gothic, arch: a, Barry Newbery's design for the hall of Solon's Castle in "The Brain of Morbius" (1976); b, a continuity photograph of the finished set. Drawing © Barry Newbery; photograph courtesy of Barry Newbery.*

horror movies and undermining the futuristic conventions of space fantasy. Evocation of mood—specifically a gothic mood—is paramount.

Our second example is drawn from "The Robots of Death" (1977). This is one of only two *Doctor Who* episodes where a well-known aesthetic from the history of design was applied wholesale to every aspect of imagery, including make-up. The script emerged from instructions to devise a "country house whodunit" in space.[23] The familiar formula was spiced up by there being not one murderer, but an army of them, in the form of rebellious slave robots on a mobile ore-mining plant. The writer had given no clear description of the environment, and the director, Michael Briant, made up his mind to avoid the stereotype of "silver sets and giant robots."[24] Briant and his designers decided to design the robots, like everything else in the mining craft, in a deceptively sensuous moderne idiom.[25]

The choice of style was extremely apt for the effete society portrayed in the script. A bastardized offshoot of cubism and futurism, moderne was rectilinear, shiny, and faceted where art nouveau had been sinuous, shimmering, and organic. This sleek, sharp-edged style bespoke confidence in the power and attractions of technology and was therefore piquantly appropriate to a robot-dependent civilization. Its fit with the narrative aside, the imagery was striking simply because of the perverse axis between brutality and beauty. This was an aesthetic world where, courtesy of the scenic designer, Kenneth Sharp, a cluster of hand grenades made up the facets of a decorative, cubistic scallop.

Elizabeth Waller's costume design for the killer robots epitomized the way in which the stylized moderne imagery was used to heighten the creeping horror of the *Ten Little Indians*-style narrative. The full-head mask used for the robots expressed serene loveliness: with its wide almond eyes, voluptuous lips, and luxuriant mane of wavy hair, the design strongly recalled the "perfect" physiognomies of ancient Greco-Roman sculpture (fig. 4.4). In true moderne fashion, the contours of these quasi-classical masks were simplified into sleek but sharply defined planes, and the hair was regularized into neat, undulating furrows. The robots' beauty of face was matched by sumptuous accoutrements, for rather than having bodies of exposed metal plating, they wore plush, quilted garments in an orientalizing mode.

The conceit was a remarkable one: in place of the iron-sided juggernauts of sci-fi tradition, Waller had created delicate, matelassé-clad ephebes. Other artistic choices followed from this evocation of androgynous grace,

FIGURE 4.4. *Dressed to kill: One of the Greco-moderne killer robots aboard the* **Sandminer** *in "The Robots of Death" (1977). Costume designed by Elizabeth Waller, set by Kenneth Sharp.* © *BBC Worldwide.*

such as the decision to have the robots speak in soft, soothing tones even when they were uttering death threats. In short, the visual and aural conceptions of the robots greatly enriched the menace of the shocker narrative, for the counterpoint between pulchritude and violence was chilling.

The eerie perversities of imagery in "The Robots of Death" were carried further still in the unusually elaborate and conspicuous make-up and dress worn by the main human characters. The actors playing the Sandminer crew had metallic paint applied to their noses and brows in carefully drawn outlines, making these human visages disconcertingly similar to the faceted forms of the robot masks. Furthermore, the crew's clothes were strongly individualized in a way that was unusual for sci-fi drama in general, and *Doctor Who* in particular. Rather than donning uniforms or dull fatigues when they went on duty, they added fantastical headgear that heightened the contrasts in their already well-differentiated garb.

In conceiving attire for each member of the crew, Waller made full use of the liberation sci-fi grants the designer from received social values; she left all contemporary standards, including those of conventional gender division, behind. For example, the tough guy, played by the tall and powerfully built Brian Croucher, was dressed in a loose, blouse-like silver satin jacket with billowing sleeves (fig. 4.5). The garment had a plethora of finicky ornament, including elaborate clasps down the front and a long row of buttons on each of the tight-fitting cuffs. As with the comeliness of the killer-robots, the studied disjunction between Croucher's "effeminate" attire and his character's belligerently macho persona created an intriguing paradox.

Doctor Who, like many sci-fi/fantasy series, allowed designers great scope to cultivate their sense of play—to toy with ideas, to tease and confound audience expectations, to overturn cliché, and to color banality. In episodes like "The Robots of Death," the design imagery almost constituted a commentary on the narrative and certainly went beyond attractive décor. Nevertheless, though some of the beautifully conceived worlds of *Doctor Who* were remote from the disorderly reality of day-to-day life, the series was never, in fact, without significant contemporary and historical referents. These were provided by the Doctor and his companions.

SKIRTING THE ISSUE: DRESS AND GENDER ROLES

Design for *Doctor Who* was not overtly informed by ideology. However, tacit promotion of a particular ideology was most powerfully expressed in the costuming of the principals. *Doctor Who* implicitly endorsed and upheld many of the values so incisively satirized in *The Avengers* and *The Prisoner*. The ideological underpinnings of *Doctor Who*, its gender stereotypes, and the evocation of myths of Englishness that made it popular at home and abroad are essentially the values of British colonialism. The Doctor, a leisured gentleman-traveler, represents the sort of self-important moral arbiter so familiar from the era when "the sun never set" on the British Empire. Thus, it is not surprising to discover that the Doctor's quaint sartorial image belongs essentially to the golden age of empire, the Victorian era; nor, for

FIGURE 4.5. *"Big Girl's Blouse": Tough guy Borg (Brian Croucher) dressed seemingly against type, with fellow **Sandminer** crew members Toos, Uvanov, and Zilda (Pamela Salem, Russell Hunter, and Tania Rogers) in "The Robots of Death" (1977). Costumes designed by Elizabeth Waller, set by Kenneth Sharp. © BBC Worldwide.*

that matter, that his girl companions were given to much screaming and fainting.

Doctor Who started out rather well in its representation of women: the first heroine was an intelligent and self-possessed schoolteacher. However, the treatment of main female characters became ever more patronizing and retrogressive. By virtue of knowledge, experience, and wide-ranging abilities, the Doctor always took an authoritative stance, while his female assistants tended to be, if not actually inept, certainly dependent and passive. Crudely summarized, the narrative function of the Doctor's girl companions was to get into trouble, and his role was to get them out of it.

There was a marked divergence in appearance between the Doctor and his companions, both male and female. The Doctor's fellow travelers and assistants were always much younger and always physically attractive, while the actors who played the Doctor were "characterful" rather than conventionally handsome. While the Doctor was recognized as being, in the words of the costume designer Barbara Kidd, a "special character"[26] whose clothing could be highly eccentric, his companions wore outfits that were generally meant to emphasize their physical appeal: these tended to be hip and of-the-moment. In short, the Doctor's companions, especially the women (who were far more numerous), were meant to be gazed upon as sex objects, whereas the Doctor was not. This is not to say that the actors playing the Doctor did not become sex symbols, because several of them indubitably did. However, the Doctor's sartorial image was not designed to accentuate his nubility, unlike the attire worn by John Steed in *The Avengers* or by John Drake in *Danger Man*.

It is worth emphasizing that we speak of a single image, rather than images, for the Doctor, notwithstanding the fact that each new actor brought with him a distinctive style of dress. In spite of the superficial differences between them, there was a much greater underlying continuity in the costumes worn by the eight successive lead players than is generally acknowledged. Of course, it is true to say that each Doctor's appeal was based on the actor's exploitation of his own personal idiosyncrasies, and that costume was in every case an expression of this heightened individuality. Nevertheless, two strong threads ran through the Doctor's style of dress from incarnation to incarnation. In the first place, the costumes all incorporated some legacy from the Victorian age, and many outfits were wholly made up of clothes from the *fin de siècle*. The second, intimately related point is that each of the Doctors wore a garment that was powerfully

FIGURE 4.6. *The Doctor as teacher: William Hartnell in "The Sensorites" (1964). Costume designed by Maureen Heneghan/ Daphne Dare. Photograph courtesy of Raymond P. Cusick.*

redolent of professional authority or the upper class: morning coats for the first two, a smoking jacket and opera cloak for the third, and frock coats for all but one of the others.

The foregoing is a slight oversimplification of the relationship between each Doctor's style of dress and his persona and should be qualified. The earliest two Doctors were not traditional heroes, which complicates the signification of their dress. For all that he affected the air of an Oxbridge don, the first and most elderly-looking Doctor, played by William Hartnell, was actually an irascible and willful mischief-maker (fig. 4.6). The paradox was intentional. Because the program was conceived partly as educational, Hartnell's Doctor was meant to be a pedagogue: moral pronouncements and ethical caveats were generally put into his mouth, and one of his characteristic gestures was to stand holding his lapels, like an old-fashioned schoolmaster. However, the naughtiness of this grumpy old man was clearly meant to appeal to the juvenile target audience.

The next Doctor, played by Patrick Troughton, performed the role as a kind of cousin to Buster Keaton's sad-faced clown,[27] muddling his way through adventures in a way that was anything but conventionally authoritative.[28] Nor did his clothes straightforwardly evoke authority—he was actually rather scruffy. His outfit was, in fact, a hobo-ish parody of Hartnell's dapper attire.[29] The first Doctor had worn a short fitted morning coat, a fine candlewick waistcoat, a wing-collared shirt with foulard tie, tapered

FIGURE 4.7. *The Doctor as clown: Patrick Troughton in "Power of the Daleks" (1966). Costume designed by Sandra Reid.* © *BBC Worldwide.*

hound's-tooth-check trousers, and cloth-top boots. In Troughton's attire, the same elements were present, but wildly distorted: the sizes of both garments and patterns had been polarized, and all that was crisp had become unformed (fig. 4.7).

The new Doctor's morning coat was several sizes too big (the tails had to be pinned up to stop them from trailing on the ground); the checks on his trousers were enormous; and the flowing cravat had been supplanted by a made-up bow tie attached with a safety pin to a soft-collared shirt. Despite his beatnik defiance of sartorial respectability and his Beatle haircut, this Doctor could not be mistaken for a working-class hero. His social affiliation, expressed in his accent and his disarming old-world courtesy, was unmistakably upper crust: he came across as the black sheep of some noble clan.

All the later Doctors, though they could sometimes be crotchety and self-ish, were unequivocally heroic, and their dress reflected this. In his third incarnation, the Doctor for the first time acquired a stylish image that would firmly underscore rather than belie his status as a superhero. Jon Pertwee played the Doctor as an implacable ultra-English hero in the Bulldog Drummond mold.[30] His extensive wardrobe was dominated by inverness cloaks, velvet jackets, and frilly shirts (fig. 4.8).

This made the Doctor a "blood" in the Regency tradition—and also made him, for the first time, bang-up-to-date in fashion terms. As discussed earlier, the end of the 1960s witnessed the flower of the Peacock Revolution in men's dress, one aspect of which was the rococo revival. The ruffled shirt, championed by one of Pertwee's preferred tailors, Mr. Fish,[31] was the

FIGURE 4.8. *The Doctor as caped crusader: Jon Pertwee in a publicity photograph for the eighth season of* Doctor Who *(1971), with,* **left to right,** *Roger Delgado as the Master, Katy Manning as Jo Grant, and Nicholas Courtney as the Brigadier. TARDIS exterior prop in background. Costumes designed by Ken Trew; Katy Manning's clothes by Biba. © BBC Worldwide.*

FIGURE 4.9. *The Doctor as belle époque bohemian: Tom Baker in "Pyramids of Mars" (1975) with Elizabeth Sladen as Sarah and Michael Sheard as Lawrence Scarman. Costumes designed by Barbara Kidd. TARDIS set redesigned by Christine Ruscoe.* © BBC Worldwide.

most obvious emblem of this trend, a far cry from the drab restraint that had characterized most menswear since the Second World War. While contemporaneity was never again to be so evident in later Doctors' costumes, Pertwee's enduring legacy was that he established the character as being not merely patrician but colorfully so.

Partly because his clothing was off-the-wall and partly because he remained much longer in the role than his two predecessors, Jon Pertwee became the first Doctor whose clothing was not merely eccentric but also truly stylized. Pertwee vigorously encouraged costume designers to extemporize around the original theme of the latter-day Regency blood, and over the course of half a decade his outfits became gradually more abstracted from both historical and contemporary precedent.[32]

This trend was repeated with Pertwee's successor, Tom Baker, who played the Doctor for seven years. In his early days, Baker had the appearance of an aging student, sporting a trailing, striped scarf very much like ones worn by Oxbridge undergraduates, a baggy red corduroy jacket, a loose thigh-length overcoat, a fedora, and tweed slacks. By the end of his tenure, the image had evolved according to its own bizarre logic and was almost as divorced from any real clothing as the traditional costumes of Pierrot or Pantaloon in a nineteenth-century harlequinade.

Stylization continued to gather momentum after Baker's departure. The creative potential and the pitfalls of this tendency can neatly be shown in relation to designers' treatment of the frock coat, a garment that became central to the Doctor's wardrobe during Baker's tenure (fig. 4.9). From the mid-nineteenth century until the end of the First World War, this long, full-skirted kind of jacket was, in many ways, the ultimate expression of respectability in the gentleman's wardrobe. This symbol of probity became something very different in designs for *Doctor Who*. The most amusing of these aberrant designs was produced for Tom Baker. Throughout his tenure, his image hovered between the velvety "aesthetic" mode of dress devised by Oscar Wilde and the tweedy Edwardian sporting gear affected by George Bernard Shaw. Baker was originally given a smart, garnet-colored velvet frock coat for an adventure set in Edwardian times, a dashingly elegant item that would not have looked out of place in the cafés of Montmartre when Toulouse-Lautrec was working there.[33]

Shortly thereafter, the velvet coat was replaced by a real oddity—a nice reflection of the Baker Doctor's negligent charm that had little to do with Victorian sobriety. The new jacket, designed by Barbara Lane, adhered in length and cut to the late-Victorian frock-coat pattern, but in texture and detailing it would have been anathema to a turn-of-the-century gentleman (fig. 4.10). Made of coarse, flecked Irish tweed, with horn buttons and with a collar and cuffs in heavy, dark brown corduroy, the coat even had leather elbow patches. Lane's conceit was a clever one. While the length and formal crispness of the frock coat were kept, thereby emphasizing Baker's authoritative presence, the rural overtones of tweed and corduroy made him a more comfortable, accessible figure.

Designers continued to play with the idea of the frock coat after Baker's departure, moving further and further away from historical precedent. The garment foisted on the sixth Doctor, Colin Baker, was the most egregious: it was unflattering, aggressively obtrusive, and at a dramatic level ultimately unsustainable. The producer's idea had been to have the new Doctor dress "in bad taste."[34] The reluctant designer, Pat Godfrey, created a frock coat in stridently colored motley, worn with yellow-and-black striped pants and other lurid garments. This ensemble negated the dignity of Victorian full dress and, more important, undermined the credibility of Baker's performance. Experimentation had degenerated into risible gimmickry. The visual spectacle of *Doctor Who* was often only a stone's throw from the vivid images of light entertainment, and none the worse for that: the problem with Colin Baker's costume was that it was, by almost any standards, too far over the line.

Earlier we briefly likened the Doctor's costumes to the clothing of characters from the harlequinade—that last, superfine theatrical manifestation of the once-rumbustious *commedia dell'arte*.[35] The comparison is apposite, for

FIGURE 4.10.
Carefully mixed messages: The Doctor wears his tweed frock coat in "The Seeds of Doom" (1975). Costume designed by Barbara Lane. © BBC Worldwide.

both the limitation and the magic of the character of Doctor Who resided in his being, like Harlequin, Scaramouche, and Columbine, an exaggerated comic type, the sum of his entertainingly repetitive and occasionally capricious actions. The development of Harlequin from a caricature of an irreverent African slave in patched rags to a dancing exquisite in lozenge-patterned body stocking and trim black eye-mask reflects a seemingly innate tendency to distill and refine abstract patterns from apparent disorder.[36] The sharp stylization of the costume image for Pertwee's and Baker's Doctors is another manifestation of this tendency.

The analogy with the *commedia* can usefully be pursued a little further. Just as the acrobatic energy of the *commedia* degenerated into the effete repetitiveness of the harlequinade, so *Doctor Who* lost its way and became trapped in a maze of self-reference. The Doctor himself came to embody this decline. The version of the character played by Sylvester McCoy, a Scot, may have represented a late attempt to make the Doctor more relevant to social changes in Britain—and for that matter to acknowledge (albeit tacitly) that Britain extended beyond London and its immediate surroundings. However, the deep-seated conservatism of the show was neatly reflected in the allusions to its predecessors that McCoy's costume image exhibited: like Tom Baker he wore a scarf, like Peter Davison (the fifth Doctor) he wore a Panama hat, and like Troughton he favored boldly checked trousers. Indeed, his potpourri image showed how much antinaturalism in this context could serve not to expand the imaginative repertoire of the series but actually to reduce it.

The unwillingness of the program to embrace social change was stressed by a basic fact: Every time the Doctor regenerated, he remained male. When Tom Baker announced his departure from the series in late 1980, he suggested that his successor might "even" be a woman.[37] This proved to be a characteristically provocative joke at the expense of the press, for Peter Davison had already been cast. However, there was no compelling reason, other than a slavish devotion to precedent, for the Doctor not to change sex. Joanna Lumley was rumored to be under consideration for the role at the time of Baker's departure, but she was invited to play the part only in a farcical spoof, "The Curse of Fatal Death," shown as part of the BBC's Comic Relief telethon in 1999. That a female Doctor was seen as a basis for comedy serves to shed light on the entrenchment of male chauvinism in the series.

The inherent misogyny of the series is even more forcefully presented in the clothing of the Doctor's companions. As society at large in the developed world engaged with feminism and strove toward some kind of gender equality, *Doctor Who* became ever more bare-faced in the way that it sexually objectified young women through their attire.

At first this was not the case. During the early years of the show, when the crew of the TARDIS made up a "family" quartet, the costumes for the Doctor's companions were studiedly uninteresting. The program's first costume designer, Daphne Dare, recalls having taken pains to ensure that, unlike Hartnell's Doctor, the other main characters were in no way sartorially remarkable; their function was to mediate between the world inhabited by the audience and the exotic goings-on in the fantastical spheres to which the TARDIS voyaged.[38]

During the first three years of the program, the chief female protagonists, though physically attractive, were consistently desexualized. For example, Vicki, a teenage girl from the twenty-fifth century who might have been accoutered in any number of striking ways, was given an austere pageboy hairstyle and clothes to match. Her plain, dark, high-collared tunic, worn with heavy, dark stockings, had unmistakable overtones of a medieval youth's cotehardie and made her seem sexually neuter. In an adventure set in the war-torn Holy Land of the Third Crusade, the Doctor actually disguised Vicki as a page, in order, as he explained, to protect her from the unwelcome attentions of warriors.[39] This dissimulation was a kind of narrative echo of the ethos of the series: the Doctor was in effect verbalizing the producers' policy apropos female sexuality.

In 1966 the new producer, Innes Lloyd, overturned this approach, introducing new characters who embodied Swinging London rather than dormitory town. Clearly eager to broaden the appeal of the program, Lloyd brought sex to *Doctor Who* in the form of Polly, played by the blond, svelte Anneke Wills.[40] Modeled on the youth icons Marianne Faithfull, Jean Shrimpton, and Julie Christie, Wills' character was a swinging dolly who might have sprung directly from the pages of the "coloursupps," the hip, glossy magazines that accompanied weekend newspapers.[41] Polly's counterpart was Ben, who, unlike his male predecessors, did not hail from the professional classes: he was an assertively cockney sailor. While Polly's antecedents were clearly middle class, she was shown from the first to be cosmopolitan in a way that rejected polite bourgeois expectations. When the Doctor met her, she worked by day as a secretary, but by night as a cocktail waitress at the suggestively named "Inferno" bar.

After Polly, there was no turning back for the representation of female nubility in *Doctor Who*. Polly brought with her the miniskirt and the permissiveness it represented, and by extension she established the Doctor's girl companions as an object of the male gaze. Polly's successor hailed from the high-Victorian era, yet after only one episode her crinoline and petticoats were gone. They were replaced not with one of the more moderate styles of the later 1960s, but with a short dress and sweater. This abrupt conversion to modern modes was narratively implausible, but credibility was clearly no longer the main criterion.

Emancipation in dress was not matched by an attempt to make the female protagonists into progressive role models. Indeed, Anneke Wills claims that she specifically wished Polly to be the antithesis of Emma Peel from *The Avengers*. Thus, Polly would go out of her way to avoid danger and always acquiesced with alacrity to suggestions that she should "make some coffee."[42] While Wills' performance was certainly amusing, it tacitly endorsed the prevailing idea that a woman's prime function is to attend to men's needs. Because of the way Polly was represented, the adoption of a miniskirt could all too easily be seen as dressing simply to please the opposite sex.

If, after Polly, there was no possibility of—or wish for—a return to desexualized female characters, it proved remarkably easy to backslide into a mode of sexism that denied women any function other than that of being purely decorative. Inconsistent treatment of female characters in the later 1960s gave way to unbridled paternalism in the early 1970s, when Jon Pertwee was the Doctor. His dizzy blonde companion, Jo Grant, was remarkable for nothing except the fact that she dressed out of the radical London fashion boutique Biba (see fig. 4.8).[43] Jo's clothing was clearly meant to be appreciated as fashion rather than merely as costume. "The Sea Devils" (1972) required Jo and the Doctor to take a variety of hazardous trips in small boats, rappel down a cliff side, climb a martello tower, dash across heathland, and even negotiate a minefield. Through all this, Jo wore a modish white "Great Gatsby" suit trimmed in black, with enormous flares on the trousers. Since the location work was shot on film rather than outside broadcast video, the impact of this white garb was optimized by the chromatic responsiveness of the medium in all the scenes where the costume was narratively most absurd.

For all that feminism was emerging as a major cultural force from about 1970 onwards,[44] references to women's lib in *Doctor Who* were at best lip-service, and at worst bespoke a barely-hidden contempt.[45] When in the late 1970s a real attempt was made to create a positive role model for girls, it backfired. The first self-sufficient action girl on the show, Leela, was a heroine supposedly in the Emma Peel vein.[46] However, whereas Mrs. Peel was a scientist, Leela was a savage. The producer, Philip Hinchcliffe, envisaged her relationship with the Doctor as being akin to that of Eliza Doolittle and Professor Higgins in Shaw's *Pygmalion,* with Leela's being gradually civilized.[47] The idea was certainly questionable, but Leela was, in the event, to suffer worse indignities.

As a warrior tribeswoman living on a jungle planet, Leela was originally dressed in skins that were extremely brief, like those of all her tribe (fig. 4.11). This costume was, predictably enough, of great interest to the press. Newspaper articles introducing the character invariably emphasized

FIGURE 4.11. *Baring almost all: The superheroine Leela (Louise Jameson) in her uniform in "Face of Evil" (1977). Costume designed by John Bloomfield. © BBC Worldwide.*

Leela's feisty, fighting spirit and then proceeded to emphasize her sex appeal. According to one journalist, Philip Hinchcliffe had said that Leela was conceived specifically to maintain the attention of "the dads" in the viewing audience.[48] Whether or not this was true, in the next few episodes commissioned by Hinchcliffe a cover-up took place, and Leela's skins were replaced by more substantial clothing appropriate to the setting (fog-bound Victorian London in one case and a fog-bound Edwardian lighthouse in the next). However, shortly after Leela's début, Hinchcliffe resigned as producer, and his plans for the character never came to fruition. There could be little doubt that the new producer saw Leela primarily as eye candy. Not only was her education forgotten, but after her Edwardian adventure she was to be seen braving the coldest of climates in her skins. Most perversely, she eventually parted from the Doctor to marry an incidental character—much to the chagrin of Louise Jameson, the actress who played Leela.

During the mid-1980s, the commodification of sexuality was rampant in *Doctor Who,* becoming most pronounced around the time of the twentieth anniversary of the series in 1983. Certain costumes nodded obliquely to sexual fetishes and gay fantasies: the girl-companion of the moment was seen in one episode wearing a leather miniskirt with a chain fob, while the boy-companion spent an entire year in a tight-fitting schoolboy outfit. More remarkable, and perhaps unintentionally comic, were the weak narrative excuses for occasionally having these young people strip to their underwear in front of the cameras.

However, the pendulum eventually swung away from this blatant "sexploitation." In the case of the Doctor's final protégée, the rambunctious teenager Ace, the characterization was surprisingly subtle and deftly handled. Ace was a brutalized working-class girl with an attitude problem, a propensity for violence, and a closet full of hang-ups that were explored in several of the stories. As regards costume Ace was the first female lead whose clothing was conceived in relation to street fashions; in this case, those promoted in the late 1980s by such hip, metropolitan youth magazines as *The Face.*[49] Seldom parted from her rucksack, and clad in Dr. Martens AirWair shoes and an oversized black bomber jacket smothered with badges, Ace's appearance conveyed her aggressive, streetwise tomboyishness.

Although superficially the student, Ace exposed cracks in the facade of the Doctor's heroism, holding him to account in an unprecedented way. She was the enemy within to a much greater extent than Leela, whose threat was circumscribed by having to play the restless native to the Doctor's sahib. Leela, in other words, could be accommodated into the ultimately imperialist worldview of *Doctor Who.* Ace, with none of Leela's Amazonian exoticism, was a much more immediate, homegrown challenge to the Doctor's authority: she stood for the disaffected and disenfranchised portion of British society that the series had generally overlooked.

This tardy internal acknowledgment of elitism in the series was perhaps brave, but it was also a kind of de facto admission that the show's time had passed. In its heyday, the series had made no such concessions to political correctness for the simple reason that its overt content was divorced entirely from the diurnal. The most interesting female character in *Doctor Who,* Romana, was emphatically not a representative of normality; and because she enjoyed the same special privileges as the Doctor, she became a character in her own right in much the way that the *Avengers* superwomen had done. Unlike Leela and, more particularly, Ace, she did not represent a threat to the basic tenets of *Doctor Who* because she was another embodiment of imperialist condescension. However, it was not really the narrative conception of the character that enabled Romana to become a successful counterweight to the Doctor. Rather, this must be attributed to two factors: the determination of the actress Lalla Ward to avoid the "Who girl" clichés and the inventiveness of June Hudson, the designer who created most of Ward's costumes. Hudson and her colleagues ensured that Romana was never the drab peahen to the Doctor's shimmering peacock.

Romana's parity with the Doctor was only partly defined by the narrative. According to statements in the scripts, she was more intellectually gifted and academically qualified than the Doctor, and it was evident that her brilliant mind was better disciplined. In practice, she was another of those strong female characters who, like the smart and highly qualified Special Agent Dana Scully in *The X-Files* (Fox/Ten-Thirteen, 1993–2002), fell foul of the problem that her erratic and capricious colleague was often more successful in solving problems with his seemingly wild leaps of faith and imagination than she with her clear head.

The first actress to take the role of Romana, Mary Tamm, seldom escaped from the Doctor's shadow. She quickly took on the typical traits of getting into trouble, screaming, and dressing inappropriately. The character came into her own only with the arrival of Ward and the simultaneous appointment of June Hudson as principal costume designer. As it turned out, then, Romana achieved distinction not by virtue of the way the character was conceived by the writers, but by virtue of how she was played—and dressed. According to Tom Baker, he and Ward wrote much of their own dialogue, which was laced with quips, puns, and knowing absurdities.[50] At the same time, Ward adopted a quirkiness that, though not as manic, was close in spirit to Baker's own. Her portrayal was complemented and enhanced by the attractive but eccentric attire designed for her by June Hudson.

Hudson's outfits for Ward became more and more daring over the course of their two-year collaboration—not for the body parts exposed, but for the witty ideas the costumes embodied. Ward was akin to the show's lead player, Tom Baker, in possessing unconventional looks but abundant charisma. Her boyish figure would not have lent itself to pin-up girl glamour, but this was anyway irrelevant to her conception of the character. Hudson recalled that Ward wanted to play Romana "like a kind of cheeky teenage boy."[51] Ward's costumes, especially those devised by Hudson, were made loci of wit and flights of fantasy in a way that had never been attempted before in *Doctor Who*—and was certainly never attempted again.

As a consequence of Ward's aversion to the "weaker vessel" stereotype for female companions, Hudson's costume designs for Romana frequently involved the adoption, or at least adaptation, of masculine garb.[52] In the second production on which Ward and Hudson worked together, Romana was given a feminized pastiche of Tom Baker's by-then famous outfit, entirely in pink and white, and in soft fabrics rather than Baker's harsh tweeds and knitted wool. She wore pink Bavarian breeches with an embroidered "bib," a frock coat in the same pink fabric, and a trailing scarf in white silk (fig. 4.12). The wit was beguiling, and the costume visually underscored the consonance of Romana and the Doctor. The insistent, not to say calculatedly excessive use of pink suggested a teasing attitude to stereotypes of femininity.

In other designs for Romana, Hudson cleverly extrapolated ideas from circumstantial details in the scripts. The elements on which she drew for inspiration were not necessarily the most obvious ones, and her best work was characterized by lateral thinking. In fact, only one of her outfits for Romana can be rationalized simply as a function of the story's action. In "The Leisure Hive" (1980), Ward wore a striped, Edwardian boy's bathing costume surmounted by a sailor-collared top and straw boater (see fig. 4.15): the adventure begins with the Doctor and Romana taking a holiday on Brighton Beach. In all other cases, Hudson's designs for Ward had discursive rather than strictly narrative resonances. For example, the plot of "The Horns of Nimon" (1979–1980) was a witty, entirely undisguised revision of the Minotaur legend. Hudson's costume for Ward played knowingly with the idea of "red rag to the bull."[53] The cocksure and haughty Romana, who in this adventure had a share of the heroics quite equal to that of the Doctor, was dressed by Hudson in hunting "pinks" (fig. 4.13). Nothing could have been more wholly removed from the demeaning image of which Ward fought shy. Indeed, this assertive outfit demonstrates the extent to which costume design could help to undermine stereotype. Far from being a damsel in distress, Romana's clothes established her as a hunter—and a sporting hunter, at that, for her "pinks" clearly signified that the bull-like Nimon was not so much a threat as a quarry.

Ward's final episode in the role of Romana, "Warriors' Gate" (1980) was a lyrical homage to Cocteau. Set in a ruined castle surrounded by a gray

"DESTINY OF
DALEKS"

Scarf
Silky Rayon
Knit in
cream
with fringe

coat edged with
dark suede
pinky-brown

leather boots

Lalla Ward
as
ROMANA

June Hudson

FIGURE 4.12. *June Hudson's design drawing for Romana (Lalla Ward) from
"Destiny of the Daleks" (1979). Courtesy of June Hudson.*

FIGURE 4.13. *Taking the bull by the horns: The Doctor and Romana (Lalla Ward) explore the Nimon's lair in "The Horns of Nimon" (1979). Tom Baker's costume designed by Colin Lavers/Tom Baker; Lalla Ward's costume designed by June Hudson. © BBC Worldwide.*

void, the story revolved around a huge mirror (clearly recalling the 1949 film *Orphée*),[54] which served as a portal between worlds. Moreover, the main protagonists were the Tharils, who inevitably begged comparison with the distinctly leonine "Beast" in *La belle et la bête* (Jean Cocteau, 1946).

In arriving at a final design for Romana, Hudson allowed her mind to wander among the ideas generated by the elegiac script.[55] At the end of "Warriors' Gate," Romana parted company with the Doctor to aid the Tharils in rebuilding their paradisal civilization in the world beyond the mirror. Hudson has said in retrospect that she half-consciously interpreted Romana's choice as a wish to seek enlightenment rather than to pursue a life of picaresque excitement with the Doctor.[56] With the notion of Romana as a pilgrim to Shangri-La at the back of her mind, the designer came up with a simple design based on the traditional garb of Manchurian peasants.[57] The main garment was a loose, mandarin-red silk tunic with long sleeves, bereft of ornament except for the self-covered buttons that ran the whole length of the front. The tunic was worn with simple black "coolie" trousers, red stockings, and soft black pumps (fig. 4.14). According to Hudson, the image was meant to be light, free, and spiritualized, an appropriate contrast to that

"Dr Who"
Wawiors Gate

Goodbye to
Romana

SILK
TUNIC +
TROS.

June Hudson

FIGURE 4.14. *June Hudson's design drawing for Romana in "Warriors' Gate" (1981).*
© *BBC Worldwide.*

of Baker's Doctor, who was physically encumbered by his heavy scarf, coat, and boots and figuratively encumbered by his restless need for adventure.[58]

We have argued throughout this book that design functions tangentially to narrative. The contrast between the "levity" of Romana's outfit in "Warriors' Gate" and the heaviness of the Doctor's offers a particularly nice example of this. While viewers might not pick up on the hints of Shangri-La in Romana's outfit, they would notice its insubstantiality in comparison with the Doctor's many-layered, wintry costume.

They would also be likely to notice that unlike several previous outfits worn by Romana, this one did not refer in any way to the Doctor's. For the immediately preceding story, "State of Decay," Amy Roberts had dressed Ward in a jacket and knickerbockers, closely echoing the Norfolk suit that Baker's Doctor wore.[59] The mirror-image effect was never more apt than in "State of Decay": not only did the Doctor and Romana demonstrate their close conformity in the usual flow of witticisms, asides to each other, and merciless put-downs directed at their opponents, but they mimicked each other to the very phrase in their expressions of mutual admiration. Hudson's design for Romana in "Warriors' Gate" sharply disrupted the two characters' unanimity, foreshadowing their parting in a way that the script—apart from a few hurried words of farewell—entirely failed to do.

Because of the close correspondence between the two characters, Romana is unique among the Doctor's companions in that she sartorially upstaged him in his own terms. Before the end of Ward's first year in the role of Romana, the Doctor's image, a forceful sign of his conspicuous individualism, was in danger of being eclipsed by the characterfulness of his companion's clothing. Romana's outfits made her just as assertive, amusing, and fascinating as the hero himself. Moreover, when it came to commanding the viewer's attention, Romana had a distinct advantage: Not only did her clothes change from episode to episode, but they were more finely honed in conception than the Doctor's ever-scruffier clothing. While in narrative terms theirs was a partnership of aristocratic equals, in visual terms the Doctor's image, though certainly outlandish, was not as imposing as Romana's.

Tom Baker had long since developed a rather unkempt, bohemian style of dress with which he was comfortable (see fig. 4.13). He had sifted the elements contributed by various designers over the years until his wardrobe contained the mix of garments that he favored. Whereas Lalla Ward actively welcomed the opportunity to dress up in a variety of different costumes, Baker, like other male stars of television series, resisted changes in his wardrobe and exercised firm control over what he wore.[60] However, the incoming producer for the 1980–1981 season, John Nathan-Turner, was determined that the Doctor's image should be revised in line with the house style that he wanted to develop for the series. Nathan-Turner admired the kind of crisp, boldly conceived costumes that Hudson had been creating for not only Lalla Ward's Romana but also a host of incidental characters, and he asked to her to reinvent Baker's look. Hudson has stated that she had grave reservations about interfering with an internationally famous image. She felt strongly that Baker's performance, and by extension the integrity of the whole series, would be ill-served by an extreme alteration. What she tried to produce was, in her own words, an "apotheosis of Tom's old image."[61]

Hudson's major innovation, which brought visual unity to Baker's bizarre costume, was to use a radically simplified color scheme for the new design. In the past, though browns and grays had been prevalent in his wardrobe, the Baker Doctor's clothing had incorporated a wide range of disparate chromatic elements and patterns, the jazziest notes being sounded by the crazy, haphazard stripes of his knitted scarf. All the principal garments in the new ensemble—long overcoat, fedora hat, Norfolk jacket, corduroy breeches, and argyll socks—were entirely or largely of one hue: plum-color (fig. 4.15). The multicolored scarf, too, was gone, replaced by one whose coloration was restricted to plum and two closely toning shades, arranged in a graduated pattern.[62]

The resolution of Baker's Pied Piper polychromy into an essentially monochrome image represented Hudson's most obvious use of stylization in the design. However, her selective intensification of the established image depended on her handling of shape as well as color (fig. 4.16). Central to her project was the design for a new overcoat, which capitalized on Baker's height and leanness. Calf-length and double-breasted, this all-enveloping garment had a huge, cape-like collar and full skirts. It managed to evoke both the princely and the pastoral. Above all, this capacious, sweeping coat, which Baker liked to wear with knee-length leather top boots, was supposed to give strong visual expression to the Doctor's status as a seasoned and dauntless traveler. Hudson wanted his attire to suggest that he was equipped to brave the most inhospitable of climes and terrains in his adventures.[63]

Dressed thus, the Doctor seemed to belong to the beautiful but awesome worlds evoked by Coleridge and Caspar David Friedrich. Hudson sought to enhance the overtones of the "Romantic Wanderer" that she saw in Tom

FIGURE 4.15. *The Doctor and Romana take a holiday on Brighton Beach in "The Leisure Hive" (1980). Costumes designed by June Hudson. © BBC Worldwide.*

Baker's Doctor.[64] The actor has independently spoken of such qualities in relation to the design:

I always adored June's work because of its tremendous, operatic panache. You see, the thing you must realize is that June and I are both essentially Romantics. That marvelous, purplish outfit, with the long, Byronian coat— that represented our common ground in Romanticism. How could I be anything other than utterly in love with it?[65]

The introduction of the plum-colored outfit prevented the Doctor from being visually outclassed by his companion but also helped to clarify the nature of their partnership in the 1980–1981 season. Romana, with her penchant for dressing up, had by this time become the quirky, quicksilver member of the duo, often courting and frequently overcoming hazards on her

FIGURE 4.16. *June Hudson's design drawing for Tom Baker's plum-colored Norfolk suit (greatcoat not shown).* © *BBC Worldwide.*

own. The Doctor, wrapped in his rich but tenebrous attire, was a more inward, often taciturn figure. He was now often content to observe situations, quietly cracking wise from the background and only occasionally taking center stage as the man of action or as a stern moral arbiter.

The Doctor also needed a bulwark against being overshadowed by the creatures and environments encountered on his travels. Because of Nathan-Turner's wish to ensure that visual imagery in the eighteenth season was consistently striking,[66] all characters were designed to be larger than life. This might have made the hero almost invisible in a sea of spectacle had his costume image not been so powerfully elemental. The sets that season saw the heaviest concentration of nonnaturalistic and stylized imagery ever in the series, some of it nearly expressionist, some downright surreal. No matter what bizarre situation the Doctor found himself in, his costume provided a strong chromatic accent, a clear focal point for the viewer's attention.

In explaining her decision to preserve and enhance the broad strokes of Baker's image rather than impose an entirely new style, Hudson emphasized that the Doctor "must be the still center in a spinning universe."[67] But the Doctor could only remain an effective "still center" if the aesthetic character of his environment remained stable. When the whole design idiom of the series altered, the Doctor's apparel would to some extent have to alter to suit—and this is effectively what happened in the 1980–1981 season under Hudson's tutelage. In the final episode of the previous season, "The Horns of Nimon," the Doctor had been the most visually quotidian element. Primary colors and bold silhouettes abounded, and compared with the quasi-graphic sharpness of his environment, the Doctor's image looked cluttered. During the next season, in his plum colored outfit, the Doctor was distinctive without seeming aesthetically out of place.

THE USES OF STYLIZATION

The decision to forge a distinctive, overall aesthetic for *Doctor Who* in 1980 was unprecedented, but idiomatic change in the design of the series was not. Only two images were substantially unaltered throughout the show's quarter-century run: the Daleks and the TARDIS. Otherwise, the design idiom underwent seismic shifts over the years; even some of the more popular monsters were updated on return appearances to suit changing tastes.

The rationales for some of these shifts offer another perspective on the changing conceptual relationship between design and the cumulative narrative of *Doctor Who.*

Every movement toward greater stylization in *Doctor Who* can be attributed to one of four causes. First, a change toward stylization in a central image like the Doctor's costume would invariably lead to similar changes in the overall visual character of the program. Second, elements of stylization might be introduced to reflect a greater incidence of irony in the series, the parodic intent being evoked, as so often in *The Avengers,* by the use of caricatural simplification. Third, a simplified idiom might be adopted in response to a shortage of funds: a logical decision for a scenic designer faced by such constraints was to use meager resources in the production of a bold effect rather than to attempt lifelike texture. Finally, antinatural design might reflect a stronger than usual preoccupation with the fantastical or the surreal, although such usage was, in fact, uncommon.

The Daleks represented the first and finest flowering of stylization in the series, while most subsequent design imagery was intended to make the fantastical appear palpably real. The most potent design image in the show, the Daleks had a decisive effect on the popularity of the series but even more particularly on audience's expectation regarding the kind and density of spectacle that *Doctor Who* would provide.

Although their enduring popularity is a tribute to the attractiveness and effectiveness of stylized design in sci-fi/fantasy series, the Daleks are perhaps best understood as examples of popular modernism within the framework of early-1960s design. While the man who conceived the unforgettable "pepper pot" shape, the scenic designer Raymond P. Cusick, never received any royalties from the large-scale commercial exploitation of his work, his achievement was appreciated by peers in the world of industrial design. Michael Wolff, writing for a 1965 edition of the *Journal of the Society of Industrial Arts,* commented that "the sort of designers in Britain who have really given people a bang in the last two years are Ken Adams [sic], Art Director of the James Bond films; Frederick Starke with his clothes for Cathy Gale [in *The Avengers*]; and Ray Cusick, with his daleks."[68] The choice of Pop images as paradigms of excellence and excitement was not fortuitous; it represented Wolff's contribution to an antiestablishment polemic directed at the ultraconservative Council of Industrial Design.[69] However, the aptness of the Daleks for his argument testifies to their potency as designed objects.

There is an eerie beauty to Cusick's original Daleks, notwithstanding the fact that their squat forms were full of latent menace. The fascination with the Daleks in the 1960s, a decade nicely (if prejudicially) characterized by one commentator as a period of "neophilia," is not hard to fathom.[70] As Wolff seems to have divined, the Daleks embodied the power of stylish design to excite—and therefore to sell. Indeed, the Daleks gave rise to a consumer phenomenon without precedent: "Dalekmania" proved to be a true juvenile equivalent to "Beatlemania" in the sheer volume of merchandise generated.[71] More important, the Daleks helped to sell *Doctor Who* to audiences and thereby definitively conditioned its orientation: Cusick's Daleks turned *Doctor Who* into "the monster program."

Aesthetically, the Daleks can be characterized as the embodiment of modernism rampant. In his script, Terry Nation had given only a summary description of the monsters, indicating that they had no human features.[72] As realized by Cusick, the Daleks were exquisitely styled monuments to functionalism, an aesthetic that still dominated industrial and architectural design in the early 1960s.[73] Jon Pertwee later complained that the creatures did not look like machines, but the Daleks that he knew in the early 1970s had been deprived of their intended context.[74] What made the Dalek image so powerful in the monsters' first appearance was that they were visually keyed into their setting, their metallic city on the planet Skaro (see figs. 4.2 and 4.17). The Dalek city that Cusick created was Le Corbusier's "machine for living in" taken to an extreme. It wholly conformed to the physical properties and visual character of the Dalek casings. Cusick himself has explained the rationale:

The Daleks themselves, when you saw them, were meant to be entirely different from human beings, with a city that was built without any regard for human concepts of scale, size and functioning. The city was designed for these machines even down to the shape of control switches on their instruments.[75]

Deprived of an environment sympathetic to their own aesthetic—as they were in their next outing in *Doctor Who*, "The Dalek Invasion of Earth," and in nearly all subsequent Dalek stories—Cusick's creations lost much of their impact. Their large, flat bases for gliding over the smooth metal floors of their city made them improbable masters of Earth or any environment other than their mechanized habitat on Skaro. This shortcoming was lampooned in a cartoon showing a group of Daleks at the foot of a flight of

FIGURE 4.17. *The Daleks at their specially designed control terminals in "The Survivors" (1963). Set and Dalek props designed by Raymond P. Cusick. Photograph courtesy of Raymond P. Cusick.*

stairs: the caption reads "Well, this certainly buggers our plan to conquer the Universe."[76]

Pertwee's objection that the Daleks did not look like machines, though unsustainable in relation to Ray Cusick's original, subtle deployment of the design, does highlight an important point about the nature of the Daleks' modernism. It is useful to compare the Daleks with their on-screen nemesis, the Mechanoids, also designed by Cusick for "The Chase" (1965). Unlike the more ruggedly functional-looking Mechanoids, which in their shape and surface articulation were intended to recall the geodetic architectural forms of Buckminster Fuller (so trendy in the 1960s),[77] the Daleks and Skaro City seem to belong to an earlier phase of modernism. In their synthesis of smoothly finished, sharply intersecting geometric elements, they could almost be products of the imagination of Oskar Schlemmer and his colleagues at the Bauhaus. It comes as no surprise to find that Cusick admired the sets in Korda's 1936 film *Things to Come,* conceived partly under the aegis of the sometime Bauhaus tutor Moholy-Nagy.[78] The Daleks embody the idea of the machine, rather than appearing plausibly and overtly functional in the manner of, say, the killer android in *The Terminator* (James Cameron, 1984).

For most viewers in 1963, the question of the Daleks' credibility as machine creatures would hardly have arisen. The issue was not meaningful; there were too few precedents against which audiences could judge any new sci-fi/fantasy design. Sci-fi films had rarely been "A" features, and the genre was virtually nonexistent on television. The most influential of the few screen exemplars, from *Just Imagine* (David Butler, 1930) and *Lost Horizon* (Frank Capra, 1937) in the 1930s to *Forbidden Planet* (Fred M. Wilcox, 1956) and *The Day the Earth Stood Still* (Robert Wise, 1951) in the 1950s, tended to represent alien, advanced, or futuristic cultures in terms of purist, monumental modernism—the modernism, that is to say, of Le Corbusier, of Gropius, and, latterly, of Lubetkin and the Festival of Britain. The adoption of such a majestically austere idiom in *Doctor Who* will, therefore, have seemed perfectly natural to audiences and designers alike.

By the mid-1970s, expectations about the look of the future, and by extension expectations about the look of the alien, were being defined along new lines. The actuality of space travel provided an index for authenticity. This new benchmark was cleverly manipulated by Stanley Kubrick in the first sci-fi film since *Metropolis* (Fritz Lang, 1927) with real pretensions to artistic seriousness, *2001: A Space Odyssey* (1968). Tony Masters, Harry Lange, and Ernest Archer, the chief designers for Kubrick's film, built their vision of future space travel on contemporary technologies, and *2001* introduced textural richness into the imagery of space travel. The abstracting tendencies of the designs for robots and machinery in *Forbidden Planet* and *The Day the Earth Stood Still* were deliberately eschewed. The late 1970s saw the "dirtying down" of futuristic technology in *Star Wars* (George Lucas, 1977) and the exaggerated texturing of environments and creatures in *Alien* (Ridley Scott, 1979).[79] After these films, which between them carved a mainstream niche for sci-fi/fantasy and set a precedent for intense visual incident, the "less is more" aesthetic of the International Style never resurfaced.

To some extent, *Doctor Who* mirrored these changes in the sci-fi aesthetic. While the Daleks survived unmodified, another set of popular adversaries, the robotic Cybermen, was repeatedly made over in line with the changing standards for futuristic imagery. One of the earliest designs for the creatures, by Sandra Reid, was heavily stylized (fig. 4.18). In their 1967–1968 outings, the Cybermen wore one-piece silver coveralls, terminating at the hands in three-digit gloves; their smoothly rounded, helmet-like heads had no facial features except discs for eyes and rectangular apertures for mouths. From

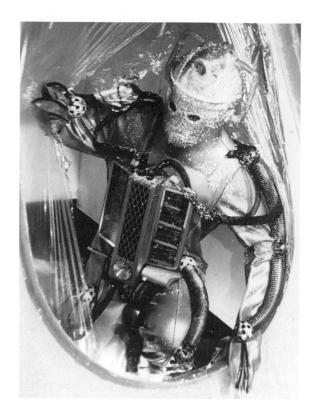

FIGURE 4.18. *From tin god . . . : A Cyberman emerges from its ice tomb in "Tomb of the Cybermen" (1967). Costume designed by Sandra Reid, set by Martin Johnson. © BBC Worldwide.*

this point on, however, the costumes became more and more highly textured. The trend reached its apogee in 1982 with a design created by Dinah Collin (fig. 4.19).

The Cybermen's coveralls, still silver, were now ridged and given a patina that made the fabric react in a complex way to studio lighting. Their helmets were burdened with fixtures and detailing, and their faces were now finickily subdivided by lines and ridges. There was even a transparent mouth/chin-piece, revealing a silvered human jaw within—an element that became mesmeric in close-up. It was hard to avoid comparing the overall effect of the new costume with that of Darth Vader from *Star Wars* (and the comparison was further encouraged by a vocal change from androgynous singsong to Vader-like basso profundo). There was no doubt where the aesthetic allegiance and aspirations of *Doctor Who* now lay.

The changing image of the Cybermen, then, is symptomatic of the way in which *Doctor Who* tried to accommodate itself to design imperatives from sci-fi films. Another such imperative, which dictated the predominant orientation of the series toward naturalism, was provided by the horror-movie tradition, and more specifically by the kind of horror exemplified in *The Thing from Another World* (Christian Nyby/Howard Hawks, 1951), *Invasion of the Body Snatchers* (Don Siegel, 1956), and the *Quatermass* adventures (BBC TV, 1953, 1955, and 1958). From the late 1960s to the mid-1970s, *Doctor Who* dealt mainly with alien menaces on Earth rather than on far-flung worlds. Shocking effects were achieved by tainting the everyday with the alien or the unexpected. This trend culminated in the creation of the Nestenes, the monsters facing Pertwee in his début *Doctor Who* episode, "Spearhead from

FIGURE 4.19. . . . *to tin-pot: Cybermen hunt the Doctor in "The Five Doctors" (1983). Costume designed by Dinah Collin. © BBC Worldwide.*

Space" (1970). The Nestenes had no corporeal form but could take possession of plastic artifacts, and their most characteristic guise was that of animated shop-window mannequins, the "Autons." The menace of these creatures depended on their appearing commonplace and anodyne. The margin for suggestive adjustment open to the costume designer Christine Rawlins was therefore extremely small. In fact, the only way the Auton dummies deviated from the real thing was in their hollow eyes and the slight hint of a cruel frown in the articulation of their foreheads. By chance, the sense of the contingent horror was increased, because the episode was shot entirely on film and on location in response to a studio strike.[80] The final edit has a correspondingly clinical, documentary feel.

Because even his Auton adversaries were studiedly drab, Pertwee stood out effortlessly in "Spearhead from Space," by virtue of his imposing face and physique and his fancy clothes. The materials were sumptuous—silk foulard tie, broderie anglaise shirt and jabot, velvet smoking jacket, and so on—but his costume was predominantly black, as it was to remain throughout his first year in the role. The following year, more chromatic variation was introduced, and this proliferation of color increased throughout his five-season tenure. This evolution in Pertwee's costumes precipitated one of those changes in overall aesthetic for *Doctor Who* that was wholly led by the key image.

As Pertwee entered his second year in the role, the Doctor was reconceptualized as a kind of comic book superhero (see fig. 4.8). This was underscored by the *Radio Times* cover announcing his return, which was a photomontage presented as a comic strip. In his sweeping inverness cloak, Pertwee's Doctor was already well on the way to being a "caped crusader." Just as Batman was regularly pitted against the Joker, the Doctor now faced his own arch-nemesis, the Master, who had an equally sharp, arresting visual image. Looking like Delacroix's Mephistopheles, the character was dressed by Ken Trew in a gray, Cardinesque, patrol-collared suit. To heighten the visual difference between the characters, the Doctor's sartorial palette immediately burgeoned to include claret and lilac. This change of costume gave rise to others. The following year saw a further expansion of color range, including the arrival of a stridently green-and-red-checked inverness. The year after that, under the initial impetus of James Acheson, Pertwee was given a series of coordinated outfits: sea-pine green velvet jacket with turquoise silk shirt and scarlet velvet waistcoat; mulberry corduroy jacket with lavender shirt and pink and orange bow tie; and so on.

After the advent of color recording and broadcast, the BBC increasingly worked to order in terms of balance of luminance (i.e., it ensured that various elements in the screen image had a reasonable measure of parity in their color values and brightness).[81] Once the Doctor began to dress in high-value, high-intensity colors, it became desirable to inject corresponding tonalities into incidental costumes and sets. In "The Mutants" (1972), the Doctor's wine-colored jacket and lilac-lined cloak were matched by blood-red and pink light effects in the caves used for location filming.

In the penultimate year of Pertwee's tenure, the creative possibilities afforded by the Doctor's bright palette were fully exploited, and designers went out on a limb in their use of stylization. For the imagery in "Carnival of Monsters," costume designer James Acheson and scenic designer Roger Liminton created images that would not have looked out of place on a light entertainment show. Strongly tinged with satire, "Carnival of Monsters" concerned a clash between immigration bureaucrats and two visiting showpeople, Vorg and Shirna, on the planet Inter Minor. The gray-skinned, bald Inter Minorians wore what were, in effect, space-age parodies of the city gent's pinstripes—all in shades of gray and insistently linear. The showman Vorg, by contrast, wore spangled clothing in bright shades: it was predominantly green (a color also prominent in the Doctor's wardrobe), but also contained splashes of pink and orange, and incorporated such singular details as a transparent bowler hat.

The Doctor, who was caught in the middle of the immigration dispute, was visually the linchpin between the quarreling parties. He was resplendently clad in olive, apple green, and brown, which ensured that he was not overwhelmed by the visual incident in his surroundings, especially the brightly clad Vorg and Shirna. His costume also had to work effectively in the other locations in the episode. On a ship in the Indian Ocean in the 1920s, the Doctor's high-intensity outfit complemented the high-value sailor's whites and light-colored linens and silks worn by the passengers. The Doctor, in miniaturized form, also visited the interior of the entertainment machine operated by Vorg. For this set, Roger Liminton freely extemporized on the idea of a printed circuit, transcending verisimilitude (figs. 4.20a and 4.20b). Here again—at least for those with color sets—Pertwee's Doctor held his own with the vibrant overall effect in a way that his predecessor, Patrick Troughton, dressed mainly in black and gray, would not have.

The flamboyant designs for "Carnival of Monsters" were partly dictated by the Doctor's style of clothing, but also came about because not every-

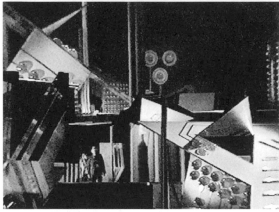

FIGURES 4.20A AND 4.20B. *Under the "Miniscope": The Doctor and Jo explore the interior of the Scope in "Carnival of Monsters." Set designed by Roger Liminton. © BBC Worldwide.*

thing in the episode was meant to be taken seriously. Greater than usual stylization was derived from the use of irony (the second reason given earlier). When the author of "Carnival of Monsters," Robert Holmes, was appointed script editor in 1974, irony and humor became consistent features in the show. Most episodes were conceived so as to satisfy at two different levels. For engaged and ingenuous spectators (i.e., children), there were thrills and horrors aplenty—often, in fact, more than watchdog organizations found acceptable.[82] For more detached spectators (i.e., adults), there were other pleasures, for the nature of the horror had changed. Rather than being based on the contingent, episodes were now knowing homages to the icons of gothic horror, many of them fresh in audience's minds from Hammer films of the previous twenty years. These included *Dr. Jekyll and Mr. Hyde* and *The Day of the Triffids.*

Irony is hard to embody in design imagery. Designs can easily be made humorous through exaggeration, but the inherent duality that characterizes irony cannot readily be expressed visually. However, the use of selective artifice, rather than self-effacing naturalism, is one means of achieving this aim, for artifice generally promotes detachment rather than involvement. The process of explicitly playing with cliché is something that we have commented upon in relation to set design for *The Avengers*. In *Doctor Who*, blatant antinaturalism could not be so openly or so extensively used since the ostensible function of *Doctor Who* was to frighten. Varied degrees of stylization were therefore used in costume and set design during the mid-to-late 1970s.

An effective compromise between spoofily drawing attention to cliché and approaching hackneyed images with seeming ingenuousness was achieved in several of the homage episodes of *Doctor Who*. Barry Newbery's sets for "The Brain of Morbius," discussed above, represent a prime example. An even more forceful conceit was seen in a *Mummy* pastiche, "Pyramids of Mars" (1975). One of the knowingly absurd ideas that occurred to Holmes was to introduce mummies that were in fact robots in disguise.[83] Brought to his Victorian gothic home by a demon-possessed Egyptologist, these automata were at one stage seen constructing a futuristic—but still pyramidal!—rocket in the stable courtyard. Christine Ruscoe's austerely modernistic acrylic-and-metal design for the rocket underscored the absurd humor, for the structure made no sense in relation to either the wrapped "cadavers" or the High Victorian architecture.

The humorous device of the robot-mummies was also exploited to horrific ends, for they were repeatedly shown to be implacable hunters and efficient killers. Few images from *Doctor Who* are as strong as that of two robot-mummies stalking an elderly poacher through the greenwoods of Middle England. Apart from the weird juxtaposition of monster and environment, the shocking impact of this scene was due to the remarkable appearance of the monsters themselves.

In her design for the robot-mummies (fig. 4.21), Barbara Kidd took the emaciated form of a disemboweled cadaver and transmuted it into something that was at once powerfully threatening and sharply stylized. Although the robots' elaborate bindings were based on those of actual mummies in the British Museum, there were necessary inconsistencies, such as the arms being free.[84] More strikingly, the contours of the skeletal framework underneath the wrappings were simplified and exaggerated. The hollow eye sockets were enlarged to occupy almost the entirety of the other-

FIGURE 4.21. *Bad wrap: A robot-mummy from "Pyramids of Mars" (1975). Costume designed by Barbara Kidd.* © *BBC Worldwide.*

wise blank faces, while the eviscerated stomach was offset by a massive thorax. Most strikingly, the ribcage was defined by a jutting shelf, which the robots used to pinion and crush their victims. Kidd's design plays with two B-movie clichés: the killer robot and the vengeful resurrected mummy. The resultant hybrid did not have to exhibit much logic: its function was to provide a frisson of raw fear for kids and wry amusement for their parents.

Neither of the stimuli for aesthetic redefinition in *Doctor Who* discussed so far produced design imagery that was extreme in its antinaturalism. Prior to 1980, heavily stylized imagery in *Doctor Who* almost always announced an episode made under severe budgetary restrictions rather than an aesthetic choice or discursive gambit. In "The Horns of Nimon" (1979–1980), scenic designer Graeme Story was given a reduced budget in order to free up money for use elsewhere in the recording block and had to produce more than half a dozen futuristic sets for next to nothing. As a result, he "concentrated on a few striking shapes and effects" and constructed his sets almost entirely from stock pieces, borrowed materials, and black drapes.[85]

The episode concerned a once-powerful race of warriors in thrall to the bull-like Nimon, which lived at the heart of their shattered civilization in a maze complex. The concourse at the entrance to the Nimon's lair was, by intent, Story's most carefully composed and striking set: a three-sided arcade giving on to a cyclorama that depicted a threatening gray sky. In fact, the set consisted of little more than a framework of uprights and lintels, light modulators arranged as arches in an upturned "V" formation (a leitmotiv in both sets and costumes for the episode, presumably referring to bulls' horns), and metal walkways that had originally served as wall panels in the recently released film *Alien*. Apart from the harsh geometry of the set, Story relied on the clanging sound made by boots on the metal walkways to create a suitably militaristic effect.[86]

The Nimon's lair consisted of a maze of corridors and a central chamber of deliberately unclear dimensions. This central control room (see fig. 4.13) was composed mainly of towers of stock machinery from the BBC store, commonly used for sci-fi dramas in the late 1960s. The mechanical elements were backed by the panels from *Alien*, again doing service as walls, and beyond that by black drapes, which augmented the sense of space. Whereas this central chamber was a riot of ingenious invention—Story even interpolated a metal music stand into the jungle of wires and tubes—the "jigsaw" set representing the corridors of the maze simply comprised rows of vacuum-formed flats.[87]

Custom-built elements were confined to a few focal props such as the Nimon travel vehicle, which was a capsule shaped like a large egg. This was a nod by Story to one of the key images in *Alien*, thereby complementing his practical debt to the film with a neat aesthetic genuflection.[88] The designer restricted the color scheme almost entirely to white and gray, allowing the expressionistic silhouettes of June Hudson's black costumes to dominate. The only visual incident in the sets that complemented Hudson's work consisted almost entirely of cheap, flexible plastic tubing of various sizes in black, white, or silver, laid copiously around the rostra and strewn over the flats that made up the walls. Story's formal vocabulary, even when it came to set-dressing, was extremely simple.

Though Story used stylization to overcome a small budget, not all designers adopted this strategy when financially challenged. A year earlier, for example, the designer of "The Armageddon Factor" (1979) struggled to maintain verisimilitude in his sets despite a shortage in funds; a year before that, "The Sunmakers," a dark satire on the British tax system, was marred by imagery that proclaimed its cheapness but was unrelieved by any distinctive formal properties.

Nor was stylization simply the last resort of the penurious. In 1980, a new producer and script editor encouraged extreme artifice certainly in costume, but also to a great extent in scenic design. John Nathan-Turner, the unit-manager turned producer, successfully argued for increased expenditure on design and favored the glamorous imagery produced for 1930s Hollywood films by the likes of Van Nest Polglase, Cedric Gibbons, and the dress designer Adrian.[89] Nathan-Turner's script editor, Christopher Bidmead was interested in exploring a range of scientific concepts in the show, and the more self-consciously philosophical and poetic approach adopted in several episodes lent itself naturally to visual experimentation.

Some of the experimentation carried out in the 1980–1981 season was radical. In "Warriors' Gate," the scenic designer—Graeme Story again—followed a suggestion in the script that certain scenes should not be shot in conventional sets, but rather should have live-action figures superimposed onto black-and-white photographic stills. One of Story's sets, a two-tier affair representing the interior of a spacecraft, had the distinction of being the first in *Doctor Who* to incorporate the lighting rig from the studio into a setting—much to the chagrin of the lighting director.[90]

"Warriors' Gate" was not an isolated case of stylization. One of the most lavish episodes of the season, "The Leisure Hive," was a dazzling display of pure formalism. Tom Yardley-Jones' sets for the "hive" of the title were among the most starkly simplified ever seen in the series. Primary colors were liberally used to offset an abundance of corrugated white plastic and chrome. The props, including those representing scientific instruments, were often no more than handheld polyhedrons made of colored glass and acrylic, "activated" by being placed on tiered trays or racks. All this unadorned geometry bordered on a "De Stijl" aesthetic, recalling the boldly shaped and colored furniture of Gerrit van Rietveld and, once again, the light-space modulators of Moholy-Nagy (see fig 4.22).[91]

Of course, Yardley-Jones' designs did not come across as being in any absolute sense antinatural. Exceptionally tight and rapid editing, the extensive use of extreme close-ups, and abrupt cuts to unexpectedly low or high camera angles meant that the studied austerity was fully apparent only in still photographs; the audience could form little more than an overall

FIGURE 4.22. *An interesting experiment. The interior of the lab from "The Leisure Hive" (1980). Set designed by Tom Yardley-Jones.* © *BBC Worldwide.*

impression of glittering splendor in the "hive." Nevertheless, by virtue of the willingness to create an aesthetic for an alien race that was so at odds with contemporary industrial design and technology "The Leisure Hive" was exceptional, if not quite unprecedented, in the design history of the series.

Design for *Doctor Who* at this time also featured the selective generalization of artistic forms to maximize their suggestive potential. The Gundan Warrior Robots from "Warriors' Gate" best exemplify this (figs. 4.23*a* & 4.23*b*). June Hudson's design managed to be rigorously disciplined in its formal simplicity and yet at the same time richly evocative. What makes the image so arresting and visually rewarding is not any particular detail, for details are few. Rather, the extreme stylization of the costume hints at various historical precedents without confirming any of them. For example, the helmet recalls the samurai kabuto, a reference the author had suggested in the script (the robots were originally designated "Shoguns"),[92] but is too head-hugging to be a true descendant. There again, the grill over the face points to Roman gladiatorial styles, while the bold crescent-moon crest recalls the heraldic symbols of Islam. Taken in its entirety, the strong silhouette and fine contouring of the armor make a powerful impression, but, like the helmet alone, could not be said specifically to evoke classi-

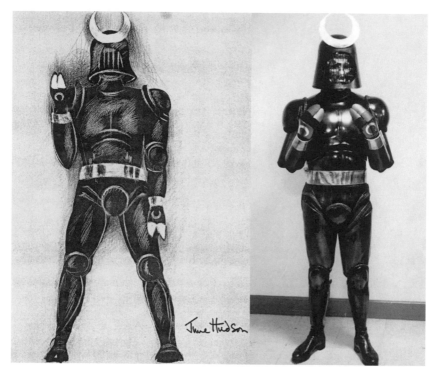

FIGURES 4.23A AND 4.23B. *Gundan Warrior Robot from "Warriors' Gate" (1981): a, design drawing by June Hudson; b, completed costume. Drawing and photograph courtesy of June Hudson.*

cal antiquity, or the medieval orient, or even the chivalric fantasies of the Pre-Raphaelites. Unlike Kidd's robot-mummies in "Pyramids of Mars" or Newbery's castle sets for "The Brain of Morbius," the image does not invite interpretation or precise intellectual appreciation: rather, Hudson's Gundan serves to stimulate the viewer's imaginative participation.

To recap: The deployment of antinaturalism and extremely simplified forms was piecemeal in the history of the series, including the relatively stylization-intensive periods outlined in the foregoing discussion. Even Nathan-Turner's sponsorship of heavily stylized imagery was short-lived. For the 1982 season, with the less adventurous Eric Saward as script editor and the volume of unusual ideas brought to expression therefore much smaller, Nathan-Turner opted to affiance *Doctor Who* with the emergent sci-fi/fantasy mainstream. Design imagery for the 1982 season, such as Dinah Collin's new, "textured" Cybermen, tended to be conspicuously related to precedents from the movies. The new look of the Cybermen, as we have already mentioned, borrowed from Darth Vader, but there are other obvious referents, such as the Stormtroopers from the same film and the Cylons from *Battlestar Galactica* (ABC/Universal, 1978–1979).

More generally, the instability of the visual idiom in the program underscored the loose-knit relationship between design and the rest of what Tulloch and Alvarado have called "the unfolding text" of the series.[93] Written guidelines seldom served as more than a springboard for the elaboration of ideas by the more inventive designers in *Doctor Who.* Safeguards against the unbridled imagination of the designer, so clearly defined in other kinds of dramatic narrative, do not apply in sci-fi/fantasy. This means that a commonplace screenplay like "The Leisure Hive" could be rendered memorable and cogent almost entirely by design, which appeals to the imaginative and evocative powers of the spectator's mind more directly than the fairly sketchy and formulaic script. On the other hand, the absence of conceptual restraint coupled with the financial vagaries of television production (i.e., uneven budgeting for successive episodes) could lead to greater visual unevenness in a series such as *Doctor Who* than in one with a contemporary setting, such as *NYPD Blue* (TCF/Bochco, 1993–).

In fact, from 1981 on producer Nathan-Turner brought a stylistic coherence to *Doctor Who* that had been missing almost since its first year. Then, visual unity had been ensured by having only a single costume supervisor and alternating scenic designers (one for the sci-fi and the other for the historical narratives).[94] Of course, there was some stylistic change during Nathan-Turner's nine-year tenure as producer. The arrival of Colin Baker with his tasteless patchwork coat required another general increase in gaudiness for both scenic and costume design to maintain parity of luminance.[95] Overall, however, design for *Doctor Who* in the 1980s hybridized the sub-*Alien* with the sub-*Star Wars:* imagery was vivid (often to the point of luridness), rich in surface detail, and expensive-looking.

The homogenizing of imagery in *Doctor Who* impoverished the special character of the series, as a series and as a fantasy. There was no great necessity for stylistic consistency in such a loose-knit and whimsical drama, and the creation of a standard look led to banality and unadventurousness. Nathan-Turner's main aim, apart from trying to woo back the wider audience that increasingly regarded *Doctor Who* as passé, was to satisfy the most devoted spectators of the series. Some fans had spoken out strongly against the "clownish" character of episodes like "The Horns of Nimon,"[96] and the superficial sophistication that Nathan-Turner brought to the series, together with the reintroduction of popular characters like the Cybermen, initially brought him into favor with this pressure group. He even took on a "senior" fan, Ian Levine, as an adviser.[97] This act in many ways epitomizes the manner in which Nathan-Turner consigned the series to the forces of ossification. As can be demonstrated in relation to the TARDIS, perhaps the central image of the series, fans' influence was, unsurprisingly, reactionary and stultifying.

BOXED IN: THE TARDIS AND THE DESIRE FOR REALISM

In a manner typical of this most singular of series, the TARDIS in itself embodied a dichotomy, for the ship was bigger on the inside than on the outside. The contrast between the exterior, shaped like a police lock-up box (still a common sight in early-1960s London) and the expansive, hauntingly alien interior, gleaming white and filled with unearthly equipment, was striking. The contrast actually went beyond mere size discrepancy. The police box was not just a recognizable, "down-to-earth" object for audiences—it was actually an old-fashioned artifact, and this emphasized the technology gap between our reality and the Doctor's "dimensionally transcendental" world beyond the blue doors. Giving the exterior of the ship the appearance of a mundane object provided viewers with a stable visual referent from week to week.[98] However, the decision also created a further entertaining anomaly, for the police box looked out of place anywhere except on a London street.

Although initial staff appointments to *Doctor Who* favored young blood,[99] the design manager insisted on allocating a senior designer, Peter Brachacki, to the first episode. His work on the pilot proved to be Brachacki's only contribution to Doctor Who; chronic ill health forced a reassignment. Barry Newbery was brought in and given responsibility for erecting and dressing the TARDIS set when a remount of the pilot was ordered. However, Newbery's involvement with the design predated his allocation to the show:

I actually remember Peter showing me his original model for the set. It was about two feet square, and he had cut the walls from the plastic which at that time was used for ceiling-light panels. These had staggered rows of circular holes in them, each of which was about three-eighths of an inch in diameter. It had occurred to Peter to use these circles as part of the decoration in the full-size set by just scaling them up, and in fact, they provided the germ idea for the whole interior. Peter's design was beautiful. I was probably too busy with my own work at the time to appreciate what he'd done properly but, looking back, I realize that it was the first-ever "hi-tech" set for television. It broke new ground, and Peter has never been given proper credit for it.[100]

The TARDIS design was a remarkable response by Brachacki to his mandate. Sydney Newman, then Head of Drama at the BBC, had specified that the ship should be bigger within than without. Brachacki made the contrast between the scale of exterior and interior emphatic, and Newbery recalls that the finished set was so large that it took up half of the floor space in the studio.[101] It was not merely in terms of scale that Brachacki's thinking was radically innovative, however, for the whole character of the interior design was without precedent. The TARDIS remains a milestone in the history of design not only for television but for screen drama as a whole.

Brachacki's stroke of genius lay in his decision to use the staggered circles on his plastic model as the principal motif for the whole interior of the ship (see figs. 4.1, 4.7, and 4.9). The interior provided a breathtaking contrast with the police-box shell in size and aesthetic. The basic formal unit of the police box was the upright rectangle, which gave it an aspect of sturdy, "masculine" dependability. These anthropomorphic overtones were presumably not accidental, for the police-box design had its basis in the trabeated forms of classical temple architecture, long related by architectural theorists to the human body.[102] The dominant forms of Brachacki's TARDIS interior, by contrast, were nonhuman in their resonances. The walls carried strong overtones of the honeycomb, for the recessed circular panels that decorated their surfaces were arranged in staggered lines that implied interlocking hexagons. The zigzag hinge ends of the double doors strengthened the association with the honeycomb.

The hexagon motif was fully realized in the central, mushroom-like control table, with its six banks of dials, lights, and switches. Metallic plates around the base of the central pedestal of the table echoed the shape, as did the hexagonal cowl containing a louvered circular lamp, which hung from the ceiling nearby. Concentric circular forms were used at the heart of the control table in the nest of transparent cylinders that rose and fell when the ship was in flight and rotated when it was stationary. Brachacki had wanted the controls on the central table to be molded to the form of the operator's hand, but this was deemed too expensive, and the designer reluctantly accepted the more commonplace solution of levers and switches.

The contrast between the TARDIS exterior and interior was echoed in the dissimilarity between the glistening control chamber and its furnishings. Brachacki decorated the set with a variety of unusual objects drawn from various periods, giving the impression that the ship's occupants had traveled widely in the Earth's past. Together with William Hartnell's well-cut, if eccentric, costume, these trappings confirmed the air of the haughty gentleman-adventurer that the actor brought to the role of the Doctor.

The contrast between the pure, "platonic" geometries of the control room and the fussy trappings of the Doctor's quasi-Victorian persona remained a constant for nearly fifteen years. Then, in 1976, Barry Newbery was asked to design a new control room. This one turned out to be even more stylized than Brachacki's hi-tech "honeycomb," partly for practical reasons. Newbery's assignment was to produce a more flexible set with fewer mechanical elements that might go wrong.[103] His response to the latter problem was uncompromising: he dispensed with the two main moving parts of Brachacki's design, the glass cylinder that rose and fell in the center of the control table and the cumbersome double doors. To avoid the necessity for the doors, his new design simply had an aperture leading to a darkened vestibule, the black backdrop of which gave the sense of a limbo existing between the room and the lock-up box exterior. Newbery got rid of most of the flashing lights on the control table and greatly reduced the size of the whole prop.[104]

None of these changes demanded a new aesthetic for the TARDIS, but Newbery, thinking to keep the series fresh, reinvented the set, much to the chagrin of some vociferous fans. Instead of the brilliantly white clinical perfection of Brachacki's TARDIS, Newbery created a wood-paneled control room appropriate to the Doctor's status as an honorary Edwardian gentleman (fig. 4.24). Thus, the control table became a davenport—albeit a six-sided one—and stood on a podium surrounded with brass rails that might have been the fittings to a yacht or ocean liner.[105] Everything else in the new interior was of polished mahogany. The walls of the set had baseboards, cornices, and dados, and among the wall discs—now framed by spindled moldings rather than being simple, sunken recesses—there were even a few circular stained-glass windows. The effect of the new set, with topical lighting from a louvered lamp that recalled Brachacki's,[106] was at once rich and chaste. Making a virtue out of practical requirements, Newbery had taken the TARDIS further away from the platitudes of spaceship design.

Although the Edwardian TARDIS interior immediately found favor with

FIGURE 4.24. *Changing the tone: The "Edwardian" TARDIS control room from "The Masque of Mandragora" (1976). Set designed by Barry Newbery.* © BBC Worldwide.

Tom Baker,[107] it was dropped from the series after only one season and never reintroduced. The following year a new producer, Graham Williams, requested a return to a white control room, in line with Brachacki's design. Newbery was, ironically, the designer called upon to approximate the original interior.

There is now no way of establishing why the late Graham Williams abandoned the Edwardian TARDIS interior, but the issue warrants a little speculation—especially as no such radical experimentation with the TARDIS set was ever carried out again until the making of the *Doctor Who* movie in 1996. Newbery subsequently formed the impression that devotees of the series objected to the wood-paneled control room:

What I didn't know at the time is that there were fans of the program who didn't like anything to change. As far as we designers were concerned, any change was good, and kept it fresh.[108]

Fan opinion may well have influenced Williams' decision to revert to a "hi-tech" control room. The first *Doctor Who* fan club had been formed recently in England, and Williams noted that he and the production crew "did our own audience research" and "became more aware of the Doctor Who Appreciation Society."[109] Indeed, Williams attended the first Doctor Who convention shortly after being appointed producer. Dissatisfaction with the Edwardian interior has been expressed by at least one vocal, influential fan, John Peel. According to him,

[the] wooden control room had warped during the break in shooting between the seasons, due to the wood used, and it was decided that reaction to the new room was too unfavourable to allow it to be rebuilt.[110]

On the basis of remarks that he made elsewhere, Peel was presumably not disappointed by the decision to revert to an old-style control-center set:

To fans brought up on the first control room (like myself), the [Edwardian] room was a dreadful travesty of the show—totally missing the juxtaposition of the old and new that Hartnell had had.[111]

If Williams responded to pressure from a fan lobby group whose views matched Peel's, or to wider expressions of such a view, then we are confronted with the irony that a designer working on a supposedly unconstricted and fantastical program was in reality hamstrung by core-audience expectations.

Apart from recycling its traditions, *Doctor Who* during the 1980s showed an increasing preoccupation with credibility, rather narrowly defined. In an over-enthusiastic attempt to refute the (generally unfair) charge that the series was blighted by "cardboard sets," new design imperatives seem to have been promulgated to excise anything that, by contemporary standards, stretched the imagination. One further revision of the TARDIS is worth mentioning in this connection, for it clearly reflected the changing tastes and imperatives for *Doctor Who* design at large.

In 1983, the control-room set underwent a makeover, a small but highly significant shift toward greater naturalism. The original control console, which had been fetched out of retirement and revivified by Newbery after the Edwardian interlude,[112] was scrapped. Visual effects designer Mike Kelt was asked to build a new one for the twentieth-anniversary special, "The Five Doctors." Because he was able to have the new prop constructed from much lighter materials (molded fiberglass and aluminum), Kelt retained the size and shape of the unit and even kept the rising-and-falling transparent cylinder in the center. However, he did seek to modernize the overall effect by replacing the levers and switches of the original with computer keyboards and monitors. This seemingly small alteration dramatically altered the TARDIS set. The previous controls—an odd assortment of panels and excrescences—were so weird that they were curiously timeless, whereas the injection of contemporary hi-tech ensured that the new design was locked irrevocably in the moment (with the effect that, by the next year, it already seemed out of date).[113]

Of course, the contemporaneity of Kelt's design was merely conforming to standards of plausibility that were increasingly—if perversely—applied to screen sci-fi/fantasy in the 1980s. In order for the audience to accept an image of the future or an alien world, it seemed more and more that the technology of this environment had to look recognizably workable. What this meant in real terms was that a design for a twenty-fourth-century computer terminal in a *Star Trek* movie could not stray too far away from the latest advances in twentieth-century computer technology.[114] Voice activation and the use of touch-sensitive screens gave the *Trek* films and Gene Roddenberry's massively popular new series, *Star Trek: The Next Generation* (Paramount, 1987–1993), an immediacy that audiences evidently enjoyed. Fantasy in the sense of unrestrained imagination really no longer had any place in this context.

If sci-fi/fantasy design had to play off contemporary reality to satisfy audiences, it also, increasingly, had to be seamlessly polished in its realization. Indeed, a high degree of realism in every genre of drama was a *sine qua non* by the mid-1970s. In 1974 Clifford Hatts, Head of Design Group at the BBC, defended rising expenditures on design in an article for *The Stage & Television Today* specifically because of the demand for naturalism in television:

You can do Softly, Softly *on the stage with canvas doors and black drapes because of the convention of the theatre. In television you're in for realism because we've just had the nine o'clock news, we've just had* Panorama, *we've just had* Man Alive *and now we've got* Play for Today. *Where the designer can be self-indulgent is in light entertainment where it has to look designed and feel contrived. You can't treat a Priestley play like that.*[115]

Nor, apparently, could you treat *Doctor Who* like that. Fans, grown increasingly powerful and vociferous in the late 1970s, certainly did not think so. Patrick Mulkern, who in 1987 wrote an article on scenic design for Marvel Comics' *Doctor Who Autumn Special,* exemplifies a prevalent mindset, evidence of which can be found piecemeal throughout the fan literature. Aesthetic judgments as such are relatively sparse in Mulkern's piece; his concern is almost entirely with credibility. Thus, "convincing mock-ups" made in the studio of such real locations as the London Underground and the sewers of Victorian London are singled out for praise, as are futuristic sets or alien environments where a believable effect was achieved with limited financial and technical means. The most enthusiastic accolade offered by Mulkern is that design work for a production "looked as if it had been given a film's budget."[116] This is how he characterizes the caverns and space-freighter cargo hold built in the studio for "Earthshock" (1982), designed by Bernard Lloyd Jones. Mulkern uses "artificial" and "stagey" to deride the unacceptable face of design in the series: the sets for "The Horns of Nimon" are condemned as representing the "nadir" of scenic design for the series, being "wobbly and noisy, in parts garish, in other respects bland."[117] For Mulkern, ingenuity is applauded only inasmuch as the finished product approaches a seamless illusion, and the beauty of even the most lavishly realized design concept is, for the most part, secondary to its realism.

SCI-FI AND LIGHT ENTERTAINMENT

Mulkern's preference for realism in design reflects the wider preoccupation of fans with narrative realism. The consolidation of the *Doctor Who* "mythos" was a central policy during the 1980s, as the appointment of the fan adviser, Ian Levine, attests. The revival of past characters was accompanied by strenuous efforts to cement the internal continuity of the series. This attempt to transform *Doctor Who* into something coherent and monolithic denied its nature as a series and, more specifically, it belied the particular kind of series that *Doctor Who* had always been. As a time-and-space-travel fantasy, *Doctor Who* was episodic to the nth degree. It offered not drama, in the sense of a portrayal of the personal development of its protagonists, but pageantry. *Doctor Who* made a cardinal virtue of its diversity of spectacle. The premise of the series would not support a continuous narrative—nor, for that matter, did it lend itself to smoothly uniform treatment in design terms. Its strength was its capacity to suggest multiple worlds of the imagination, not to provide tight-knit dramatic entertainment where design has an unobtrusively denotative function.

A brief comparison between *Doctor Who* and a sci-fi series that was in the ascendant at this time, *Star Trek: The Next Generation,* might shed some light on the reasons for the decline and cancellation of the former. The *Star Trek* films that had been released throughout the early 1980s had achieved broad audience approval, and this trend was exponentially magnified by the runaway success of the new television series. According to one survey conducted in the early 1990s, about fifty percent of television viewers in the United States described themselves as *Next Generation* devotees.

Roddenberry's new series was everything that *Doctor Who* was not. The world of the show was mapped out in detail. The physical division of the galaxy worked out by Roddenberry for the original *Star Trek* was, in essence, followed in *The Next Generation* and in its two spin-offs, *Deep Space Nine* (Paramount, 1992–1999) and *Voyager* (Paramount, 1995–2001). Its episodes were unified by an overarching soap-opera-like saga that followed the interactions of the multispecies crew of the U.S.S. *Enterprise.* In short, *The Next Generation* offered real drama, albeit of an antiseptic, heavily airbrushed kind. It was, to use old BBC Drama Department parlance, a "loyalty" program.

In its half-hearted effort to espouse something of this kind of seriousness and dramatic substance in the mid-to-late 1980s, *Doctor Who* was attempting one self-reinvention too many. Its producer might have done better to ignore the carping of over-earnest fans and pursue the course that his predecessors had steered a decade earlier—pushing *Doctor Who* more wholeheartedly into the sphere of the comedy thriller. Interestingly enough, the sci-fi/fantasy series that did flourish in Britain during the 1980s and 1990s were not those with grand pretensions, but ones conceived as light entertainment—*The Hitchhiker's Guide to the Galaxy* (BBC TV, 1981) and *Red Dwarf* (BBC TV, 1988–). Other British-based sci-fi productions such as *Star Cops* (BBC TV, 1987) and *Space Precinct* (GA-Fox, 1995) have come and gone, but *Red Dwarf* remains in intermittent production more than a decade after its inception. The great advantage of *Hitchhiker* and *Red Dwarf* for the television designer was that both series traded on sci-fi cliché, and because of their satirical premises, there was no reason for artifice to be suppressed—it could be embraced and enjoyed.

The Hitchhiker's Guide to the Galaxy exemplified the way the suggestive rather than demonstrative potential of television can be optimized in a sci-fi/fantasy that fully espouses humor. *Hitchhiker* had begun as a radio series (BBC Radio 1, 1978), and there was an obvious obstacle to translation—the long narrations that were generally extracts from the guide of the title. (Peter Jones, the voice of the guide in the radio series, actually received first billing in the television series.) Writer Douglas Adams decided to retain these sequences and add a visual text, which complemented the spoken word and even generated new humorous possibilities:

Television pictures stifle the picturing facilities of the mind. I wanted to step over that problem by packing the screen with so much information that more thought, not less, was provoked in the readers.[118]

The imagery created by Rod Lord to accompany Peter Jones' reading of passages from the "Guide" did not present real images of the diverse subjects treated in the voiceovers, but self-drawing, mock-LCD images, generally a little exaggerated in character. These graphics, which still look extraordinarily fresh after twenty years, illustrated Jones' narration, blow by blow (and generally provided a read-out of his words). As Adams had wished, these graphics created a density of visual information seldom matched in any television series.

Lord's effort, meticulous and funny in equal measure, was aptly complemented by the work of his colleagues in other design departments. The design of *Hitchhiker* not only matched the clever humor of the script but also, as in such *Doctor Who* episodes as "Carnival of Monsters," burgeoned beyond the written word to incorporate sophisticated visual jokes and fantastical imagery.

Douglas Adams had worked as a writer and script editor on *Doctor Who* during Graham Williams' tenure as producer, and he had been involved in an attempt to push out the boundaries of the program in terms of narrative and visual humor. This attempt was not entirely successful or much appreciated by fans.[119] However, his experience clearly served Adams well when he approached the task of revamping *Hitchhiker* for television. The transition was graceful and seamless partly because costume designer Dee Robson and one of the scenic designers, Tom Yardley-Jones, had already proved their ability to work in a way-out vein on *Doctor Who*.[120]

Robson's ease at developing Adams' brand of humor was exemplified by her costume for Zaphod Beeblebrox. The exuberantly egotistical, ultrahip former galactic president, Zaphod possessed an extra arm and a duplicate head. Since Douglas Adams had only ever alluded indirectly to the character's clothing, claiming in the *Hitchhiker* novel that Zaphod had been "recently voted the Worst Dressed Sentient being in the Known Universe for the seventh time," Robson enjoyed free rein in designing the character's clothes (fig. 4.25).[121] She kept to the spirit of vulgarity that Adams suggested by using a variety of strident colors. She also added refinements of her own—including a hint of yet another duplicate body part.

Zaphod's costume was essentially based on the idea of a circuit board, so you get the crossing lines and the bits stuck on like chips and diodes—we even put some of them in his hair. The idea was that he could program it to add body parts at will. As well as having an extra head and arm, we also gave his trousers two flies. It was a sort of a joke between me and Mark; I don't think anybody else noticed![122]

One other sight gag devised by Dee Robson should be mentioned here, because it provides a close similarity with *Doctor Who* but also points up the gap between what was acceptable in design for the two programs. The only Earthling seen throughout *Hitchhiker* is the story's Everyman, Arthur Dent. No reference had been made by Douglas Adams to what he might be wearing, and Robson came up with a solution that was at once logical and witty.

We worked out that he gets up in the morning, he goes outside, and he's only just got out of bed. Now, it's got to be respectable, because you're on television and we weren't parading full-frontal nudity at that point. So we had him in his pajama bottoms and a vest. He would have put his dressing gown and slippers on to go outside. Then his house is demolished and he's whisked off into space, so he hasn't got time to go back and say "Oh, I think I'll put my suit on."[123]

It had been intended that Arthur should assume new clothes when he arrived on Zaphod's spaceship, the *Heart of Gold*, but Robson resisted this idea, once again putting forward a logical objection.

I think it would have been a shame to change it. When he gets onto the Heart of Gold, *he's supposed to change into a gold spacesuit. I think it would have looked ham; it was much better to keep the dressing gown. And anyway, they didn't pass any shops en route on any planets.*[124]

The handwritten annotations on the drawing read:

ZAPHOD BEEBLEBROX.

HITCH HIKERS GUIDE TO THE GALAXY. B.B.C.T.V.

Delivery 17th Sept.

T. Shirt or knitted sweater

design of computer print out of perpendicular polarisation

Top Pkts of woven fuse wires

Zips over arm tops e around Top pkts

Corner Cube reflective strip

double

crutch, padded to give effect of 2 organs. Zipped with Brightly coloured plastic Y.K.K. Zips

Top Pkts of plaited plastic wire in bright colours

Sunglasses for Ep 3 or throughout.

Thurs 11.00 am Fitting.

self on collar, epaulet belt e pkts + yoke (plain)

self fabric

Corner Cube reflective strip

Circuit printed Combat jacket with photocells, diodes e small component parts wired randomly onto it.

corner cube reflective belt.

Pkt with components making circuit

Day glo orange trousers.

Leather boots with lacing. High soles and lifts inside

FIGURE 4.25. *Twice blessed: Dee Robson's design drawing for Zaphod Beeblebrox in* **The Hitchhiker's Guide to the Galaxy** *(1980). Courtesy of Dee Robson.*

The parallel between Arthur's night attire and the police-box exterior of the TARDIS is obvious: both stick out like sore thumbs in any environment alien to their original function. However, whereas the conceit of the blue lock-up box is merely quirky, the pajamas, because they possess connotations such as privacy (and "naffness") are likely to provoke renewed amusement in each fresh situation. If *Hitchhiker* had, like *Doctor Who,* been constructed as serious drama, Robson would surely have lost the argument over Arthur's proposed change of dress, logical as her contention undoubtedly was. Logic is often funny, inasmuch as it is no respecter of conventional notions of decorum; and comedy is, after all, essentially based on the breach of the appropriate. To put Arthur in space-worthy clothes would have lent him, and by extension the series, credibility. The absurdity of his pajamas, check dressing gown, and slippers is sustainable because credibility was not relevant to Douglas Adams' looking-glass cosmos.

Perhaps, to fulfill its fantastical potential, *Doctor Who* needed to embrace the absurd more fully, rather than resting on its dignity, for dignity and unconstrained imagination are not really compatible. The destructiveness of the over-earnest approach that emerged in the 1980s was perhaps best indicated in a remark by one of the most successful designers for the series, June Hudson. She has no doubts as to where the aesthetic affiliations of the program lay:

The best qualification you could actually have for Blake's 7 *and* Doctor Who *design is a really strong background in L.E. Sure, it's always a benefit with science fiction to have plenty of experience with period design, so that you have all those different silhouettes and textures to draw on. But really, the kind of creative originality and outrageousness and over-the-top, bare-faced cheek which breaks new ground, and which is so necessary in science fiction, is best schooled and nurtured in light entertainment. In fact, when you come down to it, that's what* Doctor Who *really is: it's variety— it's L.E.*[125]

AFTERWORD

Since this book is a first foray into the subject of design for television, and adumbrative rather than definitive, it seems slightly false to offer a formal conclusion. However, in this final section we will reel in some of the lines we have cast, reexamining our core theses in light of the material we have covered in the three case studies and suggesting ways in which our ideas could be developed in relation to other television series.

In the first chapter, we made an assertion that was as elementary as it ought to be uncontroversial, viz., that design in screen drama functions tangentially to narrative. This claim is in essence an epistemological one. Unlike narrative, design cannot be "followed" by the viewer; and while the suggestive range of design imagery may be great, its meanings are unstable and its signification hard to control. Whereas ambiguities and nuances can, of course, be written into a script, it is not easy to correspondingly "write them out" of design imagery. While a film or television narrative can be said to be *about* something in particular, design cannot be pinned down in the same way.

Nevertheless, the temptation to interpret design imagery is strong; and the more one thinks about and looks at a design, the stronger the temptation grows. The danger lies not so much in succumbing as in making unqualified assertions, especially where a very specific meaning is claimed to be found. Writers on screen drama who take no serious account of design are especially prone to this kind of *ex cathedra* statement. For example, Toby Miller, who seldom alludes to set design or decoration in his book on *The Avengers,* does note that Steed possesses "the requisite globe and telescope which establish him as sophisticated," as though this were the only logical interpretation of these objects (see fig. 2.16).[1] The implied transparency of meaning is no more than an interpreter's wishful thinking.

To say that Steed's telescope and globe signal sophistication is to deny the multiplicity of ideas and feelings that could be attached to these artifacts. For example, one credulous but perfectly reasonable interpretation might be that Steed is an amateur astronomer; another, that he has a penchant for collecting brass objects (he does, after all, also possess an old brass tuba); and so on. If we, like Miller, wish to speculate over the underlying (ideological) message that Harry Pottle meant to convey by the inclusion of the telescope, then the notion of sophistication can hardly be said to have prior claims over that of antiquarian taste. The real point, however, is that all these meanings are sustainable: to choose one in preference to the others is not only pointless but also misleading. We have tried to avoid such prescriptive and proscriptive analyses of design imagery in this book.

In stressing that design functions tangentially to narrative, we do not mean to imply that design for screen drama works independently of narrative. Design is in its own way as much an interpretation of (or, at least, an extemporization around) elements in a script as an actor's performance. Just as a subtle performer will suggest more than is overtly expressed in the scripted narrative, so design, by its very nature, hints at a rich, complex diegetical reality of which the narrative can at best offer snippets. The difference, of course, is that design imagery, unlike an actor's performance, is involuntarily evocative. It is an inherent irony that the act of establishing a frame of reference for a drama, which is perhaps the simplest function of design imagery, generally entails suggesting much more than is directly relevant to the writer's or director's purpose.

None of this is to suggest, as Tashiro and the Affrons have implied, that design has an innate tendency to be too assertive—a tendency that has to be reined in to prevent the imagery from confusing or distracting the viewer.[2]

As noted in the first chapter, an integral part of the pleasure of a film or television program is that it contains pictorial imagery. The pleasure in a story well told and imagery well realized need not be separated, even if the two are appreciated in different ways. The convenience for the scholarly analyst of categorizing divergent kinds and modes of responses should not lead us into the fallacy of imagining that the vast majority of filmgoers, untroubled by philosophical matters, have difficulty assimilating more than one element of what they are watching. Films and television programs, especially television series, are complex entities, and our responses to them are likely to be complex, too.

The tendency of design to evoke multiple ideas leads to our main summary observation. The stylized imagery considered in this study generally restricts possible interpretations in a way that naturalistic imagery does not. True, all design for the screen is selective, and the designers' art resides as much in what to omit as in what to include. However, few designs are as forcefully restrictive of possible associations as Harry Pottle's Togetherness marriage bureau for *The Avengers;* its insistence on a single motif pares away all distractions and reinforces one particular idea. This monolithic imagery created a distancing effect through its artifice and thereby encouraged a heightened intellectual response to events and ideas in the narrative—in this case, sham and mendacity. Some will, no doubt, disagree with this interpretation, but one point should stand as incontrovertible: license, in Pottle's work, did not entail exploiting the natural expressive prolixity of design imagery, but in curbing it to an extent that would be unsustainable in naturalistic screen drama. In many ways, the same could be said of the closed system of Village imagery in *The Prisoner.* Jack Shampan's motif of the globe/circle, repeated time and again in both the lower and upper worlds of the Village, may not disclose a clear range of meaning in the same way as Pottle's Togetherness, but it is calculated to focus the viewer's mind on McGoohan's "allegorical conundrum," encouraging speculation about the metaphorical significance of the conceit, and by extension, the program.

However, there is another sense in which less can be more in antinatural design. Images so austerely stylized that they contain no clear external referent, such as the Gundan Warrior Robot in *Doctor Who* (see figs. 4.22*a* and 4.22*b*), are effective because they hint at what is absent rather than being attached to a fixed set of associations. Yet here, too, stylization works upon the viewer's imagination by paring away unnecessary detail. As watchers, we would give less attention to practically any "realistic" costume design in a contemporary drama, but insofar as a present-day image did impinge on our awareness, it would almost certainly trigger associations in a more untidy fashion than June Hudson's Gundan. Stylized design almost inevitably draws the eye, and having secured our attention, the designer often has no need to be profligate with detailing. Hudson's delicately insinuated references to historical precedent are enough to spark the imagination and place the Gundans within the quasi-mythic tradition appropriate to the spirit of *Doctor Who* at the time she designed them.

For the most part, this volume has been given over to the wider ramifications of design imagery rather than to its relationship with individual episode narratives. We contended that the overall context of a series, and in some cases the overall cultural context of an image, are at least as important in determining that image's meanings as the narrative that generated it. We have identified two forms of significance for design beyond its immediate narrative-related role. One of these is passive, the other active: design can be reflexive of the changing character of a series, and it can generate interest that subsumes or transcends the limits of the series. In all three of our subject programs, the stimulative role of design had implications both for the public perception of that program and for the evolution (or, in the case of *The Prisoner,* the initial conception) of the series as a whole. Conversely, the changing tenor of *The Avengers* and *Doctor Who* can be deduced from the character of the design imagery at any given moment.

To some extent it is true that both the reflexive and the stimulative functions of design in our three series were greater than is normally the case. A design such as the Dalek or John Steed's sartorial style could not acquire synecdochic force or a shaping influence in a series that had no fantasy element because the images would never have been devised in the first place. Similarly, the bizarre imagery of the Village in *The Prisoner* could only be integral to the ethos of the series because the idea of the toy-town social microcosm was central to McGoohan's conception of the program. In a nonfantastic series, the opportunities for such landmark designs to arise at all, far less to exert a broad influence on the public imagination or on the fabric of the series itself, will be slight or nonexistent.

In light of this last point, our three case studies may seem unlikely to furnish general truths about the role of design within the television series as a form. However, inasmuch as they deviate from the norm, our subject programs have a great deal in common with other series. What follows is an attempt to suggest ways in which some of the ideas we have put forward, and some of the patterns we have discerned, might serve as the basis for future studies.

Two aspects of the use of design that we have covered can usefully be pursued in relation to other kinds of drama. The first is the phenomenon of the sartorially distinctive (generally male) protagonist whose dress and grooming serve as a kind of embodiment of the character of the series as a whole. This is strongly evident in all three of our subject series, but it can readily be found elsewhere. The second design-related phenomenon is the use of visual imagery to create a selective reflection of the real world.

Both of these aspects of design shed light on a larger issue, namely, the way that design imagery helps to clarify relationships among the various genres within the series form. A genre is a collection of motifs that repeatedly recur in conjunction with one another. Not all of these conventions are narrative structures and devices; some are visual. In other words, we orient ourselves toward a new drama series partly by how it looks and, perhaps more important, by how we expect it to look. Design is a powerful indicator of similarity and difference.

What follows is a brief examination of imagery from three further series, dealing variously with the iconic male lead, the skewed representation of reality, and the way in which the ethos of the series is shaped in relation to precedent. For the sake of coherence, the examples come from recent popular British crime-detection series: *Cracker* (Granada TV, 1993–1996), *Inspector Morse* (Central/Zenith TV, 1987–2000), and *A Touch of Frost* (Yorkshire TV/Excelsior, 1992–2000).

Crime drama has historically been predominant in the television schedules in Britain. While their forms may vary from the pedestrian to the farfetched (*The Avengers,* it may be remembered, was a crime series of sorts), all crime dramas are united in this: criminals are consistently detected and brought to account, however seemingly insuperable the hindrances to this goal. This tends to give rise to a phenomenon that we have seen in all our three subject programs—a protagonist who is extremely able and assertively individualistic. "Great Detectives," all in some measure progeny of Sherlock Holmes, abound on television. Some reveal their Holmesian lineage in the fact that they are idiosyncratic in appearance and eccentric in habits. In these cases, design plays an important role, albeit not necessarily in such an overt way as in *The Avengers* or *Doctor Who.*

Fitz from *Cracker* is a usefully moderate example of the latter-day "Great Detective"; his dress was neither as "way out" as the clothes worn by Steed in *The Avengers* nor as pedestrian as those donned by David Jason in *A Touch of Frost*. Robbie Coltrane, who played Fitz, is physically a big man, being both tall and well-fleshed. In *Cracker,* costume designers capitalized on his physique, his presence, and even on features of his established screen image. Coltrane retained his trademark 1950s-style coif, and Fitz's relaxed but dapper style of dress also subtly suggested the modes of that decade. Fitz's wisecracking, cynical persona was also in the tradition of the hard-boiled detective hero who flourished in detective and noir films of the war years and the 1950s. Moreover, the horrifically violent, often sexually charged cases on which he worked contained strong overtones of noir. The connection with the hard-boiled tradition was made clear in the main publicity image used for the series: a black-and-white still that showed Coltrane half-length, in a pool of light, leaning over a table with a plume of smoke rising from his cigarette. The image could have come from the lobby card for a Bogart movie.

Fitz's actual on-screen appearance was not as assertively based on the hard-boiled model, but his dress was singular enough to set him clearly apart from the metropolitan drear of his Manchester stamping ground. Coltrane typically wore a dark shirt, open at the neck, with a two-piece Italian-style suit in a shade such as powder blue. The cut of his outfits, with their tapered trousers and small-lapelled, unvented jackets, was by no means anachronistic: on the contrary, his clothes were decidedly modish in the early-to-mid 1990s, when *Cracker* was being made. Nevertheless, in conjunction with Coltrane's coif, these costumes conjured up the narcissistic machismo of the era of Johnny Hallyday, Elvis Presley, and Jerry Lee Lewis. This can hardly have been accidental: Coltrane had become firmly associated with rock 'n' roll on both the small and large screen in the BBC comedy series *Tutti Frutti* (1987) and the film farce *The Pope Must Die* (1991).

One might have fun trying to rationalize Fitz's mode of dress as a reflection of his egotistical, dissipated, and chaotic personality. However, the meaning of his costume within the diegesis is, ultimately, a side issue in the present context. What is important is that Coltrane's costume reinforced the aspects of the Fitz persona that made *Cracker* such a hit. His style of dress was a visible reflection of the sharp-talking gallows wit and irreverence that Coltrane portrayed with such panache. It would be excessive to suggest that Fitz's clothing presented him as a kind of latter-day Teddy Boy, but his outfits implied an unspoken resistance to conformity. When seen against the drab grays and buffs of his police colleagues' dress and working environment, Fitz is as prominent as a parrot in a chicken coop. This leads to an important point. Prominence is ultimately the raison d'être of the costuming of all such "special" characters as Fitz: dress is a visual marker of their being personally remarkable and professionally outstanding. Within Jimmy McGovern's stories, Fitz is co-opted onto police cases because of his brilliant, if maverick, powers of psychological insight and persuasion; his stylish clothes at one level embody his socially valuable form of individualism.

Scenic design for Fitz's environment was as studiedly dreary as his colleagues' attire. The series called for little visual exotica: most episodes were set in Greater Manchester, where the program was made. Designers primarily furnished consistency of mood and tone and the kind of understated effects usually accepted as naturalistic. After the first episode established Fitz and his troubled domicile, their scope for innovation or expression was severely circumscribed by the gritty content of the narratives, which generally demanded uncompromising, slice-of-life verism.

So, while scenic design for *Cracker* was "reticent," Robbie Coltrane's sartorial image, like Macnee's in *The Avengers,* was clearly a powerful synecdoche for the series as a whole—though Fitz's grooming and personal demeanor were perhaps more important to this purpose than his dress. Unlike Macnee's Steed or Tom Baker's Doctor Who, Coltrane's Fitz represents the way in which a principal player's established reputation and familiar qualities may have a significant, overriding impact on design imagery within a series. This issue, touched on in relation to Patrick McGoohan's status in *Danger Man* and *The Prisoner,* would repay extended consideration, certainly in connection with television but also in relation to films and the "movie star." Important work has already been done on the sartorial images of Marlene Dietrich and other female stars, especially of the interwar years, but the range could be extended.[3] The enduring, ultrasharp sartorial image of Cary Grant, for example, could profitably be considered in relation to the successes and failures of his career.[4]

With *Inspector Morse,* the role of scenic design is more significant than the main character's costume design. In *The Prisoner* and *The Avengers* we saw how important settings could be as bearers of ethos—and in each case a distorted, simplified vision of the world was presented. The same is true of *Morse,* one of the most successful drama series produced in Britain in the 1980s and 1990s. Even if they do not gain synecdochic meaning, the settings and props for a series can play an important role in describing wider cultural concerns. Morse, played by the late John Thaw, was a detective chief inspector who operated within the picturesque city of Oxford and was portrayed in a correspondingly safe, conservative fashion. In this respect, the screen character stood in stark contrast to Thaw's previous star role as the sharp-talking cockney Flying Squad detective, Inspector Regan, in the hugely popular 1970s police action series, *The Sweeney* (Thames TV/Euston Films, 1974–1978).

Although Thaw gave a workmanlike performance, Morse quickly became an entertaining but undemanding nonpersonality who, like James Bond or Sherlock Holmes, was really no more than the sum of his mannerisms and habits: his crustily cack-handed attempts at old-world chivalry, his love of choral music and opera, his proficiency at crosswords, and his predilection for thinking out problems with a jar of ale in his hand. Although the Morse of Colin Dexter's novels had a serious drinking problem and manifested not only ineptitude but gross misjudgment in his dealings with women, these flaws were given only lip service in the first season of the TV series. These issues were then glossed over, and even overturned, in later ones. Morse became an attractive embodiment of backward-looking elitism, and his accoutrements heavily emphasized this preoccupation with the past: the walls of his office in police headquarters were always emblazoned with posters for musical productions; he wore dapper suits and shirts; and his most immediately identifiable attribute was his bright red Jaguar 2.4, of early 1960s vintage.

Morse and the mysteries he investigated became increasingly gentrified, especially after the original novels had all been dramatized. Even during the second season, when Dexter's material was still being exploited, pretty rural locations and establishing shots of dreaming spires became ever more prominent. In the end, Morse was pretty much brought down to the level of a "Tommy and Tuppence"-style "country house" detective, whose forays into Oxford itself were largely confined to the collegiate cloisters and whose social interactions beyond the confines of his work amounted principally to hobnobbing with academics and the upper crust.[5] Oxford has long been a key site in Americans' whistle-stop tour of "Historic Britain," and *Morse* seemed calculated to provide a curiously imploded variant on the travel-guide style of *Danger Man;* the program increasingly emphasized the theme-park character of Oxford and its environs.

Where *The Sweeney* had portrayed locations whose fascination derived from their being often grotesquely inhospitable, *Morse* was the epitome of the comfortable, traditional Englishness that was promulgated as a hollow ideal (and heavily commodified through the growth of the "Heritage Industry") in the years of Conservative rule from 1979 to 1997.[6] Morse's world seemed to be populated largely by antique dealers and well-to-do professionals living in elegantly appointed cottages or detached, suburban, nineteenth-century "villas." The depiction of their lifestyles could provide as much inspiration for the affluent, middle-class, home-improving viewer as the ever-growing rash of interior-decorating programs such as *Home Front* (BBC TV, 1994–) and *Changing Rooms* (BBC TV, 1996–). The *pièce de résistance* in the cultivation of the picturesque in the series was a gratuitous and barely credible reversion to the *Danger Man* travel formula: in one episode, Morse was taken to Sydney (where he could be photographed in proximity to Jørn Utzon's Opera House), and in another to Vicenza and Verona (where he could be photographed, respectively, in Palladio's Villa Rotonda and the Roman Arena).[7]

The paramount status of the polished, genteel detective story was sustained throughout the 1980s and 1990s by the appearance of such broadly similar figures as Ruth Rendell's truly rural Inspector Wexford and by successful adaptations of "Golden Age" detective literature by authors from Conan Doyle to Margery Allingham.[8] These classics of the genre not only reinforce myths of Englishness, but are among its prime literary constituents. Allingham, Agatha Christie, Dorothy Sayers, and Ngaio Marsh all portray a world of ingratiating conservatism. Christie's England, in particular, presents a comforting, bogus image of stability, where inconvenient corpses may turn up in a gentleman's library or a village rectory, but upper lips do not tremble and the niceties of life are upheld: servants remain calmly deferential, and tea is still served at four o'clock on the dot. The nostalgia in the Christie and Marsh adaptations of the 1980s and 1990s was buoyed up by a conspicuous attention to historical detail of the kind previously reserved for prestige period dramas such as *War and Peace* (BBC TV, 1972–1973) and *Edward VII* (ATV, 1975). Indeed, the watchword of these detective-story adaptations was authenticity.

The chief significance of production design for *Morse* and other detective series of the 1980s, then, does not really reside in the way that individual images served particular narrative needs, nor, as for *Doctor Who,* in the relationship of individual conceits to the series as a whole. Rather, design for the series was refined into a reflection of contemporary consumer tastes, as expressed in magazines such as *Period Living.* More broadly, the *Morse* image upheld prevailing myths of Englishness.

By extension, it is noteworthy that crime drama as a genre began to meld, in terms of visual sensibility, with "serious" serializations of classic nineteenth-century novels such as *Middlemarch* (BBC TV/WGBH, 1994) and *Pride and Prejudice* (BBC TV, 1995), which enjoyed widespread popularity among British audiences during the 1990s.[9] The clear consonance of television series with contemporary taste is something we have touched upon in relation to *Danger Man*. A thorough examination of the influence of the "heritage" boom on imagery in British drama of 1980–2000 would, we suggest, be both interesting and revealing—and many comparable studies of the relationship between design imagery for television and contemporary cultural trends might be proposed.

Ironically enough, our last example, *A Touch of Frost*, illustrates another facet of the significance of *Morse*. As a series, *Frost* traded off the *Morse* precedent, albeit in perverse fashion. Although, *Morse* formed the hub of a sizeable constellation of polite, anodyne, middle-class murder mysteries, the image and ethos of the series has also spawned a counterculture in the detective genre. R. D. Wingfield's waspish, cussed, and ill-starred Frost and Reginald Hill's provocatively coarse Mid-Yorkshire police chief, Superintendent Dalziel, in *Dalziel and Pascoe* (BBC TV/A&E, 1996–), both became popular screen figures in the mid-1990s. *Frost,* in particular, seemed studiedly opposed to *Morse* in terms of design as well as tone and dramatic structure. The programs were scheduled in the same way—miniseasons of two or three two-hour episodes, broadcast irregularly—and were even given the same midweek, prime-time slot. They were meant to appeal to broadly similar audiences, but Frost was everything that Morse was not. This is clearly apparent in the scripting of the series. Whereas Morse, in true Holmesian tradition, had a faithful, dog-like companion, Sergeant Lewis, Frost was pointedly given a succession of different assisting officers (allowing for some delightful comic cameos). Although some proved to be returning characters, the element of unpredictability in *Frost* remained paramount and distanced the program strongly from *Morse,* and, for that matter, from *Dalziel and Pascoe* and *The Inspector Wexford Mysteries* (Southern TV/Meridian, 1987–1998).

Even more striking than the narrative differences, though, is the difference in aesthetic between *Morse* and *Frost*. With his commonplace Ford Sierra, thinning hair, and walrus moustache, and his habitual garb consisting of an unprepossessing porkpie hat, cheap suit, and ugly, padded, thigh-length raincoat, Frost's image is studiedly antithetical to Morse's quietly

elegant dress. His "patch," Denton, is a depressed industrial town of inde-
terminate location, its drab buildings far removed from the ashlared stone-
work of the famously gracious colleges of Oxford, and Frost spends very
little time in unspoiled countryside. The list of studied divergences could
be extended to cover even such details as the title sequences and signature
tunes.

Although design does not occupy center stage in series like *Morse* and
Frost in the same way as in our three subject programs, what emerges clearly
from a brief comparison of these two dramas is the potency of design as
an expressive element within the drama. For the first-time viewer of these
series, it is visual imagery that first proclaims the divergence of *Frost* from
the *Morse* formula, well before any narrative eccentricities have been disclosed. Indeed, since all detective series share so many fundamental features,
design is the area in which the most substantial variations on the formula
can be achieved. Nor is this a minor claim, for the overall aesthetic character of what we watch will play a considerable part in conditioning our
relationship with it.

In other words, as implied in the first chapter, the interplay between design idiom or imagery and genre is often as significant as the relationship
between design and narrative. Generic resonances have not been pursued
much in our book, since our three subject programs all, in varying degrees,
defy or subvert generic categorization. Nevertheless, we place a high premium on genre-based surveys of television series, and such articles as Char-
lotte Brunsdon's "Structure of Anxiety: Recent British Television Crime
Fiction" are, in our view, heartily to be welcomed.[10]

In conclusion, then, we should like to enter a plea for greater attention to design in wide-ranging studies of genre and program type. There
is a real need for a book that comprehensively examines the formal and
genre-specific properties of the police series, for example, giving design
due weight as an expressive component. To date, there has been only one
volume that paid attention to these matters, and this was devoted to only
a single series. Edward Buscombe's and Manuel Alvarado's comprehensive
and neatly compartmentalized study of the detective series *Hazell* (Thames
TV, 1978–1979) stands as an example of the usefulness and effectiveness
of examining different components of the cumulative narrative in a television series, including costume and scenic design. However, this volume
was written well over twenty years ago and has spawned no progeny. David
Buxton's otherwise excellent account of the police series and related genres,

From The Avengers *to* Miami Vice, is avowedly constructed on the principle that visual matters are secondary to the "ideologemes" embodied in a program, and the author consequently gives only passing attention to design.[11]

Influential as Buxton's book has been on many aspects of our thinking, we question his contention that the scripted content of a program can be divorced from the way in which it is mediated to watchers. As interpretative filters between the writer and the actors, and more important between the writer and the audience, costume and scenic designers are of enormous importance. We mentioned in our introduction that screen studies has coalesced into a "linguacentric" discipline. Too often, scholars speak of "reading" television, rather as though watching were in some way a partial or deficient activity. Television does not offer the same pleasures as a written story, or even a radio drama: it is spectacle—unstable, capricious, mobile spectacle. If students must insist on the idea of reading the "text" (and, by implication, subtexts) of a television program, it behooves us to remember that this particular form of narrative is as heavily illuminated as any medieval bible or psalter. When we "read" television, we are reading between designs.

INTRODUCTION

1. The only British-produced volumes devoted to the subject are handbooks by designers themselves: the locus classicus is R. Levin, *Television by Design,* London: The Bodley Head, 1961; but see also P. Seddon, *Where's the Designer?,* London: BBC Production Training, 1993, and R. L. Olson, *Art Direction for Film and Video,* London: Butterworth-Heinemann, 1998. The only scholarly study of television drama that deals with design is M. Alvarado and E. Buscombe, *Hazell: The Making of a TV Series,* London: British Film Institute Publishing, 1978, which devotes one chapter to scenic, costume, and make-up design (Chapter 9: Design, Costume, Make-up, pp. 124–145) and another to theme music and title graphics (Chapter 8: Music and Titles, pp. 117–123). We are grateful to Ian Potter of the National Museum of Film, Photography and Television in Bradford for drawing our attention to this book.

2. V. LoBrutto, *By Design: Interviews with Film Production Designers,* Westport, Conn.: Praeger, 1992.

3. B. Heisner, *Hollywood Art: Art Direction in the Days of the Great Studios,* Jefferson, N.C.: McFarland and Co., 1990.

4. C. Affron and M. J. Affron, *Sets in Motion: Art Direction and Film Narrative*, New Brunswick, N.J.: Rutgers Univ. Press, 1995.

5. C. S. Tashiro, *Pretty Pictures: Production Design and the History Film*, Austin: Univ. of Texas Press, 1998.

6. S. Harper, *Picturing the Past: The Rise and Fall of the British Costume Film*, London: British Film Institute Publishing, 1994; see also her essay "Historical Pleasures: Gainsborough Costume Melodrama" in *Home Is Where the Heart Is: Studies in Melodrama and the Woman's Film*, ed. C. Gledhill, London: British Film Institute Publishing, 1987.

7. S. Bruzzi, *Undressing the Past: Clothing and Identity in the Movies*, London and New York: Routledge, 1997.

8. For the nice conceit that scenic design provides the ethos of a production, we are indebted to Barry Newbery.

9. We are grateful to Clifford Hatts, Dick Cole, and especially David Murphy for discussing with us the problematic nomenclature for costume designers; it is a subject to which we intend to devote more attention in a forthcoming book.

10. As all-film productions have become more common, the establishment of a hierarchy akin to that in the film business has arisen, with the term "production designer" being used in preference to "supervising art director." A production designer on a drama serial now typically has at least one credited art director working under him or her.

11. The economic as well as the artistic status of the designer within the BBC will be discussed in a future volume, material for which we are currently collating.

12. Oldhamstead typically worked for a fixed fee, whereas the cost of realizing designs in the BBC workshops was calculated in terms of man-hours expended (June Hudson, interview with P. Britton, November 1993).

13. June Hudson, interview with P. Britton, August 1999.

14. June Hudson, interview with P. Britton and S. Barker, October 1994.

15. See n. 1 above. Other important examples are J. Hambley and P. Downing, *The Art of Hollywood: A Thames Television Exhibition at the Victoria and Albert Museum*, London: Thames Television, 1979 (Downing is a scenic designer); and E. Carrick, *Designing for Film*, rev. ed., London and New York: Studio Productions, 1949 [1st edition published as *Designing for Motion Pictures*].

16. See, for example, J. Ellis, *Visible Fictions: Cinema, Television, and Video*, rev. ed., London: Routledge, 1992; D. Bordwell and K. Thompson, *Film Art: An Introduction*, New York and London: McGraw-Hill, 1997; and R. Stam, R. Burgoyne, and S. Flitterman-Lewis, *New Vocabularies in Film Semiotics*, London and New York: Routledge, 1992.

17. For studies focused exclusively on the cinematographer, see L. Maltin, *The Art of the Cinematographer: A Survey and Interviews with Five Masters*, New York: Dover, 1978; P. B. Rogers, *Contemporary Cinematographers on Their Art*, Newton, Mass.: Focal Press, 1998; and V. LoBrutto, *Principal Photography: Interviews with Feature Film Cinematographers*, Westport, Conn.: Praeger, 1999. On the aesthetic ontology of film images generally, see J. Aumont, A. Bergala, M. Marie, and M. Vernet, *Aesthetics of Film*, Austin: Univ. of Texas Press, 1992.

18. Perhaps the most powerful metanarrative of screen entertainment is that of the

"star," an iconic figure who both sustains and transcends the film/TV narrative. The classic study is R. Dyer, *Stars,* London: British Film Institute Publishing, 1979.

19. See P. D. G. Britton, "Dress and the Fabric of the Television Series: The Costume Designer as Author in *Dr. Who,*" *Journal of Design History* 12, no. 4, 1999, pp. 345–356.

20. Perhaps the most notable (if also the most idiosyncratic) example of this phenomenon is the semiotician and novelist Umberto Eco. See, for example, his classic study "Casablanca: Cult Movies and Intertextual Collage" in *Travels in Hyperreality,* trans. W. Weaver, New York: Harcourt Brace Jovanovich, 1986, pp. 197–211. More directly relevant to our project is D. Buxton, *From* The Avengers *to* Miami Vice: *Form and Ideology in Popular Television Series,* Manchester and New York: Manchester Univ. Press, 1990; see especially the introductory chapter, pp. 1–20.

21. B. Barber, "Art History's Significant Other . . . Film Studies," in *The Subjects of Art History: Historical Objects in Contemporary Perspectives,* ed. M. Cheetham, M. A. Holly, and K. Moxey, Cambridge: Cambridge Univ. Press, 1991, pp. 262–287.

22. The most substantial study of the subject is *Film Architecture: From* Metropolis *to* Blade Runner, ed. D. Neumann, Munich and New York: Prestel, 1996, which contains essays by D. Albrecht, A. Vidler, and others. An excellent account of the adoption of modernism in scenic design for American cinema of the 1920s and 1930s is D. Albrecht, *Designing Dreams: Modern Architecture in the Movies,* London and New York: Thames and Hudson, 1987.

23. The critical enshrinement of modern art detached from social reality was promulgated vigorously by Clement Greenberg in his essay "Avant-Garde and Kitsch," *Partisan Review* 6, no. 5, 1939, pp. 34–49. For a reprint of "Avant-Garde and Kitsch" along with a judicious selection of responses to Greenberg's position, see *Pollock and After: The Critical Debate,* ed. F. Frascina, London and New York: Harper and Row, 1985. For an elaborate deconstruction of Greenberg's self-fulfilling critical vision, see R. E. Krauss, *The Optical Unconscious,* Cambridge: MIT Press, 1994.

24. See Greenberg, "Avant-Garde and Kitsch." On the relationship between "high" and "low" in the postmodern era, see F. Jameson, "Post-Modernism: Of the Cultural Logic of Late Capitalism," *New Left Review* 146, July/August 1984, pp. 53–92; and T. Crow, "Modernism and Mass Culture in the Visual Arts," in *Pollock and After,* ed. Frascina, pp. 233–266.

25. See P. O. Kristeller, "The Modern System of the Arts," in *Renaissance Thought and the Arts,* Princeton, N.J.: Princeton Univ. Press, 1990, pp. 163–227, especially pp. 181–184 (on the elevation of the visual arts).

26. The valorization of Vincent van Gogh, for example, began with the publication of J. Meier-Graefe, *Vincent van Gogh, a Biographical Study,* trans. J. Holroyd-Reece, London and Boston: The Medici Society, 1922.

27. See, for example, the black chalk drawing of a male figure in masquerade costume, now in the collection of Queen Elizabeth II at Windsor Castle, discussed in E. H. Gombrich et al., *Leonardo da Vinci* [Hayward Gallery Exhibition Catalogue], New Haven and London: Yale Univ. Press (for the South Bank Centre), 1989, p. 152.

28. For a brief discussion of some of Leonardo's stage designs at the Sforza court of

Milan, see M. Kemp, *Leonardo da Vinci: The Marvelous Works of Nature and Man,* London: J. M. Dent and Sons, 1981, pp. 166–169; for a more substantial account, see K. T. Steinitz, "Leonardo Architetto Teatrale e Organizzatore di Feste," *Lettura Vinciana* 9 (Florence), 1970, pp. 53–55. For a good example of the interplay between the staging of religious drama and the imagery of religious painting in the Renaissance, see J. Shearman, "Raphael's Clouds, and Correggio's," in *Studi su Raffaello,* ed. M. Sambucco Hamoud and M. Letizia Strocchi, Urbino: Quattroventi, 1987, pp. 657–668.

29. See M. Barnard, *Art, Design, and Visual Culture,* London: Palgrave, 1998; and N. Mirzoeff, *An Introduction to Visual Culture,* London: Routledge, 1999.

30. For some critiques of traditional art history and introductions to recent approaches, see *The New Art History,* ed. A. L. Rees and F. Borzello, London: Camden Press, 1986.

31. See K. Moxey, *The Practice of Theory: Poststructuralism, Cultural Politics, and Art History,* Ithaca, N.Y. and London: Cornell Univ. Press, 1994.

32. Tashiro makes a nice observation about the jaundiced attitude to popular film within the discipline of film studies: "Put simply: the academic attitude toward mass media seems to be that if it is enjoyable, there must be something wrong with it." *Pretty Pictures,* p. xvi.

CHAPTER 1

1. From 1970 to 2002, the only Oscar winners for Costume Design that were not period films were *Star Wars* (1977), *All That Jazz* (1979), and *The Adventures of Priscilla, Queen of the Desert* (1994). Oscars for Art Direction have gone to a few more non–period films: *All the President's Men* (1976), *Star Wars* (1977), *Heaven Can Wait* (1978), *All That Jazz* (1979), *Batman* (1989), and *Dick Tracy* (1990); the last of these had a period setting, even though its stylized imagery was far from authentic.

2. See Jane Gaines' discussion of the "naturalization" of particular associations of color, etc. through frequent use in "Costume and Narrative: How Dress Tells the Woman's Story" in *Fabrications: Costume and the Female Body,* ed. J. Gaines and C. Herzog, New York: Routledge, 1990, p. 191.

3. C. Bergstrom, unpublished interview from *Buffy the Vampire Slayer: Season III DVD Collection,* Twentieth Century Fox Home Entertainment, Inc., 2001, Disc Six, Special Features: Featurettes: Wardrobe.

4. Cited in N. Holder, with M. Hart and J. Mariotte, *Buffy the Vampire Slayer: The Watcher's Guide,* Volume 2, New York: Pocket Books, 2000, p. 351.

5. Tashiro, *Pretty Pictures,* pp. 13–16.

6. See Gaines, "Costume and Narrative": ". . . in the ecosystem of classical cinema, telling the story requires subordinating an especially evocative aesthetic to narrative designs" (p. 194). This issue is also discussed by Tashiro in *Pretty Pictures:* see, for example, his claim that, in history films, there is a normative assumption that "the designer should make the decor work in the background" (p. 98) and his larger assertion that an image

"at optimal saturation . . . 'works' as a designed image because the number of possible associations has been limited and structured" (p. 49).

7. R. Levin, "Television and the Designer," EBU [European Broadcasting Union] Review, No 58B, November 1959 (reprint of article), p.7.

8. On the normative importance of the "reality effect," see Affron and Affron, *Sets in Motion*, pp. 40–41; for a more penetrating argument on the limitations of artifice in film imagery, see Tashiro, *Pretty Pictures*, pp. 30–32.

9. In *Pretty Pictures*, Tashiro identifies what he calls the "conservative stylization of the History film" (p. 59) and states that History films are "with science fiction, uniquely obvious in [their] reliance" on stylization (p. 74). Yet he also claims that "a primary component of historical pleasure" is "the sense of the past having been re-created in physically tangible form" (p. 72). A definition of stylization that encompasses seeming actuality is irreconcilable with ours. Nor, for that matter, is the designer Ken Adam's definition of stylization as "heightened reality" (LoBrutto, *By Design*, p. 38) sufficiently precise.

10. See Tashiro, *Pretty Pictures*, pp. 70 and 77.

11. See Tashiro's definition of Realist History as that which attempts "to create the Realistic, plastic illusion of witnessing the past" (*Pretty Pictures*, p. 73) and see the following chapter on Realist History as embodied in *Nicholas and Alexandra* and *The Leopard* (pp. 75–94). Tashiro defines the aim of those making Realist History films as "convincing [the audience] that they have successfully recreated a Total Historical Space" (p. 75). However, compare his observation of the way that "our knowledge of past style requires that a Realistic narrative be dressed in a fashion that answers to that awareness" conflicts with "our knowledge that our reality does not appear as it does on-screen," which "immediately marks the historical image as stylized" (p. 64).

12. See Tashiro, *Pretty Pictures*, p. 56.

13. On uses of stylization, see L. Barsacq, *Caligari's Cabinet and Other Grand Illusions: A History of Film Design*, revised and edited by E. Stein, New York and Scarborough, England: Plume, 1976, p. 138. Essentially naturalistic films occasionally veer away from realism. Dream sequences, for example, sometimes incorporate antinatural imagery, as in Hitchcock's psychoanalysis-based thriller *Spellbound* (1945), for which Salvador Dali provided surreal backdrops for sequences representing one of the main character's tortured dreams. Fantasy scenes in Todd Haynes' *Velvet Goldmine* (1998) similarly made use of palpably fantastical scenic design imagery (by Christopher Hobbs). However, such instances are rare: more often, as in Danny Boyle's *Trainspotting* (1996), hallucinogenic and dream imagery are accomplished by distorting the image (through cinematography and lighting) rather than by manipulating décor.

14. *Neverwhere* was, in fact, broadcast on the arts channel BBC2 at 9 P.M. on Thursdays, September 12, 1996–October 17, 1996.

15. June Hudson, interview with P. Britton, August 1994.

16. We are extremely grateful to John Trenouth of the National Museum of Film, Photography and Television, Bradford, for detailed information on television lighting, of which the account here is greatly simplified.

17. We are grateful to Clifford Hatts for discussing this matter with us.

18. D. Rogers, *The Ultimate Avengers,* London: Boxtree, 1995, p. 57.

19. Seasons 5 and 6 (1967–1969).

20. Amies provided Macnee with a satin dress suit: see P. Macnee and D. Rogers, *The Avengers and Me,* London: Titan, 1997, p. 84. For Amies' views on shirt color, and especially his contention that white "is very off-the-peg and truly 'naff,'" see H. Amies, *The Englishman's Suit,* London: Quartet Books, 1994, p. 58.

21. See J. Bentham, "Three's A Crowd" in *Doctor Who: An Adventure in Space and Time* 69: "The Three Doctors," London: CMS, 1987, p. 9; D. Howe, J. Vincent-Rudzki, P. Moffatt, and M. Platt, *The Making of The Five Doctors,* Surbiton, England: Doctor Who Appreciation Society, 1984, p. 24 ("The Costumes").

22. The best studies of the scope of television programming, and of the economic and cultural aspects of the medium, are still J. Fiske and J. Hartley, *Reading Television,* London: Methuen, 1978, and J. Fiske, *Television Culture,* 2nd ed., London: Routledge, 1987.

23. See Fiske and Hartley, *Reading Television,* pp. 91–100; and R. Wallis and S. J. Baran, *The Known World of Broadcast News: International News and the Electronic Media,* London and New York: Routledge, 1990.

24. Having said that, soap operas often deal with topical issues (e.g., AIDS, and attitudes to those who are HIV positive, in *EastEnders*) and may encourage debate. See C. Geraghty, "Social Issues and Realist Soaps: A Study of British Soaps in the 1980s and 1990s," in *To Be Continued . . . Soap Operas around the World,* ed. R. C. Allen, London and New York: Routledge, 1995, pp. 66–80.

25. News broadcasts can, of course, focus on "human interest" and be emotionally manipulative, but this is not their ostensible function; see Fiske and Hartley, *Reading Television,* pp. 91–100.

26. On narrative structures in soaps, see R. C. Allen, *Speaking of Soap Operas,* Chapel Hill and London: Univ. of North Carolina Press, 1985, pp. 69–84.

27. This is not always the case: Narrative threads can be left trailing, and in one famous case a character in the British motel-based soap *Crossroads* (1964–1988) disappeared without explanation, supposedly having gone off-camera to borrow a wrench.

28. This is more applicable to staff designers in corporations such as the BBC, Granada, and Yorkshire TV than to freelance designers, who may be hired on the basis of reputation (e.g., for excellence in "period" drama) or, more often, because a director or producer feels comfortable working with them. We are grateful to Stuart Craig, Denise Exshaw, David Myerscough Jones, and David Murphy for discussing this issue with us.

29. Signal examples are the designs of David Myerscough Jones for *Orde Wingate* (1976) and *Bomber Harris* (1989), both produced for the BBC by Innes Lloyd and written by Don Shaw; sets for the former were quasi-abstract. Myerscough Jones has admitted to being uncompromising in his pursuit of stylized imagery against the prevailing tastes within the BBC drama department (D. Myerscough Jones, interview with S. Barker, November 1994). However, these plays, though meant to have broad appeal, were not pitched at the same level as, say, police series such as *Softly, Softly — Taskforce* (1966–1976). In serious drama, Myerscough Jones' approach could be more easily accommodated.

30. *Special Branch* and *The Sweeney,* made by Euston Films, were trailblazers in being

all-film productions made almost entirely on location; studio work was accomplished in permanent sets and re-dressed rooms in the former school where the production company was based. (We are grateful to Bill Alexander for this information, given in an interview with S. Barker, January 1995.) See M. Alvarado and J. Stewart, eds., *Made for Television: Euston Films Limited,* London: British Film Institute Publishing, 1985. From the late 1970s onward, prestige productions at the BBC were increasingly made wholly or largely on location, e.g., Jonathan Powell's much praised and award-winning production of *Tinker, Tailor, Soldier, Spy* (1979). According to Clifford Hatts, this was done on the questionable (at that time) pretext that overhead costs for location shoots were lower than for set-building in the studio (C. Hatts, interview with P. Britton, October 1995).

31. We are grateful to Damian White at BBC Information for apprising us of this; it is worth explicitly noting that Lambie Nairn does not receive a screen credit for his work.

32. N. Banks-Smith, "Last Night's TV: The Strange Story," in *The Guardian: The Guide,* January 18, 2000.

33. For the idea of differing degrees of "design intensity," see Affron and Affron, *Sets in Motion,* pp. 35–40.

34. The costume designer for *The Box of Delights* was Christine Rawlins; the scenic designers were Bruce Macadie and David Buckingham. The cost of the four-part serialization of *Gormenghast* exceeded £9 million: B. Summerskill, "Gormenghast Has Viewers Groaning," *Daily Express,* February 3, 2000.

35. The production is covered extensively in E. Daniel, *The Art of Gormenghast,* London and New York: HarperCollins, 2000.

36. *Four Weddings and a Funeral* (Mike Newell, 1994) was produced by Working Title in association with Channel 4 Films. For an excellent summary discussion of both the funding and reception of British films during the 1990s, see R. Murphy, "A Path through the Moral Maze," in *British Cinema of the 90s,* ed. R. Murphy, London: British Film Institute Publishing, 1999, pp. 1–16.

37. Hudson interview with Britton, August 1994.

38. B. Newbery, interview with P. Britton, August 1998.

39. C. Hatts, written notes to P. Britton, January 1996.

40. Ibid.

41. C. Hatts, interview with P. Britton, May 1999.

42. Ibid.

43. See Tashiro, *Pretty Pictures,* pp. 4–7.

44. C. Hatts, notes to Britton, January 1996: "Levin was admired internationally. He twisted the Corporation's arm and got money for three immensely prestigious and expensive 'Design Conferences.' Delegates swarmed in from every quarter of the globe, like bargain hunters at a sale, anxious to discover Levin's secret; how the BBC's standards of design and productivity were achieved."

45. Ibid. See P. Purser, "Richard Levin" (obituary), *The Guardian,* Monday, July 10, 2000. In his capacity as chief designer of the Land Travelling Exhibition, Levin contributed to M. Banham and B. Hillier, eds., *A Tonic to the Nation: The Festival of Britain, 1951,* London: Thames and Hudson, 1976, pp. 148–149.

46. C. Hatts, notes to Britton, January 1996.

47. Levin, "Television and the Designer," p. 7, caption to fig. 10.

48. We are grateful to Hatts and B. Newbery for discussing the formation and structure of the Studio Design Unit with us; Newbery was for a time one of its personnel (Newbery interview with Britton, August 1998).

49. Levin, "Television and the Designer," p. 7, caption to fig. 11.

50. Hatts, notes to Britton, January 1996.

51. C. Hatts, "The Rôle of the Designer in Television," *Journal of the Royal Society of Arts* 123, January 1975, p. 90.

52. Hatts, notes to Britton, January 1996.

53. Levin, "Television and the Designer," p. 7, caption to fig. 10.

54. See J. Mayne, *Cinema and Spectatorship,* London: Routledge, 1993; M. Smith, *Engaging Characters,* Oxford: Oxford Univ. Press, 1995; Fiske and Hartley, *Reading Television;* and Fiske, *Television Culture.*

55. For example, *The Old Crowd,* one of a set of six plays by Alan Bennett produced by LWT in 1978–1979. Visual anomalies in this play culminated in a total rupture of the stage illusion as the camera tracked from the action to show the studio, crew, and the director in his gallery. Unlike the other plays in the set, *The Old Crowd* was badly received; Bennett has speculated that this was due to its assertive antirealism: A. Bennett, *Writing Home,* London: Faber and Faber, 1994, p. 267.

56. M. McLuhan, *Understanding Media: The Extensions of Man,* 2nd ed., New York: Signet, 1964, pp. 273–274, 276.

57. Ibid., p. 36.

58. Ibid., p. 43.

59. Ibid., p. 44.

60. We are grateful to Ian Potter for discussing this point with us.

61. See Buxton, *From* Avengers *to* Vice, p. 16.

62. It is worth noting that Buxton's approach, defined in his introductory chapter, does not really allow for ideological shift within a series (*From* Avengers *to* Vice, pp. 16–20). His discussion of *The Avengers,* for example (pp. 96–107), treats the entire series as monolithic, for all that it ran for nearly ten years. While the issue cannot be pursued here, Buxton's assumption that all series are ideologically homogeneous is questionable.

63. Such a view was put forward, for example, by the costume designer June Hudson, who also noted that the director James Cellan Jones "used to say that costuming a play in modern dress was much more difficult than doing a period play" (Hudson interview with Britton, August 1994).

64. See E. G. Craig, *On the Art of the Theatre,* London: Heinemann, 1911; D. Kennedy, *Granville Barker and the Dream of Theatre,* Cambridge: Cambridge Univ. Press, 1985; and L. Simonson, *The Art of Scenic Design,* New York: Harper and Row, 1950.

65. Much of the humor of *The Young Ones* was visual and demanded sharp and witty contributions from costume designer Barbara Kidd and scenic designer Graeme Story. The main characters were all stereotypes, instantly recognizable from their caricatured costumes. Sets and props were conceived around sight gags. Thus, when the cord of the VCR won't reach the socket, one of the characters goes outside to push the wall closer,

and when the lentils in the cupboard are unreachable due to precariously balanced plates, the protagonists break through the wall on the other side to retrieve them. The series also contained frequent vignettes that involved zooming in on objects such as a matchbox (which proclaimed, "Don't look at me, I'm irrelevant") or the back of a cornflakes box (where family members in an ad for a tent are arguing as their picture is taken).

66. Barsacq, *Caligari's Cabinet*, p. 7; see Tashiro, *Pretty Pictures*, pp. 4–5.

67. See the references in note 55 above.

CHAPTER 2

1. A. Aldgate, J. Chapman, and A. Marwick, eds., *Windows on the Sixties: Exploring Key Texts of Media and Culture*, London and New York: I. B. Tauris, 2000 (cover designed by Graham Seamon).

2. See Chapman, "*The Avengers:* Television and Popular Culture during the 'High Sixties,'" in *Windows on the Sixties*, A. Aldgate et al., eds., pp. 38–46; and T. Miller, *The Avengers*, London: British Film Institute Publishing, 1997, pp. 10–24. The production history of the series is covered more leisurely and anecdotally in Rogers, *Ultimate Avengers*.

3. "The Frighteners" is the earliest surviving episode of *The Avengers*; the tapes of the rest of the episodes from the first season were discarded by ABC during the 1960s. See Chapman, "*The Avengers*," p. 41.

4. See Chapman, "*The Avengers*," pp. 44–45; and Rogers, *Ultimate Avengers*, p. 175.

5. For a plot summary, see D. Rogers, *The Complete Avengers*, London: Boxtree, 1989, pp. 201–202.

6. On the various trends in 1960s cinema, see R. Murphy, *Sixties British Cinema*, London: British Film Institute Publishing, 1992.

7. See Murphy, *Sixties British Cinema*, pp. 23–25 and 259.

8. See Rogers, *Ultimate Avengers*, pp. 15–27, 44–60, 78–94, 113–138, 159–178, and 201–221; and Chapman, "*The Avengers*," pp. 38–46.

9. See Rogers, *Ultimate Avengers*, pp. 129–131; and Chapman, "*The Avengers*," p. 54.

10. We are grateful to Patrick Downing for discussing his contribution to the series with us (interviews with S. Barker, October and November 1994); he is quoted briefly in Rogers, *Ultimate Avengers*, pp. 20–21. For a very brief account of some of Robert Jones' work on the fifth and sixth seasons of *The Avengers*, see Rogers, *Ultimate Avengers*, pp. 176 and 216. On Jones' and Shingleton's approach, see below, pp. 84–89.

11. P. Macnee and M. Cameron, *Blind in One Ear*, London: Harrap, 1988, p. 233; P. Macnee and D. Rogers, *The Avengers and Me*, pp. 84–85; Rogers, *Ultimate Avengers*, p. 174; and Miller, *The Avengers*, pp. 43 and 52–53.

12. See D. Rogers, The Avengers: *The Making of the Movie*, London: Titan, 1998, p. 2. The original silhouette image is widely reproduced, especially on the Internet, where it is, at the time of writing, the logo icon on *The Avengers Forever: A Virtual Encyclopedia* (www.theavengers.tv/forever). For an excellent reproduction, see *Starburst* 67, March 1984, p. 11.

13. Miller, *The Avengers*, p. 153.

14. This tag was used on the theatrical poster and also on the rear cover of Rogers, *Making of the Movie.*

15. Miller, *The Avengers,* pp. 28 and 58.

16. D. Rogers, *The Avengers Anew,* London: Michael Joseph, 1985, p. 8.

17. On the central role of haute couture in *Funny Face* and *Sabrina,* see Bruzzi, *Undressing the Past,* pp. 5–6.

18. *TV Times,* February 9–15, 1964, p. 7; cited in Buxton, *From* Avengers *to* Vice, p. 99.

19. This sequence is described, and associated photographic stills reproduced, in Rogers, *Avengers Anew,* pp. 44–45.

20. Ambren Garland, Head of the Wardrobe Department at ABC, has stated emphatically that Starke did not design Blackman's clothes. According to Garland, the link with Starke was manufactured by Marie Donaldson, who managed publicity for *The Avengers,* and Blackman's wardrobe was in fact entirely created by Garland and Audrey Liddle; see Rogers, *Ultimate Avengers,* pp. 87–88.

21. Rogers, *Ultimate Avengers,* pp. 130–132.

22. Harry Pottle, production designer on the series in 1965–1966, informed us that *The Avengers* was a British trailblazer in offering product placement to manufacturers of furniture and other household items—a clear indication of its perceived popularity (interview with S. Barker, November 1994). See Miller, *The Avengers,* pp. 26–27, which points out that the series was the first to have "a designated 'Exploitation Manager' who sold product placements."

23. See Rogers, *Ultimate Avengers,* p. 329.

24. We are grateful to Denise Exshaw for this information (interview with P. Britton, July 1998).

25. Rogers, *Ultimate Avengers,* pp. 159–161.

26. See Chapman, "*The Avengers,*" pp. 62–63; and Miller, *The Avengers,* pp. 133–138.

27. The short scene between the last commercial and the end credits.

28. Aspects of Derrida's model of deconstruction have been absorbed into thinking on the nature of the postmodern. See, for example, F. Jameson, "The Deconstruction of Expression," *New Left Review* 146, July/August 1984, pp. 53–92.

29. This is a simplification; the vicissitudes of modernism are best explained by the documents reproduced in *Art in Theory, 1900–1990,* C. Harrison and P. Wood, eds., Oxford: Blackwell, 1992; see in particular the introduction to "Part VII: Institutions and Objections," pp. 797–802.

30. See A. Huyssen, "Mapping the Postmodern" in *The Post-Modern Reader,* ed. C. Jencks, London: Academy Editions, 1992, pp. 40–72; and Chapman, "*The Avengers,*" pp. 58–64.

31. C. Jencks, "The Post-Modern Agenda," in *The Post-Modern Reader,* ed. Jencks, pp. 11–15.

32. Ibid., pp. 12–13 and 17.

33. U. Eco, "Postscript to *The Name of the Rose:* Postmodernism, Irony, the Enjoyable," in *The Post-Modern Reader,* ed. Jencks, pp. 73–75.

34. Macnee uttered this aphorism in the introduction to one of the reruns of the Macnee/Blackman episodes on Channel 4 in 1993; cited in Miller, *The Avengers,* p. 7.

35. Macnee and Rogers, *The Avengers and Me*, pp. 84–85. On Liddle's contribution, see Rogers, *Ultimate Avengers*, p. 57.

36. Macnee and Cameron, *Blind in One Ear*, pp. 213–214; and Macnee and Rogers, *The Avengers and Me*, pp. 22–23.

37. Rogers, *Complete Avengers*, p. 14.

38. See Rogers, *Ultimate Avengers*, pp. 57 and 88; and Macnee and Cameron, *Blind in One Ear*, p. 231. Macnee refers to his cutter, according to convention, simply as "Mr." James, omitting his given name even in the book's index. Bailey and Weatherhill of Regent Street was Macnee's tailor throughout the entire production period of *The Avengers*, even making the Pierre Cardin collection used in the fifth season (see Rogers, *Ultimate Avengers*, p. 174).

39. "A Surfeit of H$_2$0" (1966), "Silent Dust" (1966), and "The Man Eater of Surrey Green" (1966).

40. Cited in Rogers, *Ultimate Avengers*, p 48.

41. See F. Chenoune, *A History of Men's Fashion*, trans. D. Dusinberre, Paris: Flammarion, 1993, pp. 274–276 and 280; see also P. Cardin, *Pierre Cardin*, Paris: Flammarion, 1997.

42. J. Harris, S. Hyde, and G. Smith, *1966 and All That: Design and the Consumer in Britain, 1960–1969*, London: Trefoil, 1986, pp. 115–116.

43. Miller, *The Avengers*, p. 43.

44. See Macnee and Rogers, *The Avengers and Me*, p. 85, where Macnee states that Julian Wintle, executive producer of the show from 1965 onward, prevented him from signing with Cardin or Amies for contractual reasons.

45. Rogers, *Making of the Movie*, p. 53

46. See Miller, *The Avengers*, pp. 51 and 55.

47. Macnee and Rogers, *The Avengers and Me*, p. 123.

48. For an excellent study of the symbolism of the bowler hat, see F. M. Robinson, *The Man in the Bowler Hat: His History and Iconography*, Chapel Hill, N.C.: Univ. of North Carolina Press, 1993. On hats in costume design and consumerism, with specific reference to the hat worn by Omar Sharif in David Lean's *Doctor Zhivago* (1965), see Tashiro, *Pretty Pictures*, pp. 143–169.

49. For an account by Macnee of the shaping of the Steed character that acknowledges the role played by Sydney Newman, ABPC's Head of Drama (and the effective creator of *The Avengers*), and emphasizes that Macnee was encouraged to play the part of Steed as an extension of himself, see Macnee and Cameron, *Blind in One Ear*, pp. 213–214; and Macnee and Rogers, *The Avengers and Me*, pp. 22–23 and 70–71.

50. See, for instance, J. Coe, *Humphrey Bogart: Take It and Like It*, New York: Grove Weidenfeld, 1991, the cover of which shows Bogart at his most dapper, wearing a black dinner jacket.

51. Macnee and Cameron, *Blind in One Ear*. The image of Steed is in fact taken from a publicity still for *The New Avengers*.

52. See, for example, L. Nimoy, *I Am Not Spock*, Millbrae, Calif.: Celestial Arts Publishing, 1975; and L. Nimoy, *I Am Spock*, New York: Hyperion, 1995.

53. T. Baker, *Who on Earth Is Tom Baker?* London and New York: HarperCollins, 1998.

54. Stuart Craig, interview with P. Britton, June 1998.

55. Cited in Rogers, *Ultimate Avengers*, p. 132.

56. See Miller, *The Avengers*, p. 33.

57. See Miller, *The Avengers*, p. 81.

58. See Tashiro's observations on Omar Sharif and the "Zhivago hat": Tashiro, *Pretty Pictures*, pp. 144–148 and 158–166.

59. Miller, *The Avengers*, p. 43.

60. See Bruzzi, *Undressing Cinema*, pp. 68–69.

61. See T. Triggs, "Framing Masculinity," in *Chic Thrills: A Fashion Reader*, ed. J. Ash and E. Wilson, London: Pandora, 1992, p. 28; and A. Hollander, *Seeing through Clothes*, Berkeley, Calif.: Univ. of California Press, 1993, p. 208.

62. Bruzzi, *Undressing Cinema*, p. 88.

63. See Chenoune, *Men's Fashion*, pp. 241–250.

64. The term "Emmapeelers" was coined by Alun Hughes and referred to the various all-in-one bodysuits that he designed for Diana Rigg; see Rogers, *Complete Avengers*, p. 126.

65. Cited in K. Sutcliffe, "Making a Killing: Interview with Brian Clemens," *Primetime* 8, Spring 1984, p. 30.

66. Macnee and Rogers, *The Avengers and Me*, p. 32.

67. Rogers, *Ultimate Avengers*, p. 18.

68. Ibid., p. 24.

69. Steed's military rank is mentioned in "The Murder Market" (1965) and "Game" (1969).

70. See M. Lowry, "They Get Color Next Year, but We Get Macnee Now," *New York World-Telegram*, March 21, 1966, p. 10, cited in Miller, *The Avengers*, p. 47. For more recent uses of Edwardian to describe Steed's apparel, see Miller, *The Avengers*, pp. 43 and 128; and Rogers, *Ultimate Avengers*, p. 34. Although Macnee and the costume designer Ambren Garland have tended subsequently to stress the Regency antecedents of the image (see Rogers, *Ultimate Avengers*, pp. 18 and 37), Macnee described his clothes as having an "Edwardian look" in an article on fashions for the series in *TV Times*, "The Immaculate Avengers," by Diana Lancaster (Issue 418, November 1, 1964, p. 7). In the same article, Macnee discussed Steed's alternate, modernistic style of clothing, the principal garments of which were what he called his "Chinese admiral" blazers.

71. Reproduced in Chenoune, *Men's Fashion*, p. 232.

72. The homosexual antecedents could be traced a stage further: in later life, having abandoned his aesthete apparel, Oscar Wilde adopted the curly-brim bowler, stitched Chesterfield coat, and crisp peg-top trousers of the conventionally fashionable man-about-town. See, for example, the photograph of Wilde taken in Rome after his release from Reading Gaol, reproduced in S. Calloway and D. Colvin, *Oscar Wilde: An Exquisite Life*, London: Orion, 1997, p. 98.

73. Chenoune, *Men's Fashion*, pp. 231 and 229–233.

74. Kingsley Amis, article in *T.V. Times*, February 9–15, 1964, p. 7.

75. Macnee and Rogers, *The Avengers and Me*, p. 95.

76. "The Forget-Me-Knot" (1969).

77. Rogers, *Ultimate Avengers*, p. 212; Macnee and Rogers, *The Avengers and Me*, p. 103.

78. Rogers, *Ultimate Avengers*, p. 212; see Macnee and Rogers, *The Avengers and Me*, pp. 103–104.

79. See Harris et al., *1966*, pp. 115–116; and C. Probert, "The Era of Individualism," in *Costume and Fashion: A Concise History*, ed. J. Laver, London: Thames and Hudson, 1982, pp. 268–269.

80. Miller, *The Avengers*, p. 79.

81. See p. 47 above.

82. Macnee and Rogers, *The Avengers and Me*, pp. 105–106.

83. See Chenoune, *Men's Fashion*, p. 285 *ff.*

84. On the Peacock Revolution, see H. Amies, *The Englishman's Suit*, pp. 27–41, especially pp. 32–33.

85. Rogers, *Ultimate Avengers*, p. 18.

86. J. Pertwee, interview with P. Britton, April 1994.

87. "Quick-Quick Slow Death" (1966).

88. See Rogers, *Ultimate Avengers*, p. 220; and Miller, *The Avengers*, p. 20.

89. Exshaw interview with Britton, July 1998.

90. Miller, *The Avengers*, p. 144.

91. Ibid., p. 128.

92. "The Town of No Return" (1965).

93. Pottle, who was credited as "art director," following standard film industry designation, was in fact replaced by Robert Jones for one episode, "Too Many Christmas Trees" (1965).

94. Pottle interview with Barker, November 1994. We are grateful to John Trenouth for discussing with us the technical limitations on television broadcasting in the 1960s.

95. Pottle interview with Barker, November 1994.

96. Ibid.

97. Ibid.

98. For the relation of the gaze to screen entertainment, the classic study is L. Mulvey, "Visual Pleasures and Narrative Cinema," in *Visual and Other Pleasures*, Basingstoke, England: Macmillan, 1989, pp. 14–26. See also "Afterthoughts on Visual Pleasure and Narrative Cinema," in *Visual and Other Pleasures*, pp. 29–38.

99. See B. G. Walker, *The Women's Encyclopedia of Myths and Secrets*, San Francisco: HarperSanFrancisco, 1983, p. 294.

100. Pottle interview with Barker, November 1994.

101. On the interactions between designers and other creative personnel, see comments by the director Don Leaver and script editor Brian Clemens in Rogers, *Ultimate Avengers*, p. 83.

102. See p. 80 below.

103. "The Town of No Return" had been completed, with Elizabeth Shepherd in the role of Peel, and filming of "The Murder Market" was in progress when the decision was made to replace Shepherd with Diana Rigg (Rogers, *Ultimate Avengers*, pp. 121–124).

104. The seminal account of this view of kitsch is by C. Greenberg, "Avant-Garde and Kitsch," repr. in *Pollock and After*, ed. F. Frascina, pp. 21–33.

105. Pottle interview with Barker, November 1994.

106. On the imagery of *Caligari,* see H. G. Scheffauer's 1920 essay, "The Vivifying of Space," in *Introduction to the Art of the Movies,* ed. L. Jacobs, New York: Noonday Press, 1960. See also A. Vidler, "The Explosion of Space: Architecture and the Filmic Imaginary," in *Film Architecture,* ed. D. Neumann, pp. 13–25, especially pp. 15–16.

107. Pottle had used the same device of the low cornice, albeit in a different way and to very different effect, in a set for the Joseph Losey thriller *Blind Date* (1959), his first project as art director for Independent Artists. The climactic scene of the film takes place in the office of Inspector Morgan (Stanley Baker), a room that is clearly on a mezzanine half way up the interior of the facade of a grand Edwardian building. The floor bisects large arched windows, and the heavy cornice above it is approximately at shoulder height. Here, as in "Quick-Quick Slow Death," the effect is powerful—but because there is a clear structural logic in the *Blind Date* set, the subliminal impact is different: Morgan's office is an oppressive and saturnine space where the interrogation room is disquietingly zany. For a useful discussion of *Blind Date* and a photograph of the set in question, see Murphy, *Sixties British Cinema,* pp. 203–205.

108. This irregularity is too great to be explained away as a forced perspective intended to make the room seem larger. We are grateful to Denise Exshaw, Pottle's principal draftsman on *The Avengers,* for discussing this design with us (interview with P. Britton, July 1998).

109. See A. G. Lloyd-Smith and V. Sage, eds., *Gothick: Origins and Innovations: Papers from the International Gothic Conference Held at the University of East Anglia, Norwich,* Atlanta, Ga.: Rodopi, 1994.

110. *TV Times,* February 9–15, 1964, p. 7; cited in Buxton, *From Avengers to Vice,* p. 99.

111. Cited in Macnee and Rogers, *The Avengers and Me,* p. 76.

112. This is a simplification. For a penetrating account of the Gothick style, and its evolution into the "Gothic Revival" of the nineteenth century, see J. M. Crook, *The Dilemma of Style: Architectural Ideals from the Picturesque to the Post-Modern,* London: Murray, 1987.

113. See L. Lippard, ed., *Pop Art,* London: Thames and Hudson, 1967, pp. 27–161.

114. See Harris et al., *1966,* pp. 136 and 140.

115. R. Hamilton, *Collected Words,* London: Thames and Hudson, 1982, p. 28.

116. Ibid.

117. F. Sturges, "Video Reviews," *The Independent: The Information,* February 6–12, 1999, p. 66.

118. S. Craig, interview with P. Britton, June 1998.

119. On Wilson's "white heat," see A. Marwick, *British Society since 1945,* 2nd ed., Harmondsworth, England: Penguin, 1990, p. 111. The shifting policies and character of the Conservative Party in the last half of the twentieth century are portrayed in the documents reproduced in S. Ball, ed., *The Conservative Party since 1945,* Manchester: Manchester Univ. Press, 1998. On the rise of the New Right in Britain and its troubled relationship with traditional conservatism, see J. Gray, *Beyond the New Right,* London: Routledge, 1994.

120. See R. E. Krauss, "The Originality of the Avant-Garde," in *The Originality of the Avant-Garde and Other Modernist Myths,* Cambridge, Mass., and London: MIT Press, 1986, pp. 151–170.

CHAPTER 3

1. See C. Gregory, *Be Seeing You: Decoding* The Prisoner, Champaign, Ill.: Univ. of Illinois Press, 1999, p. 48.

2. Gregory also notes that this episode is "less about education than about television" (Gregory, *Be Seeing You,* p. 95).

3. Patrick McGoohan, interview with W. Troyer, 1977. To our knowledge, the interview is unpublished, but is available on the Internet at various sites. We consulted *Cult TV: The Home of Classic Television* (www.cultv.co.uk/mcgoohan.htm).

4. See A. Carrazé and H. Oswald, eds., *The Prisoner: A Televisionary Masterpiece,* trans. C. Donougher, London: W. H. Allen, 1990, pp. 226, 228–229.

5. Cited in Carrazé and Oswald, *Televisionary Masterpiece,* p. 6.

6. The producer of *The Prisoner,* David Tomblin, noted that McGoohan "was responsible more than anybody for the style of the series" (Interview for *Six Into One: The Prisoner File,* Channel 4 Documentary, 1984; transcript courtesy of Bruce Clark). On McGoohan's control of the series, see also Carrazé and Oswald, *Televisionary Masterpiece,* p. 211; and D. Rogers, The Prisoner *and* Danger Man, London: Boxtree, 1989, p. 131.

7. I. Raltoff, *Inside* The Prisoner: *Radical Television and Film in the 1960s,* London: Batsford, 1998, p. 166.

8. Carrazé and Oswald, *Televisionary Masterpiece,* p. 210; and Rogers, *The Prisoner,* p. 130.

9. Gregory suggests that "Dance of the Dead" "depicts the all-important will of the Individual being dangerously weakened by the inescapable mechanisms of society, embodied here in the form of psycho-sexual power games" (*Be Seeing You,* p. 111).

10. See Rogers, *The Prisoner,* pp. 10–12, 56–58; and J. Baudou, "Danger Man," in *Televisionary Masterpiece,* Carrazé and Oswald, pp. 204–207.

11. For example, in "Not So Jolly Roger" (1966), Drake proved himself hip by posing, very effectively, as a fast-talking disk jockey. See Rogers, *The Prisoner,* pp. 121–122.

12. Gregory attempts to justify No. 6's misogyny in "Never Trust a Woman," Chapter 9 of his book (*Be Seeing You,* pp. 199–208, esp. 204).

13. A. Marwick, *The Sixties: Cultural Revolution in Britain, France, Italy, and the United States, c. 1958–1974,* Oxford: Oxford Univ. Press, 1998, pp. 10–13, 15, 98–99, 483, 537.

14. Marwick, *The Sixties,* pp. 12–13.

15. Carrazé and Oswald, *Televisionary Masterpiece,* p. 205; see Rogers, *The Prisoner,* p. 11.

16. See Harris et al., *1966,* p. 45.

17. Buxton notes the "flat rejection of television by the 1970s counterculture" (Buxton, *From* Avengers *to* Vice, p. 4).

18. Marwick, *The Sixties,* p. 17.

19. The term "global village" is, of course, McLuhan's. See M. McLuhan and B. R. Powers, *The Global Village: Transformations in World Life and Media in the 21st Century,* Oxford: Oxford Univ. Press, 1989.

20. McLuhan, *Understanding Media,* pp. vii–viii.

21. See McLuhan, *Understanding Media,* pp. 245, 255–257, 273.

22. See Chapter 1, p. 33.

23. Some writers, such as Vincent Terrace, whose bizarre, literal "reading" of *The Prisoner* can be found in his *Complete Encyclopedia of Television Programs,* have "assumed [the hero] to be John Drake" (*The Complete Encyclopedia of Television Programs, 1947–1976,* South Brunswick, N.J.: A. S. Barnes, 1976, pp. 224–225); see also the speculation and rumor presented in Rogers, *The Prisoner,* p. 131.

24. Carrazé and Oswald, *Televisionary Masterpiece,* p. 6.

25. See the citation from the Troyer interview, p. 121.

26. Rogers, *The Prisoner,* p. 57.

27. Harris et al., *1966,* pp. 150–152.

28. Rogers, *The Prisoner,* p. 56.

29. On the gadgets in *Danger Man* see Rogers, *The Prisoner,* pp. 12 and 56. It is worth noting that this miniaturized equipment was the subject of a feature, "Tools for Espionage," in a U.S. comic based on the series, *Secret Agent* No. 1, Poughkeepsie, N.Y.: K. K. Publications, 1966, p. 35.

30. Pertwee interview with Britton, April 1994.

31. Interview with W. Troyer, 1977.

32. See Rogers, *The Prisoner,* p. 128.

33. Rogers, *The Prisoner,* pp. 11 and 130.

34. We are grateful to Rosemary Britton for this observation.

35. On Fuller and geodesic structures, see R. Buckminster Fuller, *Operating Manual for Spaceship Earth,* New York: Dutton, 1963; see also L. S. Sieden, *Buckminster Fuller's Universe: His Life and Work,* Cambridge, Mass.: Perseus Publishing, 2000. On the renaissance of interest in Fuller's work in the late 1960s, see K. Frampton, *Modern Architecture: A Critical History,* London: Thames and Hudson, 1980, p. 281.

36. An entertaining attempt to reconcile the studio set with the real building in Portmeirion, complete with ground-plan, is offered by Roger Langley in a short article entitled "Plan of Private Residence 6 in the Village," in *The Prisoner of Portmeirion,* ed. M. Hora, Number Six Productions, 1991, pp. 14–15. Langley acknowledges that the interior is far too big to fit in the actual space of the tiny building in Portmeirion, but does not attribute any significance to the paradox. We are grateful to Ian Potter for drawing our attention to this publication.

37. This is an idea that Gregory makes some play with in his final chapter, "The Whole Earth as the Village: *The Prisoner* as Prophecy" (*Be Seeing You,* pp. 209–214).

38. See Gregory, *Be Seeing You,* pp. 47–48.

39. Rogers, *The Prisoner,* p. 134.

40. "Living in Harmony" and "The Girl Who Was Death."

41. See Gregory, *Be Seeing You,* pp. 38–41.

42. Interestingly, McGoohan made use of this barred chamber at the press launch for the series. See Carrazé and Oswald, *Televisionary Masterpiece*, p. 236.

43. Carrazé and Oswald, *Televisionary Masterpiece* p. 226.

44. Interview with W. Troyer, 1977.

45. The script editor for the series, George Markstein, is cited as saying that the holiday camp overtones were intentional (Rogers, *The Prisoner*, p. 132).

46. Harris et al., *1966*, pp. 112–113.

47. See Gregory, *Be Seeing You*, p. 204.

48. Most of the Number 2s are shown together in Carrazé and Oswald, *Televisionary Masterpiece*, pp. 234–235.

49. Quoted in Carrazé and Oswald, *Televisionary Masterpiece*, p. 6.

50. The Prisoner is definitively given back his suit at the beginning of "Fall Out."

51. Carrazé and Oswald, *Televisionary Masterpiece*, p. 6.

52. A. Lurie, *The Language of Clothes*, London: Bloomsbury, 1981, pp. 187–193; Hollander, *Seeing Through Clothes*, pp. 365–390.

53. See, for example, J. Sternberg, "*The Prisoner*, Pioneer without Heirs," in *Televisionary Masterpiece*, Carrazé and Oswald, p. 16.

54. Carrazé and Oswald, *Televisionary Masterpiece*, p. 226.

55. See Rogers, *The Prisoner*, p. 130.

56. See R. Samuel, *Theatres of Memory*, vol.1, *Past and Present in Contemporary Culture*, London: Verso, 1996, pp. 59–79, especially pp. 59–67.

57. Buxton, *From Avengers to Vice*, p. 96.

58. One clear invocation of Pop was removed from the final credit sequence before it was aired. At the very end of the original, unscreened credit-sequence graphics, the wheels of a penny-farthing bicycle spin, one turning into the Earth and the other into a panorama of the rest of the galaxy. As the globe grows larger, an orange circle bearing the word "POP" emerges from its center and enlarges to fill the screen. There is a brief discussion of this deleted sequence, which is preserved in a first cut of "The Chimes of Big Ben," in M. White and J. Ali, *The Official Prisoner Companion*, New York: Warner, 1988, pp. 19–20.

59. The Aarnio chair should not really be considered "Pop": it is cited as an example of Sixties modernism, and more specifically as "an image of . . . [the] modernity of the Space Decade" in P. Garner, *Twentieth-Century Furniture*, Oxford: Phaidon, 1980, p. 182.

60. On the theme park and similar simulated-reality environments, see M. Sorkin, ed., *Variations on a Theme Park: The New American City and the End of Public Space*, New York: Noonday Press, 1992; and M. Gottdiener, *The Theming of America: Dreams, Visions, and Commercial Spaces*, Boulder, Colo.: Westview Press, 1997. On the Western, and specifically American, preoccupation with simulated realities, see J. Baudrillard, *Simulations*, trans. P. Foss, P. Patton, and P. Beitchman, New York: Semiotext(e), 1983, especially pp. 23–26.

61. See Gregory, *Be Seeing You*, Chapter 8: "Many Happy Returns: The Prisoner as Cult," especially pp. 193–195.

CHAPTER 4

1. Chapman, "*The Avengers,*" p. 46.

2. J. Tulloch and H. Jenkins, *Science Fiction Audiences: Watching Doctor Who and Star Trek,* London: Routledge, 1995.

3. See, for example, two episodes from the first series, "The Daleks" and "The Sensorites." See D. J. Howe, M. Stammers, and S. J. Walker, *Doctor Who: The Sixties,* London: Virgin Publishing, 1993, pp. 30–31; and J. Bentham, Doctor Who: *The Early Years,* London: W. H. Allen, 1986, pp. 83–86.

4. On fans' desire for believability in *Doctor Who,* see Tulloch and Jenkins, *Science Fiction Audiences,* pp. 153–155.

5. Interestingly, William Hartnell, the first actor in the role, claimed that he preferred to think of the Doctor as a wizard than as a scientist: see Howe et al., *Doctor Who: The Sixties,* p. 16.

6. See Howe et al., *Doctor Who: The Sixties,* pp. 3–5 and 10. On the origins of the idea of the TARDIS as being outwardly a commonplace object, see M. Hearn, "Nothing at the End of the Lane," *Doctor Who Magazine* 208 (January 1994), p. 37.

7. See Howe et al., *Doctor Who: The Sixties,* pp. 67–70. On the problems of regeneration as a means of prolonging and transforming the series, see J. Tulloch and M. Alvarado, *Doctor Who: The Unfolding Text,* Basingstoke, England: Macmillan, 1983, pp. 62–65.

8. Levin, "Television and the Designer," p. 7.

9. See Howe et al., *Doctor Who: The Sixties,* pp. 67–68; and Innes Lloyd, interview by T. Collins, in *DWBulletin* 36/37 (Summer 1986), p. 18.

10. See Howe et al., *Doctor Who: The Sixties,* pp. 83–94; Innes Lloyd, interview, pp. 19 and 22.

11. Martin Lees Baugh, interview with P. Britton, April 1995. For examples of Baugh's work, see Howe et al., *Doctor Who: The Sixties,* p. 100; and "The Abominable Snowmen," *Doctor Who Magazine* 224 (April 1995), p. 27.

12. Pertwee interview with Britton, April 1994 (and elsewhere—Pertwee was fond of the conceit and used it often in interviews). It is worth noting as an aside that a further possible reason for the increasing use of recognizable locales was an economic one, i.e., the expense involved in creating alien worlds in the studio, especially after the advent of color. We are grateful to Clifford Hatts for this suggestion (interview with P. Britton, July 1997).

13. See Tulloch and Alvarado, *The Unfolding Text,* pp. 145–154.

14. The genesis and reception of the Fox movie are meticulously documented in P. Segal and G. Russell, *Doctor Who: Regeneration,* London: HarperCollins, 2000.

15. Levin, "Television and the Designer," p. 7.

16. Roger Murray-Leach, interview with S. Barker, November 1993.

17. See J. Nazzaro and S. Wells, *Blake's 7: The Inside Story,* London: Boxtree, 1997, p. 64.

18. This shift was begun by Barbara Kidd and carried further by Dee Robson. Kidd's contribution is overlooked and Robson's dealt with only tendentiously in Nazzaro and Wells, *Blake's 7,* pp. 67–68.

19. On the flamboyant design imagery of Nicky Rocker for the third and fourth seasons, see Nazzaro and Wells, *Blake's 7*, pp. 68–72.

20. "The Brain of Morbius," *IN·VISION* 12, January 1989, p. 2.

21. Barry Newbery, interview with P. Britton and S. Barker, October 1994.

22. Ibid.

23. "The Robots of Death," *IN·VISION* 20, November 1989, p. 3.

24. "The Robots of Death," *IN·VISION* 20, November 1989, p. 5.

25. Ibid.

26. Barbara Kidd, interview with P. Britton, October 1994.

27. Troughton's Doctor bears comparison with several "Golden Age" clowns, from the chaotic Harold Lloyd to Stan Laurel: the actor himself referred to Chaplin as an exemplar (Howe et al., *Doctor Who: The Sixties*, pp. 73–74).

28. Troughton commented upon the fact that "there was an element of the uncertain in the way I played the Doctor . . . no-one could be sure whether I would ever get things right" ("The Elusive Cosmotramp," in *The Doctor Who File*, ed. P. Haining, London: W. H. Allen, 1986, p. 101).

29. See Howe et al., *Doctor Who: The Sixties*, p. 69.

30. Pertwee interview with Britton, April 1994.

31. Ibid.

32. On the renewed currency of the idea of the "blood" at this time in the fashion world, see "Masters of Men: The Blood" in *Harper's Bazaar*, Jan/Feb 1969, p. 76 *ff.*

33. James Acheson, who originally conceived Baker's costume image, cites Toulouse-Lautroo's well-known poster of Aristide Bruant, together with the "Self-Portrait with a Hat" by Wyndham Lewis (pen and ink, 1932, National Portrait Gallery, London), as stimuli for his design: James Acheson, interview with P. Britton, October 1994.

34. John Nathan-Turner; cited in P. Haining, *Doctor Who: The Key to Time*, London: W. H. Allen, 1984, pp. 254–255.

35. On the vicissitudes of the *commedia dell'arte*, see P. L. Duchartre, *The Italian Comedy*, New York: Dover, 1966; and C. Cairns, ed., *The Commedia Dell'Arte from the Renaissance to Dario Fo*, New York: Edwin Mellens Press, 1989.

36. On this tendency, the classic study is E. H. Gombrich, *The Sense of Order*, London: Phaidon, 1984.

37. H. Kingsley and P. Smyllie, "Who's Next?" *Daily Mirror*, Saturday, October 25, 1980.

38. Daphne Dare, interview with P. Britton, November 1994.

39. D. Whitaker, "The Crusade," 1965.

40. On Polly's character, see Howe et al., *Doctor Who: The Sixties*, pp. 120–121.

41. On Polly's antecedents, see "The War Machines," *Doctor Who: An Adventure in Space and Time* 29, p. 9. On the "coloursupps" as an influential purveyor of fashion and locus of trendiness in the 1960s, see N. Whitcley, "Shaping the Sixties," in Harris et al., *1966*, p. 25.

42. See S. J. Walker, "Anneke Wills" (interview), *Doctor Who Magazine* 187, June 1992, p. 11.

43. We are grateful to the late Jon Pertwee for informing us that Manning's clothes were mostly from Biba (interview with Britton, April 1994).

44. A. Marwick, *British Society since 1945*, p. 242; and Marwick, *The Sixties*, pp. 679–724 passim, but especially pp. 683, 690–692.

45. This is especially evident in relation to the first feminist on the series, Sarah Jane Smith, above all in her debut episode, "The Time Warrior," by Robert Holmes (1974). See H. Stirling, "Girl talk," *IN·VISION* 17 ("Sarah Special"), June 1989, p. 3.

46. "Face of Evil," *IN·VISION* 19, October 1989, p. 5.

47. "The Talons of Weng-Chiang," *IN·VISION* 21, December 1989, pp. 11–12.

48. See unidentified newspaper clippings reproduced in "Face of Evil," *IN·VISION* 19, October 1989, p. 4.

49. We are grateful to Ian Potter for pointing out the debt owed to contemporary street styles by Ace's image, which was conceived originally by costume designer Richard Croft for her début episode "Dragonfire" (1987).

50. Tom Baker, interview with P. Britton, September 1995.

51. June Hudson, interview with P. Britton and S. Barker, October 1994.

52. See Britton, "Dress and the Fabric of the Television Series," p. 353.

53. Hudson interview with Britton and Barker, October 1994.

54. On this celebrated film, see J. Cocteau, *Orphée,* Paris: Editions 84, 1999.

55. Hudson's first design for Romana was a distillation of the idea of dressing Ward in boy's clothes. She came up with a fantasy on late-rococo Parisian male fashions in green silk and cloth-of-gold. Romana, who had for so long been dressed like a principal boy, became in effect the story's prince. For technical reasons this green and gold design had to be abandoned.

56. June Hudson, interview with P. Britton, November 1993.

57. Ibid.

58. Ibid.

59. See text below, p. 164.

60. For example, Patrick Macnee as John Steed in *The Avengers,* discussed in Chapter 2 above, Jon Pertwee, the third star of *Doctor Who* (1970–1974), and Peter Wyngarde, who played Jason King in *Department S* (1969–1970) and *Jason King* (1971). For information on Peter Wyngarde, we are indebted to David Murphy (interview with the authors, January 1995). Baker's firmness about what he would and would not wear was confirmed by two of the designers who worked most with him, and by the actor himself (Acheson interview with Britton, October 1994; Hudson interview with Britton and Barker, October 1994; Baker interview with Britton, September 1995).

61. Hudson interview with Britton, November 1993.

62. The only variation from the red/purple tonality was provided by two relatively little-seen elements: Baker's new waistcoat, which was of black-and-gold antique figured velvet, and the predominantly green lining of the overcoat, which can really only be made out with the use of freeze-frame.

63. June Hudson, interview with P. Britton, November 1993.

64. Ibid.

65. Tom Baker, interview with P. Britton, September 1995.

66. See "The Leisure Hive," *IN·VISION* 46, September 1993, pp. 8–9.

67. Hudson interview with Britton, November 1993.

68. Cited in Whiteley, "Shaping the Sixties," in *1966,* ed. Harris et al., p. 16 (caption to fig. 5).

69. See Harris et al., *1966,* p. 16–17.

70. C. Booker, *The Neophiliacs,* London: Collins, 1970.

71. See Howe et al., Doctor Who: *The Sixties,* pp. 137–152.

72. See Bentham, *Doctor Who: The Early Years,* p. 120.

73. See Whiteley, "Shaping the Sixties," in *1966,* ed. Harris et al., p. 17; and W. J. R. Curtis, *Modern Architecture since 1900,* 2nd ed., London: Phaidon, 1987, pp. 317–342 and 355. The great champion of functionalism in Britain at this time was Reyner Banham, above all in his seminal work, *Theory and Design in the First Machine Age,* London: The Architectural Press, 1960; see especially pp. 320–330.

74. Pertwee interview with Britton, April 1994.

75. Cited in Bentham, *Doctor Who: The Early Years,* p. 139.

76. The cartoon, by Birkett, is reproduced in Haining, *The Doctor Who File,* p. 59.

77. See Chapter 3, note 35 above.

78. Raymond P. Cusick, interview with S. Barker, January 1994. On Moholy-Nagy, see note 91 below.

79. The landmark importance of design in *2001, Star Wars,* and *Alien* is acknowledged within the film design profession. See, for example, comments by Bruno Rubeo in Lo Brutto, *By Design,* p. 265.

80. J. Bentham, "Production Office," in *Doctor Who: An Adventure in Space and Time* 51: "Spearhead from Space," 1985, p. 8.

81. We are grateful to Ian Potter for this information.

82. See Tulloch and Alvarado, *The Unfolding Text,* pp. 158–159.

83. Holmes was the effective author of the script, having rewritten almost completely a screenplay by Lewis Greifer; the episode went out under the pen name Stephen Harris. See *IN·VISION* 9, October 1988, "Pyramids of Mars," pp. 2–3.

84. Barbara Kidd, interview with P. Britton, October 1993.

85. Graeme Story, interview with S. Barker, November 1994.

86. Ibid.

87. Ibid.

88. Ibid.

89. Hudson interview with Britton, August 1994. See *IN·VISION* 46, September 1993, "The Leisure Hive," p. 9.

90. Story interview with Barker, November 1994. See P. Joyce/P. Newman, "Joyce Words," *IN·VISION* 50, April 1994, "Warrior's Gate," p. 18.

91. For Moholy-Nagy's designs for the Alexander Korda film *Things to Come* (1936), see Neumann, *Film Architecture,* pp. 118–120; and Albrecht, *Designing Dreams,* pp. 162–163. On Moholy-Nagy's approach to set design, see S. Moholy-Nagy, *Experiment in Totality,* Cambridge, Mass.: MIT Press, 1969, especially p. 129.

92. See *IN·VISION* 50, April 1994, "Warrior's Gate," p. 8.

93. Tulloch and Alvarado, *The Unfolding Text,* pp. 1–4.

94. See Howe et al., Doctor Who: *The Sixties,* p. 37.

95. See p. 175 above.

96. See Tulloch and Alvarado, *The Unfolding Text,* pp. 204–205.

97. Levine acted as an unofficial adviser for several years after John Nathan-Turner's appointment as producer in 1980; we are grateful to Ian Potter for this information.

98. See Hearn, "Nothing at the End of the Lane," *Doctor Who Magazine* 208, January 1994, p. 39.

99. See Bentham, *Doctor Who: The Early Years,* pp. 38–40, 93.

100. Newbery interview with Barker and Britton, October 1994.

101. Ibid. It is perhaps worth noting that the BBC studio in question was in the very confined premises at Lime Grove, not in the much larger Television Centre at White City.

102. See, for example, J. Onians, *Bearers of Meaning: The Classical Orders in Antiquity, the Middle Ages, and the Renaissance,* Princeton, N.J.: Princeton Univ. Press, 1988.

103. Newbery interview with Barker and Britton, October 1994.

104. Ibid.

105. Ibid.

106. Ibid.

107. Baker interview with Britton, September 1995.

108. Ibid.

109. Cited in *Doctor Who Winter Special,* London: Marvel, 1983/4, p. 39.

110. J. Peel, "Doctor Who Episode Guide," *Fantasy Empire* 17 (May 1985), p. 42. The idea that the set had warped in storage was a fallacy. Contrary to appearance, it was not made of wood and was reusable when Newbery came to design "The Invisible Enemy" in 1977, for which he was asked to re-create the old, white control room (Newbery interview with Barker and Britton, October 1994).

111. J. Peel, "The Fourteenth Season Guide to Doctor Who," *Fantasy Empire* 16 (March 1985), p. 23.

112. See note 110 above.

113. It is worth noting that a later TARDIS design—albeit not for the Doctor—did incorporate beautiful antinatural imagery. In 1985, for the episode "The Mark of the Rani," Paul Trerise created a TARDIS set for the evil Rani (played by Kate O'Mara) with a central control table having no functioning buttons or keyboards, only convex and concave concentric discs and domino-like attachments arranged in an abstract pattern. The controls were operated by the Rani passing her hands over them, without actually touching; the effect, thanks in part to O'Mara's polished performance, was very striking.

114. Tashiro makes a related point about the way in which futuristic imagery in science-fiction films can rapidly become dated (*Pretty Pictures,* pp. 10–11).

115. Cited in "Rising Costs—Don't Point the Finger at Us," *The Stage and Television Today,* October 17, 1974.

116. P. Mulkern, "Designs on Who," *Doctor Who Autumn Special*, London: Marvel, 1987, pp. 6, 7, and 9.

117. P. Mulkern, "Designs on Who," p. 8.

118. Cited in N. Gaiman, *Don't Panic: Douglas Adams and the Hitchhiker's Guide to the Galaxy*, 2nd ed., London: Titan, 1993, p. 88.

119. See Tulloch and Alvarado, *The Unfolding Text*, pp. 65–67 and 151–159.

120. Robson had been costume designer on "Image of the Fendahl" (1977) and "The Invasion of Time" (1978); Yardley-Jones had been the scenic designer on "The Leisure Hive" (1980).

121. D. Adams, *The Hitchhiker's Guide to the Galaxy*, New York: Pocket Books, 1979, p. 97.

122. Cited in Gaiman, *Don't Panic*, p. 91.

123. D. Robson, interview with P. Britton and S. Barker, October 1994. It should be noted that Gaiman credits producer Alan Bell with the decision to keep Arthur in his pajamas (*Don't Panic*, pp. 91–92).

124. Ibid.

125. J. Hudson, interview with P. Britton, May 1995.

AFTERWORD

1. Miller, *The Avengers*, p. 47.

2. See Affron and Affron, *Sets in Motion*, pp. 35–37 and Tashiro, *Pretty Pictures*, pp. 5–8.

3. G. Studlar, "Masochism, Masquerade, and the Erotic Metamorphoses of Marlene Dietrich," in *Fabrications*, ed. Gaines and Herzog, pp. 229–249; and Gaines, "Costume and Narrative: How Dress Tells the Woman's Story," in *Fabrications*, pp. 180–211.

4. Grant's image is mentioned briefly in S. Cohan, "Cary Grant in the Fifties: Indiscretion of the Bachelor's Masquerade," *Screen* 33, no. 4 (Winter 1992), pp. 394–412.

5. The husband-and-wife detective team, Tommy and Tuppence Beresford, were the attractive, youthful, and upper-crust heroes of Agatha Christie's *The Secret Adversary* (1922), several later novels, and a collection of short stories entitled *Partners in Crime* (1929), the last serving as the basis for a television series in 1980.

6. See R. Samuel, *Theatres of Memory*, vol.1, *Past and Present in Contemporary Culture*, London: Verso, 1996, especially the chapter entitled "Retrofitting," pp. 59–79, which deals with the vogue for period design in interior decoration. For a trenchant critique of the heritage industry, see P. Wright, *On Living in an Old Country: The National Past in Contemporary Britain*, London: Verso, 1985. The strong overtones of "heritage culture" in *Inspector Morse* are also noted by C. Brunsdon in her article "Structure of Anxiety: Recent British Television Crime Fiction," *Screen* 39, no. 3 (Autumn 1998), pp. 228–231.

7. A relatively comprehensive if largely anecdotal account of the production history of the series is provided in M. Sanderson, *The Making of Inspector Morse*, London: Pan Books, 1995.

8. *The Adventures/Return/Casebook/Memoirs of Sherlock Holmes*, Granada TV, 1984–

1994; *Miss Marple,* BBC TV, 1984–1992; *A Dorothy L. Sayers Mystery (Strong Poison, Have His Carcase, Gaudy Night),* BBC TV, 1987; *Campion,* BBC TV, 1989–1991; *Poirot,* 1989– ; *The Inspector Alleyn Mysteries,* BBC TV, 1993–1995.

9. See Brunsdon, "Structure of Anxiety," *Screen* 39.

10. See Brunsdon, "Structure of Anxiety," *Screen* 39.

11. Buxton, *From* Avengers *to* Vice, p. 20: "I would argue for the logical priority of the type of ideological analysis attempted here over formal aesthetic devices which pose problems of a different order"; on the notion of "ideologemes," see p. 16.

B
I
B
L
I
O
G
R
A
P
H
Y

Adams, D. *The Hitchhiker's Guide to the Galaxy.* New York: Pocket Books, 1979.

Affron, C., and M. J. Affron. *Sets in Motion: Art Direction and Film Narrative.* New Brunswick, N.J.: Rutgers Univ. Press, 1995.

Albrecht, D. *Designing Dreams: Modern Architecture in the Movies.* London and New York: Thames and Hudson, 1987.

Aldgate, A., J. Chapman, and A. Marwick, eds. *Windows on the Sixties: Exploring Key Texts of Media and Culture.* London and New York: I. B. Tauris, 2000.

Allen, R. C. *Speaking of Soap Operas.* Chapel Hill and London: Univ. of North Carolina Press, 1985.

Alvarado, M., and E. Buscombe. *Hazell: The Making of a TV Series.* London: British Film Institute Publishing, 1978.

Alvarado, M., and J. Stewart, eds. *Made for television: Euston Films Limited.* London: British Film Institute Publishing, 1985.

Amies, H. *The Englishman's Suit.* London: Quartet Books, 1994.

Aumont, J., A. Bergala, M. Marie, and M. Vernet. *Aesthetics of Film.* Austin: Univ. of Texas Press, 1992.

Baker, T. *Who on Earth Is Tom Baker?* London and New York: HarperCollins, 1998.

Ball, S., ed., *The Conservative Party since 1945.* Manchester: Manchester Univ. Press, 1998.

Banham, M., and B. Hillier, eds. *A Tonic to the Nation: The Festival of Britain, 1951*. London: Thames and Hudson, 1976.

Banham, R. *Theory and Design in the First Machine Age*. London: The Architectural Press, 1960.

Banks-Smith, N., "Last Night's TV: The Strange Story," *The Guardian: The Guide*, January 18, 2000, p. 22.

Barber, B. "Art History's Significant Other . . . Film Studies." In *The Subjects of Art History: Historical Objects in Contemporary Perspectives*, edited by M. Cheetham, M. A. Holly, and K. Moxey. Cambridge: Cambridge Univ. Press, 1991.

Barnard, M. *Art, Design, and Visual Culture*. London: Palgrave, 1998.

Barsacq, L. *Caligari's Cabinet and Other Grand Illusions: A History of Film Design*. Revised and edited by E. Stein. New York and Scarborough: Plume, 1976.

Baudou, J. "Danger Man." In The Prisoner: *A Televisionary Masterpiece*, edited by A. Carrazé and H. Oswald. Translated by C. Donougher. London: W. H. Allen, 1990.

Baudrillard, J. *Simulations*. Translated by P. Foss, P. Patton, and P. Beitchman. New York: Semiotext(e), 1983.

Bennett, A. *Writing Home*. London: Faber and Faber, 1994.

Bentham, J. *Doctor Who: The Early Years*. London: W. H. Allen, 1986.

———. "Production Office. In *Doctor Who: An Adventure in Space and Time* 51: "Spearhead from Space." London: CMS (1985): p. 8.

———. "Three's A Crowd." In *Doctor Who: An Adventure in Space and Time* 69: "The Three Doctors." London: CMS (1987): pp. 8–9.

Bergstrom, C. Interview. *Buffy the Vampire Slayer: Season III DVD Collection:* Disc Six, Special Features: Featurettes. Twentieth Century Fox Home Entertainment, Inc., 2001.

Booker, C. *The Neophiliacs*. London: Collins, 1970.

Bordwell, D., and K. Thompson. *Film Art: An Introduction*. New York and London: McGraw-Hill, 1997.

Britton, P. D. G. "Dress and the Fabric of the Television Series: The Costume Designer as Author in *Doctor Who*." *Journal of Design History* 12, no. 4 (December 1999): pp. 345–356.

Brunsdon, C. "Structure of Anxiety: Recent British Television Crime Fiction." *Screen* 39, no. 3 (Autumn 1998): pp. 228–231.

Bruzzi, S. *Undressing Cinema: Clothing and Identity in the Movies*. London and New York: Routledge, 1997.

Buxton, D. *From* The Avengers *to* Miami Vice: *Form and Ideology in Popular Television Series*. Manchester and New York: Manchester Univ. Press, 1990.

Cairns, C., ed. *The Commedia Dell'Arte from the Renaissance to Dario Fo*. New York: Edwin Mellens Press, 1989.

Calloway, S., and D. Colvin. *Oscar Wilde: An Exquisite Life*. London: Orion, 1997.

Cardin, P. *Pierre Cardin*. Paris: Flammarion, 1997.

Carrazé, A., and H. Oswald, eds. The Prisoner: *A Televisionary Masterpiece*. Translated by C. Donougher. London: W. H. Allen, 1990.

Carrick, E. *Designing for Film*. Rev. ed. London and New York: Studio Productions, 1949.

Chapman, J. "*The Avengers:* Television and Popular Culture During the 'High Sixties'." In

Windows on the Sixties: Exploring Key Texts of Media and Culture. Edited by A. Aldgate, J. Chapman, and A. Marwick. London and New York: I. B. Tauris, 2000.

Chenoune, F. *A History of Men's Fashion.* Translated by D. Dusinberre. Paris: Flammarion, 1993.

Cocteau, J. *Orphée.* Paris: Editions 84, 1999.

Coe, J. *Humphrey Bogart: Take It and Like It.* New York: Grove Weidenfeld, 1991.

Cohan, S. "Cary Grant in the Fifties: Indiscretion of the Bachelor's Masquerade." *Screen* 33, no. 4 (Winter 1992): pp. 394–412.

Craig, E. G. *On the Art of the Theatre.* London: Heinemann, 1911.

Crook, J. M. *The Dilemma of Style: Architectural Ideals from the Picturesque to the Post-Modern.* London: Murray, 1987.

Crow, T. "Modernism and Mass Culture in the Visual Arts." In *Pollock and After: The Critical Debate.* Edited by F. Frascina. London and New York: Harper and Row, 1985.

Curtis, W. J. R. *Modern Architecture since 1900.* London: Phaidon, 1987.

Daniel, E. *The Art of Gormenghast.* London and New York: HarperCollins, 2000.

Duchartre, P. L. *The Italian Comedy.* New York: Dover, 1966.

Dyer, R. *Stars.* London: British Film Institute Publishing, 1979.

Eco, U. "Casablanca: Cult Movies and Intertextual Collage." In *Travels in Hyperreality.* Translated by W. Weaver. New York: Harcourt Brace Jovanovich, 1986.

———. "Postscript to *The Name of the Rose:* Postmodernism, Irony, the Enjoyable." In *The Post-Modern Reader.* Edited by C. Jencks. London: Academy Editions, 1992.

Ellis, J. *Visible Fictions: Cinema, Television, and Video.* Rev. ed., London: Routledge, 1992.

Fiske, J. "Popularity and Ideology: A Structuralist Reading of *Doctor Who.*" In *Interpreting Television: Current Research Perspectives.* Edited by W. Rowland and B. Watkins. London: Sage, 1984.

———. *Television Culture.* 2nd ed. London: Routledge, 1987.

Fiske, J., and J. Hartley. *Reading Television.* London: Methuen, 1978.

Frampton, K. *Modern Architecture: A Critical History.* London: Thames and Hudson, 1980.

Frascina, F. *Pollock and After: The Critical Debate.* London and New York: Harper and Row, 1985.

Fuller, R. Buckminster. *Operating Manual for Spaceship Earth.* New York: Dutton, 1963.

Gaiman, N. *Don't Panic: Douglas Adams and the Hitchhiker's Guide to the Galaxy.* 2nd ed. London: Titan, 1993.

Gaines, J. "Costume and Narrative: How Dress Tells the Woman's Story." In *Fabrications: Costume and the Female Body.* Edited by J. Gaines and C. Herzog. New York: Routledge, 1990.

Garner, P. *Twentieth-Century Furniture.* Oxford: Phaidon, 1980.

Geraghty, C. "Social Issues and Realist Soaps: A Study of British Soaps in the 1980s and 1990s." In *To Be Continued . . . Soap Operas around the World.* Edited by R. C. Allen. London and New York: Routledge, 1995.

Gombrich, E. H. *The Sense of Order.* London: Phaidon, 1984.

Gombrich, E. H., et al. *Leonardo da Vinci.* [Hayward Gallery Exhibition Catalogue] New Haven and London: Yale Univ. Press (for the South Bank Centre), 1989.

Gottdiener, M. *The Theming of America: Dreams, Visions, and Commercial Spaces.* Boulder, Colo.: Westview Press, 1997.

Gray, J. *Beyond the New Right.* London: Routledge, 1994.

Greenberg, Clement. "Avant-Garde and Kitsch." In *Pollock and After: The Critical Debate.* Edited by F. Frascina. London and New York: Harper and Row, 1985.

Gregory, C. *Be Seeing You: Decoding* The Prisoner. Champaign, Ill.: Univ. of Illinois Press, 1999.

Haining, P. *Doctor Who: The Key to Time.* London: W. H. Allen, 1984.

———, ed. *The Doctor Who File.* London: W. H. Allen, 1986.

Hambley, J., and P. Downing. *The Art of Hollywood: A Thames Television Exhibition at the Victoria and Albert Museum.* London: Thames Television, 1979.

Hamilton, R. *Collected Words.* London: Thames and Hudson, 1982.

Harper, S. "Historical Pleasures: Gainsborough Costume Melodrama." In *Home Is Where the Heart Is: Studies in Melodrama and the Woman's Film.* Edited by C. Gledhill. London: British Film Institute Publishing, 1987.

———. *Picturing the Past: The Rise and Fall of the British Costume Film.* London: British Film Institute Publishing, 1994.

Harris, J., S. Hyde, and G. Smith. *1966 and All That: Design and the Consumer in Britain, 1960–1969.* London: Trefoil, 1986.

Harrison, C., and P. Wood, eds. *Art in Theory, 1900–1990.* Oxford: Blackwell, 1992.

Hatts, C. "The Rôle of the Designer in Television." *Journal of the Royal Society of Arts* 123 (January 1975): pp. 81–92.

Hearn, M. "Nothing at the End of the Lane." *Doctor Who Magazine* 208 (January 1994): pp. 36–39.

Heisner, B. *Hollywood Art: Art Direction in the Days of the Great Studios.* Jefferson, N.C.: McFarland and Co., 1990.

Holder, N., with M. Hart and J. Mariotte. *Buffy the Vampire Slayer: The Watcher's Guide.* Vol. 2. New York: Pocket Books, 2000.

Hollander, A. *Seeing through Clothes.* Berkeley, Calif.: Univ. of California Press, 1993.

Hora, M. *The Prisoner of Portmeirion.* Number Six Productions, 1991.

Howe, D. J., J. Vincent-Rudzki, P. Moffatt, and M. Platt. *The Making of The Five Doctors.* Surbiton, England: Doctor Who Appreciation Society, 1984.

Howe, D. J., M. Stammers, and S. J. Walker. Doctor Who: *The Sixties.* London: Virgin Publishing, 1993.

Huyssen, A. "Mapping the Postmodern." In *The Post-Modern Reader.* Edited by C. Jencks. London: Academy Editions, 1992.

Jameson, F. "The Deconstruction of Expression." *New Left Review* 146, July/August 1984: pp. 53–92.

———. "Post-Modernism: Of the Cultural Logic of Late Capitalism." In *Pollock and After: The Critical Debate.* Edited by F. Frascina. London and New York: Harper and Row, 1985.

Jencks, C. "The Post-Modern Agenda." In *The Post-Modern Reader.* Edited by C. Jencks. London: Academy Editions, 1992.

————, ed. *The Post-Modern Reader.* London: Academy Editions, 1992.

Kemp, M. *Leonardo da Vinci: The Marvelous Works of Nature and Man.* London: J. M. Dent and Sons, 1981.

Kennedy, D. *Granville Barker and the Dream of Theatre.* Cambridge: Cambridge Univ. Press, 1985.

Kingsley, H., and P. Smyllie. "Who's Next?" *Daily Mirror,* Saturday, October 25, 1980.

Krauss, R. E. *The Optical Unconscious.* Cambridge: MIT Press, 1994.

————. *The Originality of the Avant-Garde and Other Modernist Myths.* Cambridge, Mass., and London: MIT Press, 1986.

Kristeller, P. O. "The Modern System of the Arts." In *Renaissance Thought and the Arts.* Exp. ed. Princeton, N.J.: Princeton Univ. Press, 1990.

Lancaster, D. "The Immaculate Avengers." *TV Times* 418 (November 1, 1964).

Levin, R. "Television and the Designer," *EBU [European Broadcasting Union] Review* 58B (November 1959) [reprint]: pp. 2–15.

————. *Television by Design.* London: The Bodley Head, 1961.

Lippard, L., ed. *Pop Art.* London: Thames and Hudson, 1967.

Lloyd, Innes. Interview by T. Collins. In *DWBulletin* 36/37 (Summer 1986): pp. 18–24.

Lloyd-Smith, A.G., and V. Sage, eds. *Gothick: Origins and Innovations. Papers from the International Gothic Conference Held at the University of East Anglia, Norwich.* Atlanta, Ga.: Rodopi, 1994.

LoBrutto, V. *By Design: Interviews with Film Production Designers.* Westport, Conn.: Praeger, 1992.

————. *Principal Photography: Interviews with Feature Film Cinematographers.* Westport, Conn.: Praeger, 1999.

Lowry, M. "They Get Color Next Year, but We Get Macnee Now," *New York World Telegram,* March 21, 1965: p. 10.

Lurie, A. *The Language of Clothes.* London: Bloomsbury, 1981.

Macnee, P. and M. Cameron. *Blind in One Ear.* London: Harrap, 1988.

Macnee, P. and D. Rogers. The Avengers *and Me.* London: Titan, 1997.

Maltin, L. *The Art of the Cinematographer: A Survey and Interviews with Five Masters.* New York: Dover, 1978.

Marwick, A. *British Society since 1945.* 2nd ed. Harmondsworth, England: Penguin, 1990.

————. *The Sixties: Cultural Revolution in Britain, France, Italy, and the United States, c.1958–c.1974.* Oxford: Oxford Univ. Press, 1998.

Mayne, J. *Cinema and Spectatorship.* London: Routledge, 1993.

McLuhan, M. *Understanding Media: The Extensions of Man.* 2nd ed. New York: Signet, 1964.

McLuhan, M., and B. R. Powers. *The Global Village: Transformations in World Life and Media in the 21st Century.* Oxford: Oxford Univ. Press, 1989.

Meier-Graefe, J. *Vincent van Gogh, a Biographical Study.* Translated by J. Holroyd Reece. London and Boston, Mass.: The Medici Society, 1922.

Miller, T. *The Avengers.* London: British Film Institute Publishing, 1997.

Mirzoeff, N. *An Introduction to Visual Culture.* London: Routledge, 1999.

Moholy-Nagy, S. *Experiment in Totality*. Cambridge: MIT Press, 1969.

Moxey, K. *The Practice of Theory: Poststructuralism, Cultural Politics, and Art History*. Ithaca, N.Y., and London: Cornell Univ. Press, 1994.

Mulkern, P. "Designs on Who." *Doctor Who Autumn Special*. London: Marvel, 1987.

Mulvey, L. "Afterthoughts on Visual Pleasure and Narrative Cinema." In *Visual and Other Pleasures*, Basingstoke: Macmillan, 1989.

———. "Visual Pleasures and Narrative Cinema." In *Visual and Other Pleasures*. Basingstoke, England: Macmillan, 1989.

Murphy, R. *Sixties British Cinema*. London: British Film Institute Publishing, 1992.

———, ed. *British Cinema of the 90s*. London: British Film Institute Publishing, 1999.

Nazzaro, T., and S. Wells. *Blake's 7: The Inside Story*. London: Boxtree, 1997.

Neumann, D., ed. *Film Architecture: From* Metropolis *to* Blade Runner. Munich and New York: Prestel, 1996.

Nimoy, L. *I Am Not Spock*. Millbrae, Calif.: Celestial Arts Publishing, 1975.

———. *I Am Spock*. New York: Hyperion, 1995.

Olson, R. L. *Art Direction for Film and Video*. London: Butterworth-Heinemann, 1998.

Onians, J. *Bearers of Meaning: The Classical Orders in Antiquity, the Middle Ages, and the Renaissance*. Princeton N.J.: Princeton Univ. Press, 1988.

Peel, J. "Doctor Who Episode Guide." *Fantasy Empire* 17 (May 1985).

———. "Fourteenth Season Episode Guide to *Doctor Who*." *Fantasy Empire* 16 (March 1985).

Probert, C. "The Era of Individualism." In *Costume and Fashion: A Concise History*. Edited by J. Laver. London: Thames and Hudson, 1982.

Purser, P. "Richard Levin" (obituary). *The Guardian*, July 10, 2000.

Rakoff, I. *Inside* The Prisoner: *Radical Television and Film in the 1960s*. London: Batsford, 1998.

Rees, A. L., and F. Borzello, eds. *The New Art History*. London: Camden Press, 1986.

Robinson, F. M. *The Man in the Bowler Hat: His History and Iconography*. Chapel Hill, N.C.: Univ. of North Carolina Press, 1993.

Rogers, D. *The Avengers Anew*. London: Michael Joseph, 1985.

———. The Avengers: *The Making of the Movie*. London: Titan, 1998.

———. *The Complete Avengers*. London: Boxtree, 1989.

———. The Prisoner *and* Danger Man. London: Boxtree, 1989.

———. *The Ultimate Avengers*. London: Boxtree, 1995.

Rogers, P. B. *Contemporary Cinematographers on Their Art*. Newton, Mass.: Focal Press, 1998.

Samuel, R. *Theatres of Memory*. Vol. 1, *Past and Present in Contemporary Culture*. London: Verso, 1996.

Sanderson, M. *The Making of Inspector Morse*. London: Pan Books, 1995.

Scheffauer, H. G. "The Vivifying of Space." In *Introduction to the Art of the Movies*. Edited by L. Jacobs. New York: Noonday Press, 1960.

Seddon, P. *Where's the Designer?* London: BBC Production Training, 1993.

Segal, S., and G. Russell. *Doctor Who: Regeneration*. London: HarperCollins, 2000.

Shearman, J. "Raphael's Clouds, and Correggio's." In *Studi su Raffaello*. Edited by M. Sambucco Hamoud and M. Letizia Strocchi. Urbino: Quattroventi, 1987.

Sieden, L. S. *Buckminster Fuller's Universe: His Life and Work.* Cambridge, Mass.: Perseus Publishing, 2000.

Simonson, L. *The Art of Scenic Design.* New York: Harper and Row, 1950.

Smith, M. *Engaging Characters.* Oxford: Oxford Univ. Press, 1995.

Sorkin, M., ed. *Variations on a Theme Park: The New American City and the End of Public Space.* New York: Noonday Press, 1992.

Stam, R., R. Burgoyne, and S. Flitterman-Lewis. *New Vocabularies in Film Semiotics.* London and New York: Routledge, 1992.

Steinitz, K. T. "Leonardo Architetto Teatrale e Organizzatore di Feste." *Lettura Vinciana* 9 (Florence), 1970: pp. 53–55.

Sternberg, J. "*The Prisoner,* Pioneer without Heirs." In The Prisoner: *A Televisionary Masterpiece,* edited by A. Carrazé and H. Oswald. Translated by C. Donougher. London: W. H. Allen, 1990.

Stirling, H. "Girl talk," *IN·VISION* 17 ("Sarah Special"), June 1989.

Studlar, G. "Masochism, Masquerade, and the Erotic Metamorphoses of Marlene Dietrich." In *Fabrications: Costume and the Female Body.* Edited by J. Gaines and C. Herzog. New York: Routledge, 1990.

Sturges, F. "Video Reviews," *The Independent: The Information,* February 6–12, 1999.

Summerskill, B. "Gormenghast Has Viewers Groaning," *Daily Express,* February 3, 2000.

Sutcliffe, K. "Making a Killing: Interview with Brian Clemens." *Primetime* 8 (Spring 1984): pp. 29–31.

Tashiro, C. S. *Pretty Pictures: Production Design and the History Film.* Austin: Univ. of Texas Press, 1998.

Terrace, V. *The Complete Encyclopedia of Television Programs, 1947–1976.* South Brunswick, N.J.: A. S. Barnes, 1976.

Triggs, T. "Framing Masculinity." In *Chic Thrills: A Fashion Reader.* Edited by J. Ash and E. Wilson. London: Pandora, 1992.

Tulloch, J., and M. Alvarado. Doctor Who: *The Unfolding Text.* Basingstoke, England: Macmillan, 1983.

Tulloch, J. and H. Jenkins. *Science Fiction Audiences: Watching* Doctor Who *and* Star Trek. London: Routledge, 1995.

Vidler, A. "The Explosion of Space: Architecture and the Filmic Imaginary." In *Film Architecture: From* Metropolis *to* Blade Runner. Edited by D. Neumann. Munich and New York: Prestel, 1996.

Walker, B. G. *The Women's Encyclopedia of Myths and Secrets.* San Francisco: HarperSanFrancisco, 1983.

Walker, S. J. "Anneke Wills." Interview in *Doctor Who Magazine* 187 (June 1992): p. 11.

Wallis, R., and S. J. Baran. *The Known World of Broadcast News: International News and the Electronic Media.* London and New York: Routledge, 1990.

White, M., and J. Ali. *The Official Prisoner Companion.* New York: Warner, 1988.

Whiteley, N. "Shaping the Sixties." In *1966 and All That: Design and the Consumer in Britain, 1960–1969.* J. Harris, S. Hyde, and G. Smith. London: Trefoil, 1986.

Wright, P. *On Living in an Old Country: The National Past in Contemporary Britain.* London: Verso, 1985.